The Reception of Cleopatra in the Age of Mass Media

IMAGINES – Classical Receptions in The Visual and Performing Arts

Series Editors: Filippo Carlà-Uhink and Martin Lindner

Other titles in this series

Ancient Greece and Rome in Videogames: Representation, Play, Transmedia,
by Ross Clare

The Ancient Mediterranean Sea in Modern Visual and Performing Arts,
edited by Rosario Rovira Guardiola

Ancient Violence in the Modern Imagination: The Fear and the Fury,
edited by Irene Berti, Maria G. Castello and Carla Scilabra

Art Nouveau and the Classical Tradition, by Richard Warren

Classical Antiquity in Heavy Metal Music, edited by K. F. B. Fletcher
and Osman Umurhan

Classical Antiquity in Video Games, edited by Christian Rollinger

*Geographies of Myth and Places of Identity: The Strait of Scylla and Charybdis
in the Modern Imagination,* by Marco Benoît Carbone

A Homeric Catalogue of Shapes, by Charlayn von Solms

Orientalism and the Reception of Powerful Women from the Ancient World,
edited by Filippo Carlà-Uhink and Anja Wieber

Representations of Classical Greece in Theme Parks, by Filippo Carlà-Uhink

Screening Love and War in Troy: Fall of a City, edited by Antony Augoustakis
and Monica S. Cyrino

The Smells and Senses of Antiquity in the Modern Imagination, edited by
Adeline Grand-Clément and Charlotte Ribeyrol

Women in Classical Video Games, edited by Jane Draycott and Kate Cook

The Reception of Cleopatra in the Age of Mass Media

Gregory N. Daugherty

BLOOMSBURY ACADEMIC
LONDON • NEW YORK • OXFORD • NEW DELHI • SYDNEY

BLOOMSBURY ACADEMIC
Bloomsbury Publishing Plc
50 Bedford Square, London, WC1B 3DP, UK
1385 Broadway, New York, NY 10018, USA
29 Earlsfort Terrace, Dublin 2, Ireland

BLOOMSBURY, BLOOMSBURY ACADEMIC and the Diana logo are trademarks
of Bloomsbury Publishing Plc

First published in Great Britain 2023
This paperback edition published 2024

Copyright © Gregory N. Daugherty, 2023

Gregory N. Daugherty has asserted his right under the Copyright, Designs and Patents Act, 1988, to be identified as Author of this work.

For legal purposes the Acknowledgements on p. xi constitute an
extension of this copyright page.

Cover image: 1910s USA Palmolive Magazine Advert
Retro AdArchives / Alamy Stock Photo

All rights reserved. No part of this publication may be reproduced or transmitted in any form or by any means, electronic or mechanical, including photocopying, recording, or any information storage or retrieval system, without prior permission in writing from the publishers.

Bloomsbury Publishing Plc does not have any control over, or responsibility for, any third-party websites referred to or in this book. All internet addresses given in this book were correct at the time of going to press. The author and publisher regret any inconvenience caused if addresses have changed or sites have ceased to exist, but can accept no responsibility for any such changes.

A catalogue record for this book is available from the British Library.

Library of Congress Cataloging-in-Publication Data
Names: Daugherty, Gregory N. (Gregory Neil), 1948– author.
Title: The reception of Cleopatra in the age of mass media / Gregory N. Daugherty.
Description: London ; New York : Bloomsbury Academic, 2023. | Series: Imagines–classical receptions in the visual and performing arts | Includes bibliographical references and index.
Identifiers: LCCN 2022022114 | ISBN 9781350340725 (hardback) |
ISBN 9781350340763 (paperback) | ISBN 9781350340732 (ebook) |
ISBN 9781350340749 (epub) | ISBN 9781350340756
Subjects: LCSH: Cleopatra, Queen of Egypt, –30 B.C.–Influence. |
Cleopatra, Queen of Egypt, -30 B.C.–In mass media. | Cleopatra, Queen of Egypt, -30 B.C.–Public opinion. | Popular culture–United States–History–20th century. | Popular culture–United States–History–21st century. | Mass media–United States–History–20th century. | Mass media–United States–History–21st century.
Classification: LCC DT92.7 .D38 2023 | DDC 932/.021–dc23/eng/20220531
LC record available at https://lccn.loc.gov/2022022114

ISBN:	HB:	978-1-3503-4072-5
	PB:	978-1-3503-4076-3
	ePDF:	978-1-3503-4073-2
	eBook:	978-1-3503-4074-9

Series: IMAGINES – Classical Receptions in the Visual and Performing Arts

Typeset by RefineCatch Limited, Bungay, Suffolk

To find out more about our authors and books visit www.bloomsbury.com
and sign up for our newsletters.

This book is dedicated to Cathy – my wife of infinite variety – for indulging in my obsession with another woman for so many years. A lass unparalleled.

Contents

List of Illustrations		x
Acknowledgements		xi
1	'A Lass Unparalleled'	1
	1.1 Scope and thesis of this study	1
	1.2 The 'real' Cleo and her known associates	2
	1.3 Her beauty and her race	6
	1.4 Her early receptions	10
2	The *Femme Fatale*	15
	2.1 Cleopatra at the *fin de siècle*	15
	2.2 Silent Cleopatras	26
	2.3 Pulp fiction	36
	2.4 Demise of the vamp	38
3	A Kinder, Gentler Cleopatra	41
	3.1 Advertising and Palmolive Soap 1909–29	42
	3.2 Cleopatra laughs	53
	3.3 *Femme fatale* to flapper	58
4	Thoroughly Modern Cleopatra	69
	4.1 *Caesar and Cleopatra* (1945)	70
	4.2 Postwar novels	71
	4.3 Pepla	75
	4.4 Pulps	82
	4.5 Comic and graphic novels prior to Lizpatra	85
	4.6 Television pre-Lizpatra	88
	4.7 Cartoons pre-Lizpatra	88

5	Lizpatra and Its Aftermath	89
	5.1 Mankiewicz (1963) aka Lizpatra	89
	5.2 Historical fiction after Lizpatra	93
	5.3 Historical fiction for children and young adults	93
	5.4 Science fiction	93
	5.5 Comedy	94
	5.6 Comics	95
	5.7 Manga and anime	99
	5.8 Pornographic films	105
	5.9 Musical theatre	106
	5.10 Television	106
6	Eighties' Ladies	109
	6.1 *Maxie* – Glenn Close	109
	6.2 Barbara Chase-Riboud	114
	6.3 Science fiction and fantasy	123
	6.4 Anne Rice, *The Mummy* (1989)	123
7	The Fantasy Queen of the Nineties	127
	7.1 Traditional historical fiction	127
	7.2 Film and TV	128
	7.3 Science fiction and fantasy	131
	7.4 Prose fantasy fiction	134
	7.5 Graphic novels	136
8	The Twenty-first-Century 'Authentic' Cleopatras	139
	8.1 Sources for the increased interest in Cleopatra	139
	8.2 Miniseries and films	140
	8.3 Historical novels	153
	8.4 Historical novels about Cleopatra's children	156
9	The Twenty-first-Century Fantasy Cleopatras	161
	9.1 Horror and science fiction	161
	9.2 Comics and graphic novels	165
	9.3 Video games	170
	9.4 Animation	172

10 'Her Infinite Variety'   175
   10.1 Trends 1889–2022   175
   10.2 Primacy of Plutarch and Shakespeare   178
   10.3 Endurance of Orientalism   179
   10.4 Changing role of film in influencing other reception genres   179
   10.5 As a reflection of changing gender roles   180
   10.6 As a reflection of changing racial perceptions   180
   10.7 Gal Gadot in a snake bra?   180
   10.8 Video games and graphic novels   181
   10.9 A modest pitch for a TV series   182

Notes   183
Appendices   205
   A: Brief chronology of Cleopatra VII Philopator   205
   B: Bibliography of secondary works cited in the text   206
   C: Bibliography of Cleopatra in prose fiction   215
   D: Bibliography of Cleopatra in films and TV shows   219
   E: Bibliography of Cleopatra in comics and graphic novels   221
   F: Bibliography of Cleopatra in animation   224
   G: Bibliography of Cleopatra in electronic games   224
   H: Bibliography of Cleopatra on the stage   224
   I: Bibliography of Cleopatra in poetry, recordings and music   225
Index   227

Illustrations

1.1	Postcard of Gertrude Eliot as Cleopatra	12
2.1	Cleopatra wielding a knife	18
2.2	Theda Bara with knife and snake bra	34
2.3	Helen Gardner as Cleopatra	39
3.1	Palmolive ad '3000 years ago …', c. 1916	45
3.2	Palmolive ad 'Cleopatra's vision', c. 1916	49
3.3	Palmolive ad 'Cleopatra Had Nothing on Me', 1942	51
3.4	Comparison of the Barrington cover and the Palmolive ad	63
4.1	Rhonda Fleming in *Serpent of the Nile* (1953)	76
4.2	Cover of *Detective Comics* 167 (1951)	86
5.1	Detail of ad for *Cleopatra* (Mankiewicz 1963)	90
5.2	Robot Cleopatra, *Astro Boy* manga (Tezuka 1969)	100
6.1	Screen shot of Glenn Close as Cleopatra in *Maxie* (Aaron 1985)	110
6.2	*Cleopatra's Door*, Barbara Chase-Riboud, 1984	117
7.1	Screen shot of Leonor Varela, *Cleopatra* (Roddam 1999)	129
7.2	Screen shot of Elisa Moolecherry as Cleopatra (Bradshaw 2000)	131
8.1	Screen shot of Lindsey Marshal in HBO's *Rome*, episode 8 (Heller 2005)	141
8.2	Screen shot of Lindsey Marshal in HBO's *Rome*, episode 22 (Heller 2007)	151
10.1	Fanny Davenport as a stage Cleopatra (1894)	176
10.2	Screen shot of Beyoncé as Cleopatra in *Dreamgirls* (2006)	178

Acknowledgements

I would like to acknowledge my gratitude to several colleagues for their generous assistance throughout this long process which began with a modest CAMWS paper in 1994, but which realized its full scope when Tom Sienkewicz invited me to give the Monmouth College Fox lecture in 2001. The critical importance of a welcoming venue was not lost on me. That was expanded when two of my staunchest allies in Reception Studies – Meredith Safran and Roger Macfarlane – joined me and others to form Antiquity in Media Studies (AIMS) to provide a consistent forum for our new field. Throughout the last thirty years I have been fortunate to have the advice and support of my dear friend and colleague, Monica Cyrino, the indefatigable champion of Reception Studies even before it got that label. I was especially blessed to have known Duane Roller, whose scholarship and counsel have been essential. I would also like to thank the brilliant Barbara Chase-Riboud for her own obsession with Cleopatra and her generous responses to my questions. Finally, I must thank my many students and my wife Cathy for their patient forbearance and willingness to help me navigate the labyrinth the Queen and her chroniclers left for us.

1

'A Lass Unparalleled'

1.1 Scope and thesis of this study

This study examines the reception of Cleopatra from around the beginning of the twentieth century to the present day as it has been reflected in popular culture, primarily in the United States of America. It is a reception history of an actual historical figure as opposed to fictional characters or legendary events, although many aspects of her story have been altered, enhanced and ignored since her own lifetime. It is intended as a scholarly resource for researchers in that it seeks to document receptions from this period, but since it treats them as genres and themes it should also serve as a textbook for students in courses on reception and film studies and even for the amusement of the general reader. It will include not only film and novels, but also comics, cartoons, TV shows, music, advertising, erotica and all manner of art, fine and otherwise. Dolls and toys are dealt with in passing as they would require extensive illustrations. Since it would require a book of its own by someone better versed in the genre, opera has been omitted. This book will focus on receptions intended to reach a large and non-elite audience and therefore reflects the changing tastes and concerns of the culture in which it thrived. The reception of Cleopatra's actual life began during her own lifetime in the vicious propaganda campaign waged by Octavian against his rival Antony. Her subsequent reputation was collateral damage from that civil conflict but when combined with a life which was already quite remarkable, a rich legend was born.

At the outset I must acknowledge my debts to several scholars who paved the way for the modern study of the reception of Cleopatra. Lucy Hughes-Hallett opened our eyes to looking at both elite and popular culture receptions.[1] Mary Hamer brought intellectual excitement by 'reading' Cleopatra as a political, philosophical and aesthetic icon.[2] On the artistic and archaeological side, I have profited greatly from works by Susan Walker and Sally-Ann Ashton.[3] In the area of film studies, I will in fact have little to quibble with the conclusions of Diana Wenzel Fragata[4] and Maria Wyke.[5] This study would not have been possible without their pioneering work and thoughtful analyses. I hope my own observations will help to place those films in their popular culture context.

Fuelled by Plutarch, Boccaccio and Shakespeare, Cleopatra's image endured and grew through the Middle Ages and the Renaissance, morphing with every cultural and political shift. The process and the image changed drastically and swiftly with the advent of mass media, itself a rapidly evolving phenomenon. Cleopatra was elevated in American popular culture when British pulp fiction and French melodrama made her fodder for the infant film industry. My purpose is to examine how and why various forms of mass media popularized and altered the reception of a Ptolemaic dynast into a metaphor for the female experience in the rapidly changing contemporary American pop culture. She could be a Victorian 'New Woman', a deadly monster or a laughing flapper. The process reveals more about us than the Queen herself.

1.2 The 'real' Cleo and her known associates

The narrative of the life of Cleopatra VII of Egypt displays the same 'infinite variety' which Enobarbus so eloquently ascribes to the Queen herself.[6] The nature and transmission of the source material leave open a multitude of interpretations. As Sally-Ann Ashton remarked in her quest for the 'real' Cleopatra, 'What I have subsequently realized and accepted is that by "real" I meant "my" Cleopatra.'[7] And the quantity of factual details is quite low. Students and non-specialists are often shocked to learn how little we know for certain about the events of her life, especially when crucial episodes in her reign do not happen to intersect with the adventures of certain particularly toxic Roman males.

There has been a welcome resurgence in interest in Cleopatra on the part of historians to which I credit the pioneering work of Grace Harriet Macurdy[8] culminating in Duane Roller's authoritative volume.[9] My conclusions as to facts will not differ from his in any substantial way. I have no intention of attempting to replicate his analyses or those of our equally talented peers, but for the sake of non-classicists I will offer a brief discussion of the sources for her life, take sides on a few intractable aspects and propose a minimalist version of what I think we can safely assert is true.[10]

A brief biography might be in order.[11] All dates are BCE. Cleopatra VII Philopator (69–30) was the last Macedonian monarch and a direct descendant of Ptolemy I Soter of Egypt, a fact which she highlighted in her coinage with her prominent nose, a family trait. Her father Ptolemy XII Auletes (d. 51) was illegitimate and her grandmother was a concubine and unknown. That prompted many Europeans to assume that concubine equals slave which equals Black, when in fact she could just as well have been Syrian, Greek or Macedonian. Her mother is also unknown and may have been Egyptian from a priestly family, for which there is a compelling albeit circumstantial argument.[12] Although according to Auletes' will, she was supposed to rule jointly with her brother/husband Ptolemy XIII, they fell out (50–49) while the Roman patron of Egypt, Gn. Pompeius Magnus, was mired in a civil war. After his defeat at Pharsalus, Pompey fled to Egypt in search of money and ships but was murdered by Ptolemy's advisors (48). Cleopatra was smuggled back into the palace concealed in a sack or bedding to plead her case with C. Julius Caesar. Although angered by the treatment of his former son-in-law, Caesar attempted to collect on Roman loans and enforce the will but ended up trapped and besieged. After the death of her brother and the arrest of her sister Arsinoe, Cleopatra ended up with the throne and Caesar's unacknowledged child, Ptolemy XV Caesar or Caesarion (47 or 44).[13] She visited Rome and may have been present for Caesar's triumph in 46 and the assassination in 44, but the evidence for one or two trips is not conclusive. In the civil wars which followed the death of Caesar, Cleopatra disposed of her younger brother/husband Ptolemy XIV and appears to have been a diligent if beleaguered ruler. She may have tried to play both sides before the defeat of the Tyrannicides at Philippi (42), prompting Marcus Antonius to summon her to Tarsus to prove her loyalty to the Triumvirate (41). She seems to have prevailed since he returned with her to Alexandria on the golden barge, gave her the twins Alexander Helios and Cleopatra Selene (40), assigned her the former Ptolemaic dominions and killed Arsinoe, the last of her siblings, whom Caesar had pardoned and exiled to Ephesus. In spite of Antony's marriage to

Octavian's sister Octavia, she financed his ill-starred attacks on Parthia and bore him another son, Ptolemy Alexander (36). Antony in turn celebrated his triumph in Alexandria and made Cleopatra and her four children client kings of most of the Roman east.

The reaction back in Rome was one of the most effective propaganda campaigns in Western history, preserved for us in the Augustan poets, Plutarch and lesser historians, which focused on her corruption of a noble Roman and her dastardly plans for global emasculation (34–30). It portrayed her as the antithesis of the typical patriarchal, Roman, republican ideal of what constituted a proper role for a woman – such as Octavia. She was from the East, alternatively Greek or Egyptian. She was a monarch and a woman with absolute power over free males. She was portrayed as a sexually predatory *femme fatale* who manipulated and destroyed good Roman males with her beauty, prowess and wiles. As with all effective propaganda, there was sufficient factual basis to make it credible. Nevertheless, the most outrageous of the calumnies have become permanently ensconced in her legend. The only ancient documents about Cleopatra untainted by Octavian's attacks are her own propaganda in the form of coins and Egyptian inscriptions. Of course, it was her end which made her reception more attractive to posterity. The failure at Actium was the beginning of the end (31), but Antony and Cleopatra held out in Alexandria for about a year before Octavian was able to invade. They committed suicide rather than be marched in a triumph in Rome. Three of their children were sent to be raised by Octavia, at least one of whom survived and became the Queen of Mauretania.[14]

The preceding roughly parallels the account in Plutarch's *Life of Antony*, written in the second century CE and culled largely from contemporary sources such as Asinius Pollio, Quintus Dellius and others. But he also includes details from his own family oral history. He had chosen Antony as a horrible example of flawed and failed leadership and in this context told most of what we know of the life story of the enabler of his destruction.[15] Plutarch could not help but take some Greek pride in the tale of the 'Queen of Kings'. He found the tale cautionary, but also touchingly romantic. On the negative side, he did record and give credence to many of the propaganda items in circulation.

Many of these references and episodes have made their way into various receptions. There are also numerous episodes derived from general knowledge about Cleopatra's youth, her struggles with her brother and her actions between 44 and 41, all of them subjected to highly creative massaging. Another more recent category of potential fictionalization are events documented by inscriptions, coinage and archaeological discoveries in Alexandria. Some of the more common episodes include Auletes' trip to Rome, the palace coup and subsequent execution of Berenice the eldest child, her education, the relationship with her siblings and their advisors, her participation in the Buchis bull ceremony and her exile prior to the arrival of Caesar. Some receptions provide a narrative for one or more visits to Rome, frequently focusing on Cicero's documented hostility. Cleopatra's actions between Caesar's death and her meeting with Antony at Tarsus were no clearer then than now and the treatments in her receptions are all over the map.

Some of the events outside Plutarch cannot be placed chronologically or even confirmed as historical but still crop up in many receptions. From early on, Ptolemaic kings embraced aspects of Egyptian religion and pharaonic divinity to bolster their hold on the native population, taking particular interest in the cult of Isis. Cleopatra is frequently depicted as the goddess and undoubtedly dressed as Isis for the same purposes. This has encouraged the thesis that she actually believed in her own divinity, which appears prominently in many receptions as a fact. She was also credited with a treatise on cosmetics which did not survive, but this and the references to her beauty in Roman attacks have contributed to her depiction as a highly sexualized figure. This trend extends to stories about lovers other than Caesar and Antony and to a very late claim that she slept with slaves and put to death numberless one-night stands. She is also alleged to have experimented with poisons on prisoners and built up immunity by consuming small doses, but this could have been adapted from an identical tale about Mithridates of Pontus. None of these assertions are particularly credible but have become mainstays of her reception.

Such a dramatic life requires a large cast of supporting characters. In addition to Cleopatra's relatives, lovers and their supporters, there were some key figures mentioned in the ancient sources, mainly Plutarch, who will emerge frequently in the receptions under study here. A glance at the *dramatis personae* in a playbill of *Anthony and Cleopatra*, *All for Love* or *Caesar and Cleopatra* will demonstrate the range of possibilities. Dramas and novels depend on diverse characters for exposition, conflict and commentary to move a story along. Although real people, little is known about them, which is quite convenient for creativity. Characters invented from whole cloth will abound, but at the very least we can outline what is known about Apollodorus, Olympos, Charmion, Eiras and a figure I choose to label the 'Designated Sympathetic Roman'.

Plutarch refers to Apollodorus as a Sicilian and he is credited with smuggling Cleopatra into the presence of Caesar in besieged Alexandria. Roller believes he must have been a trusted associate and perhaps the source of the story.[16] He is never mentioned again. Olympos was a court physician and apparently wrote a biography of Cleopatra. Charmion and Eiras were with her to the very end, sharing her means of death. Plutarch, Shakespeare and everyone else give Charmion the moving final words of the drama. They usually act as a team and appear so frequently in the narrative that they are often described anachronistically as ladies in waiting. Since they have Greek names, many assume they could not have been slaves, but since Charmion's last act was to arrange her diadem, their role may have been more menial. Their diverse depictions and roles in the reception display great, if not infinite, variety. There were several Romans who aided and abetted Cleopatra at various points in her career, usually associates of Caesar like Rufio, or of Antony like Ahenobarbus or even of Octavian like Proculeius. Most notable was Quintus Dellius. Dellius had a checkered career, famed for his penchant for switching sides – *desultor bellorum civilium* – from Dollabella to Cassius to Antony to Octavian and not only surviving, but prospering. He was the one who convinced Cleopatra to come to Tarsus and was undoubtedly Plutarch's source for the barge description. He is also supposed to have written *epistolae lascivae* to the Queen. None of these Romans were likely to have been quite the soft-hearted souls with a secret crush on the Queen, but their names and their presences have been invoked over the years.

1.3 Her beauty and her race

Up until about seventy-five years ago, most biographers would have accepted the prevailing pop culture image of Cleopatra as beautiful and white. This image sat well not only with our Shakespearian tragic queens, but also with our readings of Augustan poets like Propertius and historians of the Roman era such as Dio Cassius. But since the publication of several not so flattering coins and portrait heads said to be of her, the disastrous reception of the Liz Taylor movie and the impact of the British Museum/Chicago exhibition,[17] the reception has taken an ugly turn.

In the hands of specialists, the epigraphical evidence from Egypt itself is helping to clarify Cleopatra's role in religion and the Ptolemaic administration, but since the images are stylized and cultic in nature, they do little to address the question at hand. Coinage[18] is the most reliable evidence for almost any aspect of Cleopatra's life and career, since the coins are usually dateable and convey titles and other data of actual historical value, but they represent isolated periods and several were minted in Cyprus and Askalon and may not have circulated widely. Regrettably, we have no examples of a gold coin issue which are generally more detailed and artful, but some of the bronze coins reveal some her signature profile with a prominent nose, headdress or diadem and hair style dubbed as a Melonenfrisur. None are ugly and some are more flattering than others. The same cannot be said for coins of her later years. These were from her thirties and were intended to bolster her image as a Queen in the Ptolemaic tradition and a worthy ally of a Roman general. The hair style and Greek style clothing are consistent with the older versions, with the addition of 'Venus rings' at her neck. Some of them are quite unflattering. But these coins did enable twentieth-century scholars to identify some busts as possible Cleopatras, but as Peter Higgs warns us, 'A snake, a hooked nose, large eyes and a melon-hairstyle do not a Cleopatra make.'[19] We should recall that for the study of her reception during antiquity, it does not matter so much what she looked like as what people thought she looked like and how that affected their perceptions of her, her actions and her impact on history.

There are a few possible artefacts which would point to an Augustan era reception of Cleopatra's image apart from coinage and sculpture. Susan Walker has advanced an intriguing thesis that the Portland vase was intended to represent Augustan propaganda themes about Cleopatra.[20] She dates it to the reign of Augustus. To summarize her bold thesis, she posits that Figure A[21] is Antony being driven by Eros (Figure B) into the arms of Cleopatra (Figure C) who is accompanied by a sea monster alluding to her as the source of his navy and her death; while Anton (Figure D) looks on in despair of his descendant as the eastern whore literally drags him down to her level. On the opposite side, Figure E is Octavian, concerned for his grieving sister Octavia (Figure F), while Venus Genetrix (Figure G) attempts to console her. The ideology of the scene is quite Horatian in casting Cleopatra as the *fatale monstrum*, but one every bit as lovely as Octavia and Venus.

Whatever her actual appearance, it seems clear from the visual record that Cleopatra was being recalled as a beautiful woman as early as the reign of Augustus himself. Both Caesar and Cicero knew Cleopatra and wrote about her but neglected to describe her or rate her beauty.[22] There may have been a few still alive who had seen her when she visited Rome in the 40s, and her gilded statue may have been on display in the Forum of Julius. Given that she had caused Antony to reject one of the great beauties of the day – Octavia – and that her coinage would not have circulated in the west, it is not unreasonable to posit a reputation for some beauty. Horace too neglected any comment on her looks in either *Epode* 9 or *Ode* 1.37, even though he could have had a second-hand account of her from Quintus Dellius whom he addresses in *Ode* 2.3. Since Dellius was in high favour with Augustus for deserting to him right before Actium with Antony's plans, he was clearly a known figure in Horace's circle. It is not unreasonable to conclude that his observation on Cleopatra could have come to the attention of two in that circle who did comment, at least indirectly, on her beauty – Virgil and Propertius.

In Virgil's case the attribution was indirect. As Janice Benario demonstrated, Virgil is drawing a comparison of Cleopatra and Dido.[23] Dido is lovely indeed and the inference for the other *regina* is undeniable. Propertius too offers no explicit assertion of her beauty, but since he includes her in a list of famous beauties, the inference is clear. Thus, it appears more than likely that at the time of the intense propaganda against Cleopatra, there was a clear assumption that among her many allurements was her physical beauty. It is useful to remember that effective propaganda does not have to be true, just plausible. Since the overall effect of the campaign was to cast Cleopatra as a prostitute, why would this be an effective part of a propaganda campaign? Because, in the words of Lucy Hughes-Hallett, Octavian needed for her

> [...] to stand for everything that a man who wishes to be truly great, truly manly, must reject. Like any temptation worthy of the name, Cleopatra, she-who-must-be-renounced, is all but irresistible. She is femininity, exoticism,

sex and self-indulgence. She is also luxury, pleasure and peerless beauty. She is Woman epitomized. [...] Octavius and his allies laboured the point of Cleopatra's difference – sexual, ethnic, cultural and moral – from the ideal Roman male.[24]

The superficial element of beauty seems to point to a genealogy of the Cleopatra reception. An eyewitness such as Quintus Dellius brings to Rome a testament to Cleopatra's devastating impact on men in general and Antony in particular. This becomes one of the main talking points of the Augustan spin doctors. By the time it is expressed in the art and writings of the Augustan circle, Vergil and Propertius can include her among the greatest beauties of history. Livy apparently followed this line in the lost books. When Lucan, Dio and others turned their attention to Cleopatra years later, they had ready at hand an established reception of a Cleopatra who did not resemble her now non-circulating coinage. Since this was the consensus of Latin authors, most writers of the Middle Ages followed the premise of Bocaccio: 'She gained glory for almost nothing else than her beauty [...].'[25]

But there was an opposing tradition during antiquity, which endures today for various reasons including racism, opportunities for irony, comic *paraprosdokeia* and familiarity with Cleopatra's coinage or Plutarch. Jeff Tatum is on target:

> I should like to add an observation on this passage, because modern handbooks so frequently misinterpret it – a habit which I attribute to academic bitchiness: we classicists are jealous even of the long dead! By no means does Plutarch describe Cleopatra as physically unattractive, or even plain. In his view, she was simply not a stunner, which is hardly the same thing.[26]

I am not certain that we will ever know exactly what Cleopatra looked like, but I am certain that knowing will not in any way affect an historical understanding of her life. Following the thread of assessments of her beauty does help us to understand that in attempting to reconstruct the events and motivations of her career we must be aware where we are employing authentic sources and where we are sifting through the complex cross-fertilization of the reception of her legend. That legend and its reception started before Actium and has never stopped. As Prudence Jones put it:

Post-antique writers, artists and filmmakers have made Cleopatra's appearance her most significant attribute. She rapidly becomes known primarily for her irresistible beauty and her story transformed from one of political strategy to something more closely resembling Helen of Troy. Cleopatra becomes the ultimate temptation and prize for Roman leaders rather than a ruler in her own right. Indeed, in artistic representations from the renaissance onwards, physical beauty becomes the primary source of Cleopatra's power over men, perhaps because this attribute lends itself to visual expression.[27]

The race of Cleopatra is still hotly debated,[28] especially between those who see her as culturally, if not genetically, 'a mostly Greek thing' as in the *Lizpatra* line and many Afrocentrists who claim that she is Black. The recently announced film starring Gal Gadot has once again sparked the internet trolls to weigh in.[29] Since the nineteenth century, as Scott Trafton shows, Cleopatra has become a 'raced' figure especially for Americans. It is possible that Cleopatra had only 25 per cent Macedonian blood since her grandmother was an unidentified concubine. Huss offers convincing, if circumstantial, evidence that her mother might have been Egyptian,[30] and Shelley Haley's observations on race puts her unknown grandmother in quite another light.[31] There is no compelling evidence to consider her genetically Black or negro, but she was born in the cultural mixing bowl of Alexandria and she lived her life on the continent of Africa. This wide spectrum of possibilities is reflected in her reception. The racial and even racist overtones in her receptions are more reflective of the times in which they were formulated than her own.

1.4 Her early receptions

Cleopatra was hardly dead when the legend took on a life of its own. Horace wrote two poems about the victory at Actium, the first before anyone at Rome knew about her death (*Epode* 9). In the second, the famous Cleopatra Ode (*Ode* 1.37), he begins by echoing the propaganda spin, but midway he takes an ambiguous turn, calling her a *fatale monstrum* (deadly monster) or prodigy of predestination and ends with a definite tone of sympathetic admiration. Horace seems to have appreciated spunk.

Most of the Latin writers who mentioned Cleopatra in passing echoed the imperial line, but also added details about the sordid, the salacious and the sanctimonious. Some of these, especially the propaganda narratives attributed to Augustus and Asinius Pollio, an erstwhile Antonian lieutenant, were the principal sources for the second-century Greek biographer and moralist Plutarch. Since he was working from written documents for the most part, he cannot be considered a primary source, but an early reception.[32]

Since he had written in Greek, Plutarch's narrative was unknown in the European Middle Ages. But Cleopatra's story was well known from the Latin poets and the epitomators of Roman history.[33] Dante placed her in Inferno along with other wanton women, and Boccaccio uses her to show how love of lustful women can undo a man, but also paints a sympathetic portrait in the *Elegy of Fiammetta*. Chaucer includes her among the *Legends of Good Women* as a passionate lover who faces a martyr's end by throwing herself, naked of course, into a pit of snakes.

The Renaissance began officially when Petrarch read Plutarch in Greek, piquing his and other's interest in Cleopatra's story. Interest in her tale exploded in the sixteenth century when Amyot translated Plutarch into French, and North translated the translation into English. This inspired dozens of 'Senecan' dramas in Italy, France, Germany and especially in England. Shakespeare was neither the first nor the last British playwright to tell the story of this 'tragick Queene'. There will be myriad subsequent variations, but no treatment of her is totally free of his influence, especially those that try to deal with both the private passions and the political failures. The Restoration drama of John Dryden, *All for Love*, plays better even though he had reduced it to a pure love story. Indeed, these two competing themes re-echo in the dozens of eighteenth- and nineteenth-century dramas and operas that probe Cleopatra's life and loves. Like Shakespeare and Dryden, they shed much light on the concerns of their own times, but they contributed relatively little to the development of the 'Cleopatra Theme'.

On the other hand, the close of the nineteenth century and changing political and social atmospheres seemed to have sparked a renewed and differently focused attitude toward the Queen. Shaw's 1898 play *Caesar and Cleopatra* is more a study of Caesar as a European liberal versus the hypocrisy of British middle-class conventions, but he also applied his mischievous

Figure 1.1 Postcard of Gertrude Eliot as Cleopatra. From the author's collection.

originality to the figure of Cleopatra. Reacting to the romantic and sentimental tendencies of Victorian literature, he ignores her sexuality and plays up the vain, murderous and sadistic side of the teenager who would be queen. She has a winsome charm, but her petulant histrionics reveal a young girl who can be cruel, capricious and cowardly. Only the impatient tutelage of the Shavian 'old gentleman' starts her on the path to power and passion.

Separating the real from the received, Cleopatra has always been challenging because we know less about her actual life than we would like. Roller and others have done what they can with what we have, but there are still gaps, contradictions and fabrications in the evidence from antiquity. Up until the end of the nineteenth century her reception was primarily conveyed through works intended for the elite: drama, opera and fine art, for example. Only rarely did something appear that was intended for popular culture alone.

There were many other Cleopatra eruptions in the nineteenth century, but in the next chapter we will illustrate the extent to which she had re-entered the popular imagination with the old baggage of the archetypal foreign 'other' and some new pieces of cultural luggage. She once again became a sign for liberated female sexuality and active engagement in public life, but it is a symbol both desired and feared. The difference was going to be the new media that were engaged to advance the scope of her reception.

2

The *Femme Fatale*

The late nineteenth century saw an increased interest in Cleopatra in fiction, drama and art sparked by rising Egyptomania, scholarly reassessment of the Queen and the rise of the 'New Woman'. The most influential writers were George Bernard Shaw,[1] Victorien Sardou and H. Rider Haggard, especially on the emerging field of motion pictures. All three were part of a massive reaction to and revision of Shakespeare's interpretation of North's Plutarch, but neither of the playwrights matched the popularity and reach of Haggard. While not taken very seriously now, he did place two of his novels amongst the *Classics Illustrated* line-up billed as 'the greatest stories by the world's great authors'.[2]

2.1 Cleopatra at the *fin de siècle*

Sir Henry Rider Haggard KBE, the eighth of ten children of a barrister and poet, showed little early promise.[3] Relegated to a grammar school, he failed to qualify for the army or the Foreign Office but did develop a lifelong interest in psychic phenomena. His father got a friend to take him to South Africa as an unpaid assistant. The adventure never led to a career, but it made him into a champion of agricultural reform and a diehard imperialist. Back in England he quickly turned to writing as a career which he would continue to his death. His early works, including *Cleopatra*, are considered his best and were the most successful.

Haggard mastered the lost civilizations/swashbuckler romantic adventure. He recycled his hero and alter ego Allan Quartermain several times. Those were made into films six times and Allan is the prototype for Indiana Jones and numerous spoofs, including Lionel Hardcastle in the TV series *As Time Goes*

By. His work embodies an unabashed enthusiasm for the British Empire in the traditions of his friends Robert Louis Stevenson and Rudyard Kipling.[4]

She (1886) has had almost as great a cultural impact. 'She who must be obeyed' is frequently used, but most frequently out of context. Because of an ill-conceived article attacking fellow writers, Haggard attracted vitriolic criticism and charges of plagiarism which would trail him for the rest of his life. His friend, noted classicist Andrew Lang, came to his defence, and the two would work together on at least three books.[5] Haggard not only wrote a sequel (tricky since Ayesha is a pile of dust at the conclusion of *She*), but also published *She and Allan* in 1921. According to Ellis, there were eleven film versions of the story, but the best known is the 1935 version with Helen Gahagan even though it is set in the Arctic.[6] Classicists can find much to ponder in this tale. It foreshadows *Cleopatra* in its Egyptian back story, imperialist themes, focus on the dangers of the Oriental and especially on Haggard's obsession with what Richard Reeve calls 'the figure of the sexually voracious *femme fatale*'.[7]

Haggard did not treat Cleopatra in a vacuum, nor was he overly indebted to Plutarch or Shakespeare. She was a familiar topic in the nineteenth century, as witnessed by the artworks of Delacroix (1838)[8] and Sir Lawrence Alma-Tadema (1883),[9] and poems by Swinburne (1866)[10] and O'Shaughnessy (1870).[11] Along with Swinburne, Pushkin (1825)[12] and Gauthier (1838)[13] had explored Aurelius Victor's assertion of prostitution.[14] The obsession with her race is reflected in Charlotte Bronte's *Villette* (1853)[15] and in William Wetmore Story's sculpture of 1858,[16] which is described in Nathaniel Hawthorne's *The Marble Faun* (1860).[17] The character of this reception is reflected in a quote from Trafton's excellent book *Egypt Land*: 'Cleopatra was to be for Hawthorne and Story the best kind of Negro of all: almost nude, almost white, almost tamed, almost irresistible, almost dead, completely silent, and very much for sale.'[18] Jacob Abbott's biography[19] undoubtedly increased interest in Cleopatra in America.

It should be obvious that there are several convergences between nineteenth-century obsessions, the psychosexual history of the author and real and/or imagined events from the life of Cleopatra, which can be treated in three broad themes: imperialism, Orientalism and sexuality. Haggard was a lifelong Tory supporter of the Empire and the notion of the 'white man's burden'. His experiences in Africa and his love of ancient Egypt brought an obsessive fascination with all things non-Western. His romantic disappointments perhaps attracted him to manifestations of dangerous sexuality.

Haggard's close friend and consultant was the noted classicist Andrew Lang. The relationship has been carefully documented by J. L. Hilton.[20] Hilton sees Lang's influence primarily in *She* (1886) and in their joint venture *The World's Desire* (1890), an adaptation of Euripides' Helen. He believes that *Cleopatra* was relatively independent of Lang because of the decidedly pro-Egyptian plot[21] and because of the letters from Lang preserved in Haggard's memoirs.[22]

> You will loathe me for the advice, but if I were you I'd put "Cleopatra" away for as long as possible, and then read it as a member of the public. You will find, I think, that between chapters 3 and 8 it is too long, too full of antiquarian detail, and too slow in movement to carry the general public with it. I am pretty certain of this. The style is very well kept up, but it is not an advantage for a story to be told in an archaic style (this of course is unavoidable). For that reason I would condense a good deal and it could be done. You'll find / that/ when you come fresh to it again. [...] I am writing with perfect frankness because, of course, I want it to be A1 in its /genre/ – a dreadfully difficult /genre/ it is. [...] I know you hate altering, so it is /*a prendre ou a laisser*/, this long screed of opinion. Of course I see it is a book you have written for yourself. But the B.P. [British Public] must also be thought of.

Sound advice but ignored by Haggard.

It is a first-person narrative from the point of view of the fictional Harmachis. Charmion, the hand maid, gets more attention than Cleopatra who does not even appear until page 90 in the first chapter of Book Two. Harmachis is a priest of Isis and the direct descendant of the Pharoahs. Like Moses, he barely escapes a purge of all possible golden ones. Crowned in secret, he is to lead the assassination of Cleopatra and the restoration of the kingship. One of the primary agents of the conspiracy is the 'mole' Charmion, who had been planted to manage the coup.

Before her actual appearance, Harmachis's uncle Sepa fills in Cleopatra's back story up to this point (post-Phillipi and pre-Tarsus *c.* 42 BCE) and winds up describing the threat of the 'New Woman' as embodied by the Queen.

> For Woman, in her weakness, is yet the strongest force upon the earth, She is the helm of all things human; she comes in many shapes and knocks at many doors; she is quick and patient, and her passion is not ungovernable like that

of man, but as a gentle steed that she can guide e'en where she will, and as occasion offers can now bit up and now give rein. She has a captain's eye, and stout must be that fortress of the heart in which she finds no place of vantage.[23]

The plan was for Harmachis to gain admission to court as an astrologer/magician, kill the Queen and launch a rebellion. Opportunely he thrashes a

Figure 2.1 Cleopatra wielding a knife. Plate facing p. 152, Haggard 1889.

Nubian gladiator, making way for Cleopatra's procession, when the brute manhandles a spectator. And then he saw her. Haggard spared no adjectives: first he describes in detail her entourage, carriage, clothing (including I believe the source for Theda Bara's bra)[24] and a thorough survey of every feature of her face. And then, Harmachis notes:

> All those wonders I saw, though I have small skill in telling them. But even then I knew it was not in these charms alone that the might of Cleopatra's beauty lay. It was rather in a glory and a radiance cast through the fleshly covering from the fierce soul within. For she was a Thing of Flame like unto which no woman has ever been nor ever will be. Even when she brooded, the fire of her quick heart shone through her. But when she woke, and the lightening leapt suddenly from her eyes, and the passion-laden music of her speech chimed upon her lips, ah! then, who can tell how Cleopatra seemed? For in her met all the splendours that have been given to woman for her glory, and all the genius which man has won from heaven, and with them dwelt every evil of that greater sort, which fearing nothing, and making a mock of laws, has taken empires for its place of play, and, smiling, watered the growth of its desires with the rich blood of men.[25]

As he becomes royal astrologer and gigolo, the plan advances. Alas, Charmion falls for him, is rebuffed and betrays them all. This part is all Haggard and makes sense only in the context of what Reeve calls 'the sexual imperative'. Harmachis is sworn to love only Isis, but Charmion loves him and betrays him to their mutual enemy who loves no one. Harmachis secretes his phallic dagger only to lose it in bed and utterly fails to consummate the rebellion. Cleopatra then keeps him in her thrall as lover and seer.

Meanwhile, back in Plutarch, the despicable Q. Dellius arrives with Antony's summons to Tarsus. Desperate for advice and cash, Cleopatra turns to Harmachis whose Plan B is to destroy her and the Roman threat by driving them together and tempting her to desecrate a Pharoah's tomb and mummy. With enough money for the barge, she and Antony meet. Distressed by the abandonment and Charmion's confession about the betrayal, Harmachis flees only to emulate an Odyssean shipwreck and sit out a few chapters of Plutarch on Cyprus. Returning battered, altered and posing as a healer named Olympus, he turns the tide at Actium by remote control. His vengeance begins. Within fifty pages, Cleopatra and Antony will be dead.

At first Harmachis remains disguised as Olympus as he manoeuvres both to their dooms. The events are largely Plutarchan, but the *agent provocateur* is Harmachis, such as when he lures Antony away from his hermitage in the Timonium. He is there at the end to whisper his name and his vengeance in the Roman's ear. Since this is not actually her story, Cleopatra dies in the antepenultimate chapter, after a confessional banquet and handy plot summary. 'Olympus' provides the fast-acting painless poison which dispatches Iras. But Harmachis watered Cleopatra's dose so that he can not only reveal himself but also confront her with her crimes and the terrifying shades of her victims. Charmion dies there too, but Harmachis goes on to face the judgement of his fellow priests and to finish his account – almost.

There was little about Haggard's *Cleopatra* that could not be found elsewhere during the nineteenth century. She was the *femme fatale*, a sexual predator, beautiful, Greek (i.e., white), amoral, political and anti-Semitic. But due to his popularity in Britain and America, the image tended to rival that of Plutarch, Shakespeare and Dryden.

The novel clearly influenced Haggard's equally popular contemporary, the French dramatist Victorien Sardou, who among other things added Haggard's new character of Olympus. Starring Sarah Bernhardt in France and Fanny Davenport in the American road show and used as the basis for 1912 Helen Gardner film, it too reinforced a similar image.

Victorien Sardou (1831–1908) was a prolific French playwright who enjoyed considerable success with his well-crafted and visually compelling productions. Many of his plays were made into operas, lyrical dramas and films. However, George Bernard Shaw ridiculed Sardou's flamboyant style and dearth of serious intent as 'Sardoodledom' in a review of the playwright.[26] The review did not address the 1890 production *Cleopatre* but did include its star Sarah Bernhardt in the diatribe.

Sarah Bernhardt (1844–1923) led a colourful life on and off the stage. She was the illegitimate daughter of a Dutch-Jewish courtesan, and her bold choice of roles – many of them male – scandalized and titillated international audiences. Although rather slender and not particularly beautiful, her remarkable stage presence, enchanting voice and gracefully effective gesturing captivated audiences throughout Europe and the Americas. Sardou's melodrama (co-written with Emile Moreau) played to Bernhardt's strengths. It had elaborate sets, sumptuous costumes, music and songs by Xavier Leroux, emotional and actual fireworks and her specialty – a death scene with live snakes. As Dubar notes:

> No-one, neither Rostand nor Catulle-Mendes or any other, better directed and celebrated her person, her style, her silhouette, her delivery, her 'golden voice', her mastery of gesture and acting, her taste (which he shared) for beautiful sets, crowd movements and *tableaux vivants* [...] Sardou places a woman at the heart of his great historical machines – always the same woman: exotic, sovereign and loving, both a mistress to love and a slave to it.[27]

The play, as was the case with *Fedora* (1882), was probably written with Bernhardt in mind.[28] She also appeared in five other Sardou plays: *Theodora* (1884), *La Tosca* (1887), *Gismonda* (1894), *Spiritisme* (1897) and *La Sorciere* (1903). At the time, *Cleopatre* of 1890 was not an overwhelming success, but was staged in America.[29]

Even before the play opened, critics were labelling it as a mere adaptation of Shakespeare's *Antony and Cleopatra*, citing the Messenger scenes in particular.[30] Guy Ducrey makes an excellent argument for Sardou's originality and independence in his introduction to a recent and valuable critical edition of the play which makes the text readily accessible to a new generation.[31] He sums up the difference thus: 'La femme en elle etait toujours reine. Chez Sardou, la reine est toujours femme.'[32]

Sardou's *Cleopatre* was first performed at the Theatre de Porte-Saint-Martin on 24 October 1890. It joined a long list of elaborate productions featuring Egyptian scenery, spurred by Napoleon's campaigns and the general Egyptomania inspired by archaeological discoveries, admirably detailed by Jean-Marcel Humbert. Most were operas, including about fifty Cleopatras.[33] Each of the six tableaux are described in detail in the existing text of the play and some are illustrated in contemporary engravings.[34] Posed illustrations of Mme Bernhardt's Cleopatra costumes are easily found on the internet.

Act 1 opens in Tarsus in 41 BCE where a crowd awaits the arrival of Cleopatra in hopes that she will forestall their punishment for aiding Brutus. Four Roman officers provide exposition. This allows several allusions to Cleopatra's early reign without flagrant violation of the unity of time. Demetrius characterizes the mercurial and contradictory nature of Antony, while Dellius retells Cleopatra's introduction to Caesar and delivers a briefer version of Enobarbus' description, ending with 'Voila Cleopatre'. Sardou's debts to Shakespeare are clear, but the differences are telling. Cleopatra arrives in a chest, not a carpet, carried by Kephren not Apollodorus.[35] The new character Thryseus is clearly a spy from Octavian and the historical Q. Dellius actually deserted Antony on the eve of Actium. They are in stark contrast to the loyal holdovers from Shakespeare, Dercetas and Demetrius. This tension between image and reality sets the atmosphere for the appearance of the principals of the piece. That is heightened by the actual appearance of the barge on stage, replicating many of the elements described in Plutarch (Plut *Ant* 26). They are then left alone on the stage to act out the process whereby Cleopatra transforms herself from accused to seductress, playing to every one of Antony's shortcomings as she reveals her political talents and her passionate nature.[36] It was a role Bernhardt loved to play. The act ends with the acquittal of the locals and Thryseus' realization that he has underestimated the Queen.

Act 2 opens in Memphis around 40 BCE, since the death of Antony's Roman wife Fulvia is pivotal. The setting is a great hall with a view of the Nile and the couple is the very image of the 'inimitable livers'. The idyllic locale and intimate liaison are about to be shattered by some harsh Roman realities. The illusion is darkened immediately by the foreshadowing of Cleopatra's death by a serpent when Antony calls for a snake charmer to which she cries 'Non. Pas de serpents!' and calls for dancers. Antony calls them 'Autres reptiles!' for their supple movements, allowing the Queen to quote Shakespeare's words, 'Serpents du Nil', while introducing a dance sequence. The fragility of this idyll is highlighted by the silly banter between Iras and Charmion. They have convinced themselves that Thyrseus's constant questioning of Charmion and the voluminous notes he takes are a sign of his love. When they read his purloined journal they fail to see that he is a spy for Octavian. Thyrseus's slimy character is underscored by a brief appearance of the hyper loyal Kephren, a stand-in for Plutarch's Apollodorus. The scene concludes with another foreshadowing as Cleopatra explains her desire for a beautiful death.

Here enters a character not from Shakespeare but from H. Rider Haggard! Olympus the doctor and master of magic and poisons was the disguise for

Harmachis after his shipwreck.[37] As in Haggard, he conveys an instant non-disfiguring poison, but this time it is disguised in a pearl, a not-so-subtle allusion to the story told only in Pliny the Elder.[38] There are further intimations of doom when Cleopatra recounts a dream in which Thryseus summons an eagle to rip off her diadem. To distract her, Antony begs her to sing and dance the tale of Nitocris, full of similar foreboding images. Trusty Dercetas and Demetrius arrive with the momentous news that Fulvia is dead and Octavian is on the ascent. Thryseus and the others urge Antony to return to Rome and assert his rights, but he only relents when Cleopatra joins them and even promises grain for Rome. She even insists on strapping on his armour, speeding him on his way and dismissing everyone as she weeps alone by the Sphynx, saying 'Jusqu'a son retour, je suis veuve' ('Until your return, I am a widow').

The third tableau was greatly admired by critics and scholars.[39] Although Act 3 references and condenses the events of 40–32 BCE, it is the shortest of the five acts. Cleopatra and her entourage are languishing on the terrace when they hear joyful songs from a wedding. Her melancholy turns to verbal assaults on Kephren, Olympus and an astrologer until the Messenger from Rome with his news of Antony's marriage to Octavia earns himself an epic stage thrashing so impressive it was commemorated in several engravings. The climax continues to build when a message arrives from Antony ordering Cleopatra to gather her fleet and meet him at Actium.

Act 4 features another elaborate tableau of a Greek house at Actium with a dramatic view of the gulf, a giant signal pyre and a curtained-off bed. Once again, a group of Roman officers await the arrival of Cleopatra and the resolution of a conflict. This time, the focus is on Octavia and her union with Antony. Cleopatra is smuggled onto the bed in a tapestry and concealed there. She observes and comments on the Roman wife who clearly loves Antony. Together they conceive a compromise which Octavia will convey to her brother. Thryseus tries to drive Antony further from Cleopatra by linking her to a series of other lovers after Caesar but goes too far when he invokes first Herod and then the faithful Kephren. As they all argue against her, Antony wavers and demands she be brought to him from the arriving fleet.

Cleopatra parts the curtains and Antony dismisses them all. Hurt, jealousy and recriminations abound, climaxing in Antony's demand that Cleopatra execute the innocent Kephren. She agrees and gives him the poisoned pearl. Antony knocks away the cup, agreeing to reject Octavia and her peace mission. Cleopatra lights the pyre as all cheer the declaration of war it symbolizes. As they do so they remove from the scenery assorted fasces, standards and weapons which reveal a hidden trophy of victory.

The last act has two tableaux, both in Alexandria. The first is a peristyle in Cleopatra's palace overlooking a garden and the sea. The Egyptian fleet has returned in defeat, with Octavian in hot pursuit, thus compressing the events of 31–30 BCE. In the hasty preparations, Kephren assigns the spy Thryseus to defend the most vulnerable gate. Kephren is left to narrate the battle to Olympus, until Antony enters raging at the flight of Cleopatra just described. She declares that she did it because a victory would have led to the defeat of their love![40] Even after this melodramatic sophistry and with a mob in the garden howling for her blood, she rallies all with her planned sorcery and a choral prayer (with stage effects) invoking Typhon who arrives with thunder, rain, lightening and a waterspout!

The sixth tableau opens in a room in the palace in the silence of predawn. Iras and Charmion are aroused to admit a slave bearing the asp in a basket of figs. They and Kephren realize the palace is surrounded by Romans who have not only survived the storm but have been let into the compound by Thryseus the spy. As a desperate last resort, Kephren proposes to murder Octavian in her chambers after she tricks him into sending off his entourage. The descriptions are close to the several paintings and sculptures depicting Cleopatra's failed attempts to seduce Octavian.[41] Antony bursts in, mortally wounded by Thryseus, and dies in her arms. Cleopatra retrieves the asp (portrayed by two live garter snakes) and meets her end.

Audiences loved it, while critics were not kind. Apparently aside from a road tour, there was no revival in France.[42] It was pure theatre and a star vehicle for Sarah Bernhardt. As Dubar notes, 'What prevails for Sardou as much as with Sarah is indeed the taste for exceptional situations, technicalities of the theatre, decorative inventions, external music, in short for all that is not essential.'[43] The play did have a second life in English and in America and was novelized in English in 1891.[44] The British actress Fanny Davenport reprised the role in New York in 1890 and Boston in 1891.[45]

Fanny thus joined a long list of actresses who portrayed Cleopatra on American stages in the nineteenth century. Most of these appear to be versions of Shakespeare's *Antony and Cleopatra* and included the likes of Lily Langtry. Since the Bard was very much part of popular, rather than elite, culture in that century, Cleopatra was a well-known figure. While this is outside the scope of this study, it should be noted that the Victorian period abounded in diverse receptions of the Queen. For general assessments, one should consult Hughes-Hallett, Hamer and especially Wyke.[46]

In his excellent study of American Egyptomania and race in the nineteenth century, Scott Trafton devotes an entire chapter to the reception of Cleopatra, entitled 'Undressing Cleopatra: Race, Sex and Bodily Interiority in nineteenth-Century American Egyptomania'.[47] His detailed analysis of the works of William Wetmore Story, Nathaniel Hawthorne and Edmonia Lewis help to contextualize some of the early twentieth-century notions about Cleopatra.

It may seem odd to pass over *Caesar and Cleopatra* by George Bernard Shaw. The 1898 play created quite a stir as 'Shaw reclaimed her for modern Western society, desexualized her, infantilized her and made fun of her.'[48] But it remained a reception for the elite audience until it was made into a film in 1945. It is hard to consider him an influence on American popular imagination until then and that perhaps owed more to the star power of Vivien Leigh than to Shaw's contrarian portrait. The film will be discussed in Chapter 4.

Of greater impact was the evolution of the 'New Woman' during the *fin-de-siècle* period. This is rather hard to define since it was both a real social/political movement and a literary motif.[49] The image was frequently formulated in a fictional context and/or by virulent critics. As Matthews notes,

> By the turn of the century, magazines and newspapers were filled with discussions of a new type of female personality: The 'New Woman'. The actual term seems to have been coined around 1894, but the type was instantly recognizable, and the name immediately caught on. As a type, the New Woman was young, well educated, probably a college graduate, independent of spirit, highly competent, and physically strong and fearless.[50]

It is not surprising that the historical Cleopatra and her fictionalizations at the hands of Haggard and Sardou could transform her into a representative

2.2 Silent Cleopatras

With the tremendous interest in Cleopatra toward the end of the nineteenth century, it is not surprising that there were some twenty-four silent films about her life and loves, including one of the very first films made. The first talkie did not appear until 1928.[51] Diana Wenzel has done a magisterial job of cataloguing and analysing the ninety-five film versions which had appeared by 2003.[52] She discusses eight of these films in detail, but also includes thematic, social and historical analyses. My debt to her work, as well as to that of Hughes-Hallett, Hamer and especially Wyke, will be apparent.[53] I will restrict myself to a discussion of four of these silent era films in the context of my thesis. Two are lost but deserve our attention and two are not American made. Those films are:

- Georges Melies, *Le vol de la tombe de Cleopatre* (*Robbing Cleopatra's Tomb*), 1899 = Wenzel, no. 1;
- Charles L. Gaskill, *Cleopatra*, 1912, starring Helen Gardner = Wenzel, no. 11;
- Enrico Guazzoni, *Marcantonio e Cleopatra*, 1913, starring Gianna Terribili Gonzales = Wenzel, no. 12;
- J. Gordon Edwards, *Cleopatra*, 1917, starring Theda Bara = Wenzel, no. 16.

The very first Cleopatra film was produced by the father of the medium, Georges Melies. It is notable that it was a horror film – a mummy picture in fact – a genre frequently revisited by the Cleopatra reception in recent decades. The film was only two minutes long and featured an archaeologist who desecrates and attempts to burn a mummy. From the fire emerges a reanimated and vengeful Cleopatra, probably played by Jeanne d'Alcy. Regrettably, no verifiable stills survive of this lost film or even of the actress in costume, but she was quite attractive and appeared in many of her future husband's films. Cleopatra's portrayal as a youthful European beauty will have a long run ahead of it.

Since this was a French production only a few years after the debut of Sardou's play and Haggard's novel, the similarities are probably not accidental. Cleopatra is still beautiful and when her eternal rest has been disturbed, she reacts with violence and power. A French audience could easily envisage Sarah Bernhardt on that screen, while readers of English pulp fiction would have recognized a formidable and familiar *femme fatale*. Although we have very little to go on, it is clear that the incipient film industry was in tune with many aspects of the reception of Cleopatra in nineteenth-century Europe.[54] These traits will also follow the industry to America and Hollywood.

The first stop on that journey was the 1912 version starring Helen Gardner, so overshadowed by the Theda Bara blockbuster that it was revised and reissued in 1918.[55] After her success in short Vitagraph films (especially as Becky in *Vanity Fair*), Gardner formed her own production company and opened a studio in Tappan-on-the-Hudson, about twelve miles north of New York City on the west side of the river. In addition to being a film pioneer, she produced, edited, designed her own costumes, and starred. She left the direction to Charles L. Gaskill, also her lover. Gaskill adapted Sardou's play for the screen with some additions from Shakespeare, perhaps also Plutarch, and certainly his own imagination in the case of the new characters of the slave Pharon and the vengeful Diomedes.[56] It was one of the first feature length films made in America but has until recently been neglected by critics,[57] perhaps because it was not as readily available until TCM restored it around 2000.[58] Since Wenzel has provided a very complete and descriptive narrative of the plot, including a transcription of most of the English title cards, I will limit myself to detailing the influence of earlier sources and receptions, especially Sardou.[59]

The first six or seven scenes are a departure from Sardou's scheme but do reflect a theme he shared with Gauthier and others who followed the reference in Aurelius Victor to Cleopatra's practice of giving a man a night of sex in return for his death.[60] Here it is a slave named Pharon, a fisherman who is madly in love with the Queen and himself the object of the unrequited affections of the handmaiden Iras. Condemned to death for presenting flowers to the Queen, she offers him ten days of pleasure. He accepts, but on the fifth day his master (and Cleopatra's cousin) Diomedes proposes marriage to the Queen. Gaskill is not only rejected but whipped and defects to the Romans and Antony. On the tenth day, Pharon dutifully drinks the poison, but Iras gives him an antidote.

When a message arrives from Antony summoning Cleopatra to Tarsus, Pharon decides he must live in order to protect her. None of this is in Sardou, but it all reflects the general nineteenth-century reception of Cleopatra as well as some specific elements already noted. Most importantly it fills in the traditional descriptive elements found in Haggard and his predecessors, but especially the poetic description passages uttered by Enobarbus in Shakespeare and Quintus Dellius in Sardou. A silent film title card can only carry short quotes, such as when Diomedes warns Ventidius in Tarsus, 'It were better for Antony did she never come – for his army is not as powerful as her eyes.' Instead, Helen Gardner has the task of putting Cleopatra's infinite variety on the screen through costumes which she designed, Gaskill's opulent settings and props, and especially through her stylized gestures and exaggerated facial expressions. The static sets and fixed camera put even more burden on the actors. The classical style of stage and silent film acting from this period is an acquired taste, but one can readily see that Miss Gardner was a master of her craft. She manages to convey to a contemporary audience the *femme fatale* described by previous authors. The Pharon storyline is primarily a vehicle for the onscreen characterization and moral assessment of Cleopatra. It also added another name to the growing cast list of known associates, destined to reappear in multiple later receptions, including the one starring Theda Bara.

This process is beautifully illustrated in the Tarsus episode where the film returns to Sardou's scenario. It becomes clear that the Pharon episode has replaced the lengthy exposition and character sketches in Sardou (not to mention Haggard and Gauthier), because we only see the public and political face of Cleopatra as she masterfully mollifies then overwhelms Antony. As the scene opens, the renegade Diomedes warns a fretful Ventidius of Cleopatra's allure. Antony is the majestic Roman triumvir sitting in his chair of power dispassionately dispensing harsh justice on the recently rebellious locals. At the moment of their execution, the barge arrives in the background, just as in Sardou's play, only smaller to accommodate the fixed camera and the small studio of the Helen Gardner Picture Players. The scale might be diminished, but the design is very reminiscent of the well-known Alma-Tadema painting.[61] Although the audience has been shown that Cleopatra is a cruel, arbitrary and vicious maneater and steeped in oriental luxury, decadence and deceit, she descends with slow dignity holding a transparent veil until she stuns the triumvir with her revelation. She strikes a pose reminiscent of pharaonic statues, a defiant suppliant admitting no guilt. When she fixes Antony with her gaze, Diomedes' words prove prophetic. Cleopatra's gestures and looks become less subservient and more seductive, first replacing Antony in his chair, then bringing him to her side (but seated lower) and finally leading the besotted Roman to her ship and on to Alexandria.

The film continues on, conveying a faithful, if condensed, adaptation of the Sardou play when they return to Egypt. The debauched life of the inimitable lovers is portrayed with the omission of the subplot about Octavian's spy and the presence of the Pharon arc. One addition is quite remarkable, however: Cleopatra dances. This is apparently the only instance in surviving films where the character dances as Cleopatra.[62] When she receives the news of Antony's marriage to Octavia, Cleopatra briefly assaults the Messenger in the tradition of Sarah Bernhardt.

At Actium, the homage to Sardou continues with the intercession of Octavia, whose simple make-up and gestural self-control put her in sharp contrast to her rival. Gaskill keeps Sardou's device of transferring the carpet trope from Caesar, has Diomedes repeat the tale of Cleopatra's promiscuities and finally uses the signal pyre that indicates the final battle. Sardou's play did have some American performances, so these may have been anticipated by a portion of the movie audience. Due to budget and logistical issues the film was only able to depict the battle with close-ups of Antony and Cleopatra, although in fairness it should be noted that even Sardou narrated it in retrospect back in Alexandria.

The remainder of the film follows Sardou in broad outline. Antony attempts to kill himself on false news of Cleopatra's death. He is then delivered to Cleopatra in her mausoleum where he can die in her arms. Octavian meets with her where she attempts to kill and/or seduce him. In a major departure from Sardou, a disguised Pharon delivers the fatal serpent as a final service to his beloved Queen, still wearing his slave clothes under his disguise. Finally, Gardner dies in a writhing agony worthy of Sarah Bernhardt herself.

Cleopatra was not unknown to American popular culture at the turn of the twentieth century. Stage performances of Shakespeare's Tragick Queen were enjoyed by the general public at least in urban theatres and her image abounded in sculpture and painting, often with a racial twist. Gardner's Cleopatra becomes even more pivotal in this context. The Plutarchan narrative remains intact, but gone are assumptions that she is Black, a mother or shackled by constraints of virtue or reason. She is now the dangerous Oriental, a threat to male hegemony and a sharp contrast to the decorous Octavia or even her amorous maids. Cleopatra is the Victorian nightmare, the *femme fatale*, straight off the pages of H. Rider Haggard and the stage of Victorien Sardou. Helen Gardner was the first American film actress to attempt to transfer the allure of Edmonia Lewis's sculpture and the golden voiced passion of Sarah Bernhardt to the silent screen. While the primitive camera work, the tinted static scenes and the early and highly stylized acting are a barrier to full modern appreciation, Gardner almost singlehandedly made Cleopatra into a screen vamp for American audiences.

Although successful, Gaskill's *Cleopatra* was quickly overshadowed by Enrico Guazzoni's *Marcantonio e Cleopatra* (1913).[63] Guazzoni's film is on a much grander scale, with lots of extras, elaborate sets, sumptuous costumes, live leopards and pythons, more advanced lighting, outdoor scenes and lots of action. There are processions, battles, boats and triumphs throughout. Since Guazzoni produced, directed, wrote and arranged the sets and costumes, there is an unmistakable artistic unity to this film. The attractive star, Gianna Terribili Gonzales, gives an emotional and highly sexualized performance of the now familiar Oriental *femme fatale*. In spite of the title, the film is not an adaptation of Shakespeare, used Plutarch sporadically and does not show any obvious influences from the likes of Haggard or Sardou. A more probable source might be parts of the Italian play (*poema drammatico*) *Cleopatra* (1876) by Pietro Cossa,[64] but for the most part it seems to have sprung from the imagination of its auteur.[65]

Marcantonio e Cleopatra is not an accurate or even sympathetic portrait of the Queen and her liaison with Mark Antony. The meeting at Tarsus and the Battle of Actium are reimagined in Egypt. The non-Plutarchan stories about Cleopatra's experiments with poisons and deadly nights with doomed lovers are included. Pearls abound, but she never drinks one. Octavia's visit to Antony, Charmian's infatuation with him and the Egyptian plot against him are also fabricated or expanded. The portrait is of an archetypal *femme fatale*,[66] as Maria Wyke notes:

At the close of the film, like the nineteenth-century, sexually voracious *Killer-Kleopatra*s of Alexander Pushkin, Pietro Cossa, Victorien Sardou, Theophile Gautier, or Rider Haggard, she has become a murderous sorceress (returning to the witch to obtain poisons which she proceeds to test out on her slaves).[67]

Wyke also explores the relationship between the *Killer-Kleopatra*[68] and the nineteenth-century obsession with Orientalism.[69] Closely linked with European colonialism and racism, it portrayed the East as inferior but dangerously alluring. The dangerous female (*femme fatale*, vamp or *la belle dame sans merci*) is depicted as literally or symbolically an Oriental. In spite of her Macedonian blood lines, this was applied easily to Cleopatra thanks to Augustan propaganda and Shakespeare. As Wyke notes:

> Appropriated for nineteenth-century orientalism, Cleopatra authorizes the articulation of the Orient as Woman, as separate from and subservient to the Occident. Feminized, the Orient can take on, under the gendered western gaze, a feminine allure and penetrability. The colonialist project is provided with an ancient and successful precedent and geographical conquest of a land is naturalized as sexual possession of a woman's body.[70]

Wyke further extends this line of criticism to the film's association with Italian imperialistic expansion in North Africa at the expense of the Ottoman Empire.[71] Whatever the merits of that line of criticism,[72] it would have been largely lost on its American audiences, where the film was very successful. A key factor in that success was the George Kleine Attractions (GKA) organization and its all-out effort to distribute and market the film in North America. GKA recognized the potential market for the longer European films, with their enhanced production values, and decided to market them in larger, upscale venues, with enhanced advertising and promotions and with specially composed music.[73]

Music historian James Doering unearthed the score for this film during his research in the Library of Congress on the composer George Colburn.[74] He has been able to study the piece and to restore enough to actually perform it in accompaniment to the existing film preserved in several different forms. The print at the Library of Congress appears to be from the Kleine version. I can attest that the performance of this score greatly enhances the viewing experience. The score was designed either to be played by an orchestra or in its piano only arrangement. The discovery has brought light to the importance of the study of silent film music, but also given us a clearer picture of how this film might have been received by an even wider audience.

By playing in larger venues – even actual theatres – and attracting a more sophisticated audience with the lure of well-played relevant music, GKA greatly expanded its market and potential for profits in the United States. Cleopatra had always been popular in nineteenth-century productions of Shakespeare and various opera, but with this film she actually became known to a popular as well as an elite audience. The Cleopatra they were going to see was going to be the *fin-de-siècle* version, the *femme fatale* or 'Killer Kleopatra' nurtured by Haggard, Sardou and Pucci – a vamp. *Marcantonio e Cleopatra* certainly laid the foundations for the most famous American version.

Although only a few seconds have survived, the 1917 film starring Theda Bara is usually discussed as one part of the great trilogy including the 1934 Claudette Colbert and of course the 1963 Elizabeth Taylor versions to the exclusion of the ninety-two other attempts.[75] It had an impressive pedigree: produced by William Fox, directed by J. Gordon Edwards and screenplay by Adrian Johnson. Theda Bara was at the height of her brief career and already locked into the vampire type by the emerging star system in the new home base of American filmmaking: Hollywood, California.

Born Theodosia Goodman, Bara was reputedly a nice Jewish girl from Cincinnati but was quickly cast as the nineteenth-century stage type of the *femme fatale*.[76] Her breakthrough film was *A Fool There Was* (1915) which was introduced by Rudyard Kipling's 1897 poem, 'The Vampire', perhaps inspired by his cousin's painting of the same name exhibited that same year.[77] As Wyke notes, 'Bara was the first American film actress to have a star image manufactured for her by studio press agents and this image was heavily invested in nineteenth-century Orientalist constructions of Egypt.'[78]

The Fox publicity office created an elaborate, outrageous and utterly fictitious backstory for Bara and her role as Cleopatra and she seems to have played her part, going so far as to claim to the press, 'I know that I actually am a reincarnation of Cleopatra. It is not a mere theory in my mind. I have positive knowledge that such is the case. I live Cleopatra, I breathe Cleopatra, I *am* Cleopatra.'[79] Perhaps Dan Marquis was parodying this when he had the cat Mehitabel declare that she was a reincarnation of the Queen.[80] The vamp persona was rapidly becoming, as did Bara herself, a joke, but in the early silent era it could still pack theatres. A vamp is hard to define with precision and easier to describe in detail,[81] but for a succinct characterization, I offer F. Scott Fitzgerald: 'She was got up to the best of her ability as a siren, more popularly a "vamp" – a picker up and thrower away of men, an unscrupulous and fundamentally unmoved toyer with affections.'[82] Dye (2020) has a wide-ranging discussion of this genre in his recent book.

There were other actresses playing vamps in silent films, while its predecessor, the *femme fatale*, had long been associated with Cleopatra. Theda Bara and this film, however, linked the two and stoked the fires for the acceptance of or resistance to another *fin-de-siècle* phenomenon: the 'New Woman'.

The 'New Woman' was a term that began to circulate in the United States from the 1890s, its coinage signalling a recognition of (and debate about) an evident shift away from the nineteenth-century conception of woman's place of operation as properly limited to the home, marriage and the family. Concern about women's demands for the right to vote, to limit their fertility and actively to express their sexual desires was linked to concerns about immigration and expressed by eugenicists in terms of the dangers of miscegenation.[83]

Although the film is lost, there is general agreement on the broader outlines of the plot based on the studio press packets, publicity stills and other evidence.[84] Remarkably, the film covers Cleopatra's relationship with both Julius Caesar and Mark Antony. Of all the silent films, only one even features Caesar.[85] This film sets the standard for the reception of Cleopatra on film and in many novels. From now on, her story must be told from the beginning of her reign. Since none of the alleged sources of the plot (Shakespeare, Haggard or Sardou) include Caesar, it is likely to be the original contribution of the screenwriter Adrian Johnson.[86]

The film opens with Cleopatra planning to regain her throne after being expelled from Alexandria. They are deadly enemies headed for a confrontation, but when she emerges from the carpet, Caesar succumbs completely to Cleopatra's charms and her dreams of empire. While Caesar is in Rome, Pharon, a priest of Osiris and a direct descendant of the Pharoahs, plots the overthrow of Cleopatra and restoration of Egypt. Borrowing the name of a slave in the Gaskill film, this character is virtually identical to the protagonist of Haggard's novel named Harmachis. Meanwhile back in Rome, Caesar is assassinated.

Pharon (Harmachis) arrives in Alexandria disguised as an astrologer in order to kill Cleopatra. He attracts her attention when he assaults one of her guards for manhandling onlookers. She appoints him court astrologer, he falls in love with her and reveals he knows of a fortune in a Pharoah's tomb, all plot points from Haggard's novel. This connection can explain the origin of the iconic snake bra which Theda Bara wears.[87] When Harmachis meets her, we find this description: 'Her breast was bare, but under it was a garment which glistened like the scaly covering of a snake, everywhere sewn with gems.'[88] When he finally attempts to kill her, she literally disarms him and threatens him with his own knife, which I think explains the publicity still where she is wearing the snake bra and brandishing a dagger (see Fig. 2.2).[89] I think that this costume was inspired by a reading of Haggard. Dye attributes the costumes to Clare West and the jewellery to Adolph Feil.[90]

After Philippi, Antony summons Cleopatra to Tarsus, but she needs cash. She convinces Pharon (Harmachis) to betray both his ancestors and his co-conspirators to rob the tomb by promising to marry him. Once she has the

Figure 2.2 Theda Bara with knife and snake bra. From the author's collection.

money, the plot can return to the traditional Plutarchan narrative, so she drops Harmachis, ensnares Antony and leads him to Alexandria where they embark on the inimitable life until he has to return to Rome and wed Octavia. Even that cannot keep him from the arms of Cleopatra. They are portrayed as genuinely in love. There are no children, but those are rare in a vamp narrative.

Octavian declares war and they meet at an actual naval battle off the coast of California. When she gets an erroneous report of Antony's death, Cleopatra abandons the battle and Sardou's plot line. Antony pursues her back to Egypt, hears a false report of her death and stabs himself ineffectually. He is carried to her as she is pleading with Octavian for his life and expires. Pharon returns to bring the asp to his beloved as in the Gaskill version. Cleopatra now joins Antony in death. In Haggard, Harmachis deceived her with a slow-acting poison.

The Bara film enjoyed great success, reportedly one of the top releases of 1917. No data survives, but Bara herself claimed that the epic grossed a million dollars,[91] quite an achievement since it reportedly cost $500,000 to make.[92] It certainly gave the historical Cleopatra a higher profile, setting off another round of Cleomania,[93] though she had never completely fallen off the radar. Even a pop philosopher like Elbert Hubbard could include a story about Caesar and Cleopatra among his musings to illustrate his aphorism 'When power and beauty meet, the world would do well to take to its cyclone-cellar.'[94] But since the hype was more about the star than the subject, it could not be taken too seriously, as Wyke notes:

> [Female audiences . . .] understand with Bara that her brand of femininity is playfully performative and therefore, if anything, it is more appealing. Divested of any real danger or sin, her masquerade as Cleopatra offers a momentary escape from the everyday domestic constraints of a traditional femininity into an Orient figured (both on and off screen) as home to a woman of formidable power and sexual passion.[95]

This detachment is perhaps reflected in humorous takes on the film and its star. I have already mentioned the allusions in the 'archie and mehitabel' series, where Bara's claim to reincarnation is spoofed. In Chick (Ukulele Ike) Endor's popular song of 1924 ('Who Takes Care of the Caretaker's Daughter') there is a line, 'I know that [...] Cleopatra was a Vamp.' Bara's image and career were becoming a campy joke evoking laughter.[96] By the time Bara died, she had been spoofed by Marilyn Monroe, Lucille Ball and Spike Jones.[97]

As has been so admirably demonstrated by Hughes-Hallett and her successors, the interest in Cleopatra and her reception in all forms of art and literature have hardly waned since her own lifetime. The Cleopatra legend began halfway through the *Cleopatra Ode* (Horace *Ode* 1.37) and has never stopped evolving. She was well known in the nineteenth century through sculpture, painting, novels, opera and the stage. Much of this was confined to what we consider to be elite culture, although Shakespeare, for example, could be considered a form of popular entertainment in nineteenth-century America. But things began to change toward the end of that century. Novels such as those written by Haggard were also pulp fiction, often serialized in periodicals. Theatre began to appeal to the masses with the ascendancy of stage stars such as Sarah Bernhardt, Fanny Davenport and Lilly Langtry. None of the above could reach the mass audiences and/or every corner of a large country like the United States of America until the advent of motion pictures. After that, a performance could be frozen in time and opened in any venue with a projector – piano optional. Cleopatra was a ready commodity for distribution in the two dozen silent films about her that were produced. The fact that several of the more successful owed their origins to nineteenth-century popular hacks like Haggard, Sardou and their colleagues indicates that like the Roman mob and the Elizabethan groundlings, there was a market for the tarted-up tale of this complex woman. Gardner brought her story to long-form film narratives; Guazzoni lured audiences with high production values and stirring music; and Bara assaulted the sensitivities of her audience with her sexuality, tragedy and power. There could not have been very many residents of the USA who did not know of her by 1918. And that could only lead to change.

2.3 Pulp fiction

Such good material could not be restricted to just the genre of film. The earliest serious attempt is little known[98] but notable. C. Edith Ironmonger's *Cleopatra, A Narrative Poem* (1924) conveys, as Hughes-Hallett noted, 'an atmosphere of eroticized violence',[99] but clings closely to the Plutarchan narrative with numerous echoes of Shakespeare. In Ironmonger's own words, 'History in the mantle of Romance appears.'[100] While no clear connections to contemporary writers can be drawn, Ironmonger does reflect a general trend toward the emphasis on Cleopatra's intellect, as seen in these lines:

> Nature in lavish mood sometimes designs
> A perfect body, and with this combines
> A mind of rare proportions, balancing
> With due carefulness the whole, allowing
> The claims of each upon the other just,
> The body suffering not from the brain's lust,
> Nor the brain starving at the body's feast.[101]

Talbot Mundy (William Lancaster Gribbon, 1879–1940) was a British-born American writer of pulp fiction who became a Christian Scientist and a follower of the Theosophical Society movement. Although little known and less regarded now, he was quite popular as a writer of adventure fiction for the pulp magazines and is the subject of two well documented biographies.[102] Before moving to America, he spent time in India and East Africa, experiences on which he drew for his early fiction. His breakthrough came in 1912 when *The Soul of a Regiment* earned him a cover illustration on *Adventure*,[103] followed by the publication of *King of the Khyber Rifles* in 1917. The latter brought comparisons with Rudyard Kipling and H. Rider Haggard[104] – odd, since he did not share their enthusiasm for colonialism.[105]

Mundy's debt to Haggard was more stylistic than substantive. His recurring character Yasmini owes much to Haggard's Ayesha ('She who must be obeyed'),[106] but he avoided direct comparison by limiting his novel to Cleopatra's relationship with Caesar, while Haggard focused on her final years. One of his strengths was 'in creating believable, multi-dimensional women'.[107] Mundy clearly had this in mind when he wrote in a 1924 letter to his publisher:

> Cleopatra is shaping up no end well. You'll like her. So will the public. She is evolving as a human being possessed of intelligence, courage and charm, well loved by her friends and cordially hated by her enemies. She was not by any means the lecherous, treacherous she-devil that historians have made

her out to be, but a most royal lady pitched into the cauldron of intrigue and handicapped by the Ptolemy heritage and reputation, which was murderous, incestuous and unreliable.[108]

Mundy also made his Cleopatra more spiritual as a vehicle to express his own Theosophical beliefs, as he did in many of his Eastern stories.[109] Since his publisher insisted on draconian cuts to the manuscript, it did not get published until 1929 to mixed reviews.[110] By then, Barrington's novel was appearing as a serial in *The Delineator*.[111] Mundy briefly revisited Cleopatra with less success in *Purple Pirate* (1935).[112]

It is clear from his correspondence that Mundy used Weigall extensively, most probably the 1914 edition, although he did not follow him in every detail.[113] Mundy did commend Weigall in one particular area – his emphasis on Roman interests in India for trade and conquest.[114] Given Mundy's professional and literary connections with India, this is hardly surprising. For example, he has Caesar proclaim, 'I will conquer India.'[115] Cleopatra encourages Caesar to study and lust for India in order to divert him from Egypt.[116] Later she suggests a sea assault on India by building the Suez Canal![117]

Mundy's most significant contribution to the popular conception of Cleopatra was to follow Weigall's lead away from the Eastern whore of Augustan propaganda. There was to be substance behind the glamour:

> Because she was young and for ever apparently gay, most gloriously dressed and bent on having the most splendid court the world had ever known, it escaped men's observation that behind that mask of gaiety and scented luxury she was a thinker, with a lightning intuition that could read most hidden motives and with a smile that concealed her knowledge.[118]

2.4 Demise of the vamp[119]

The vamp or *femme fatale* or maneater was about to lose her appeal with American film audiences. Theda Bara had lots of competitors such as Helen Gardner, Olga Petrova, Nita Naldi, Pola Negri and others. With the possible exception of Myrna Loy, none of them were able to escape the label. It was very frustrating to Bara when her audiences could not accept her in any other role. The image of the *femme fatale* had been around since antiquity under many

Figure 2.3 Helen Gardner as Cleopatra. Screen shot from Gaskill 1912.

guises and would reappear later especially in *film noir* and pulp fiction novels, but after Bara's last film for William Fox in 1919 her career went into decline along with public fascination with bad girls. Unfortunately, most of these films are now lost due to the instability of nitrate film and lack of interest in silent films after the advent of sound. Since even Bara's own personal copies were unusable, few of them were even available to be rediscovered. Changing film styles were perhaps not the sole reasons for evolution. Postwar culture changed and the status of women with it. America was exposed to the wider world, especially India, the Orient and Eastern philosophies. The image of Cleopatra as a representative of feminine power, Eastern mysticism and the 1920s American flapper was about to burst onto the pages of magazines, novels and talkies.

3

A Kinder, Gentler Cleopatra

Although the Cleopatra as vampire theme began to wane along with the film careers of Theda Bara and her rivals, it never completely disappeared – as evidenced by the cases of Talbot Mundy and Edith Ironmonger – but began to be replaced by a less fearsome but still highly sexualized Cleopatra. In part this reflected the continuing influence of the 'New Woman' movement, which was evolving to include a broader perspective on sexuality. As Matthews notes:

> Women were indeed human beings, but they were also sexual beings, and should not that sexuality be given full recognition and freedom? Like older women activists, they bitterly attacked the sexual 'double standard'; but instead of insisting, like their mothers' generation, that men must be held to the same strict standards of sexual continence and fidelity as women, a few feminists were beginning to think that some degree of sexual latitude might be good for both sexes.[1]

The interwar period (roughly 1918–34) reflected these changes with the inevitable contradictions and exceptions in a number of areas. A number of factors contributed to the societal shifts which gave way in general to the 'Roaring Twenties'. In simplified terms, the causes of this are frequently attributed to the relief felt at the end of the horrors of the 'Great War', to the passage of the constitutional amendment giving American women the vote and to the almost Thucydidean reaction to the influenza pandemic that killed millions worldwide. This 'kinder, gentler' Cleopatra first manifested herself in the USA in print advertising by encouraging American women to emulate Cleopatra's beauty regimen. This shift was also reflected in some more flattering biographies, humorous fiction and glamorous films during this period.[2]

3.1 Advertising and Palmolive Soap 1909–29

'Everybody's Making Like Cleopatra' is the title of an article in *Colliers* in 1954,[3] celebrating yet another round of Egyptomania in American popular culture. The range of that influence is boldly displayed on the first page, with a Helena Rubenstein model in stark contrast to comedienne Imogene Coca who 'goes Egyptian'. This particular layout embodies the 'Mid Century Modern or Peplum Cleopatra' as it had been shaped by the images of the previous forty years and shows where it was to lead in the next half-century. It is no surprise that Cleopatra would be invoked in the advertising of all sorts of products throughout the twentieth century. Given her image, using her to sell fragrance, beauty and luxury items is not surprising, although some of the other choices are puzzling.[4]

In the DVD commentary to HBO *Rome 2*,[5] James Purefoy noted that he and Lindsay Marshall had decided to focus on the moist food they were consuming as a reflection of their characters' hedonistic natures. This can help to explain the number of ads for candies, fruits (Mission Citrus), bourbon (Jim Beam), a Cleo Cola, Dr Pepper (with Judy Tenuta),[6] sparkling water (Scweppes), Ovaltine and beer (Budweiser). Since tobacco and cigarettes were an important export from modern Egypt, Cleopatra was featured in several tobacco ads, in collectible Leibig meat extract cards and various brands of cigarette cards that were once quite popular, as well as in *Antonio y Cleopatra* cigars.

Increasingly Cleopatra's image and name were used to market products to women. The story told by Pliny the Elder that she dissolved a pearl in vinegar and drank it to win a bet with Antony encouraged an association with jewellery as in a Cartier pearl ad. The story of her opulent barge trips to Tarsus and up the Nile inspired an association with travel reflected in ads such as those for Northwest Orient Airlines when air travel could still be considered a luxurious pleasure. As an icon of luxurious travel since Shakespeare and reinforced by films, cars such as the Plymouth, Packard and Huckins could pitch themselves through Cleopatra.

Perhaps Cleo was not 'a nightmare dressed like a daydream',[7] but there were stories about her preference for near transparent Coan silk, so the association with fashion is a natural one, especially with stockings and other lingerie. She is called upon to market Fantasia Furs, Marquise shoes, hosiery by Belle

Sharma, Silktrique and Hanes and bras by Goddess, Warners and, most familiarly, Maidenform, which referred to 'playing' Cleopatra on the stage or screen.

There was a loose miscellany of other products targeted primarily for women. Needles, both sewing and phonograph, were probably suggested by the Obelisk erroneously named 'Cleopatra's needle'. A Blu-White detergent ad was part of a *Caesar and Cleopatra* film tie-in campaign. The fairly recent Poise television ad featuring Whoopie Goldberg is a hilarious short feature which actually broaches several themes in the Cleopatra reception including race, gender and sexuality.[8]

One product in particular seems to have been at the forefront of this trend, although Palmolive was not the first or only beauty product to invoke Cleopatra. A lost treatise on cosmetics was attributed to her, but as with her treatise on poisons, it is likely a spurious attribution.[9] Her reputation as a beauty (in spite of Plutarch's assertions) perhaps makes this inevitable. The Goya perfume and Revlon eye shadow ads reflected the many movie tie-in promotions around the 1963 film. There had been many similar campaigns associated with the Colbert version.[10] But there were also independent perfume ads from Rigaud and Quinlan and talc from Cleopatra's Rose, deodorant from Desert Dri and Summer's Eve, African American hair products from Posner and quite recently Cover Girl make-up featuring singer Katy Perry in full Cleopatra regalia.

Given the wide range of products which evoke beauty, luxury or feminine elegance, bath items, such as Ramses soap, were a natural association. Bathing in asses milk was actually associated with Claudette Colbert playing Poppaea in DeMille's *Sign of the Cross* (1932), but bathing is also featured in *Lizpatra* and other films, so the association with Cleopatra is not unexpected. What was remarkable was the almost eighteen-year campaign which tied Palmolive Soap to the Queen. By the time it concluded it had also helped to change and soften her image, though only temporarily.

The Palmolive Soap campaign of 1911–29 is perhaps the longest running and most successful Cleopatra-related advertising campaign.[11] As part of a nationwide trend away from harsh but cheap homemade lye and animal fat soap, the BJ Johnson Soap Co. of Milwaukee had developed a vegetable oil-based cleanser using palm and olive oils.[12] It was mild enough for facial use, but was green and had an odd but not unpleasant odour. There was also a lot of competition. BJ Johnson took it to admen Albert D. Lasker and Claude Hopkins of the Lord and Thomas Agency in Chicago, who suggested selling it not as a cleanser, but as a beauty product and marketing it via coupons, tokens and their revolutionary concept 'the reason why' style of salesmanship in print.[13] The market test paid for itself before the printing bills came in. Part of the 'reason why' text drew a connection between palm oil, olive oil and the Mediterranean, especially Egypt. By 1916 the ads were including images and text about Cleopatra and sales rocketed. The rationale was that it was an effective beauty product because of its association with a well-known historical beauty. In the process the campaign also dramatically altered the popular image of the Queen, making her seem less threatening and dangerous.

On the surface this could have been a risky choice. The *fin-de-siècle* Cleopatra was a dangerous Oriental man-eating vampire, especially as portrayed in the novel of H. Rider Haggard (1889) and the play of Victorien Sardou and Émile Moreau (1890), as discussed above. According to Diana Wenzel,[14] there were fifteen films featuring Cleopatra between 1903 and 1917, and in the US, Helen Gardner in *Cleopatra* (1912), Gianna Terribili Gonzales in *Marcantonio e Cleopatra* (1913) and Theda Bara in *Cleopatra* (1917) had made the image of the tragic Queen part of popular culture.[15] But Cleopatra had already acquired a solid reputation in the nineteenth century (largely due to Shakespeare) for extraordinary beauty, as attested to in the art and sculpture of that century, for example the Alma-Tadema painting. Since it was part of her legend that Cleopatra had a near scientific interest in cosmetics and perfumes,[16] it was a natural progression for the ads to claim first that the formula for Palmolive was known to the ancient Egyptians and then to link it to the most famous Egyptian known to Americans.

The company, and its admen, exploited this effectively. The Egyptian tie was not a radical shift for the company or the public. This campaign turned out to be pivotal in several contexts: the history of soap and hygiene in America, the evolution of advertising and the transformation of Cleopatra in popular culture from vampire to victim. In the nineteenth century, soap was made cheaply at home, but the lye and potash mixture, although an effective cleanser, was brutal on the toughest skin. Around the turn of the century, many manufacturers began to use vegetable oil bases. Sapolio was one of the first, but

Figure 3.1 Palmolive ad '3000 years ago . . .', c. 1916. From the author's collection.

there was considerable resistance to purchasing it in stores at many times the homemade cost. Sanitation was an important pitch and Lifebuoy went further to claim health benefits and to convince consumers that 'Body Odor' made one a social pariah. About the time BJ Johnson was trying to market its formula, Woodbury dominated the market with premium prices and a little sex.

The genius behind the Woodbury campaign, was a copywriter at J. Walter Thompson who introduced the concept of 'atmospheric advertising' to promote Woodbury as a luxury item which would insure a woman's sexual allure. Lasker called this ad one of the three most significant landmarks in the history of advertising because it broke the taboo against sex in ads.[17] The line 'A skin you love to touch' is still very risqué for 1910, but the brilliant choice of the pronoun 'you' keeps it this side of prurient. Palmolive was to copy this approach with the line 'Keeping that Schoolgirl complexion', adding the element of fear of losing one's youth. That genius behind this approach was Helen Resor.

Helen Landsdowne Resor[18] was a pioneer in American advertising. By 1908 she had become the first female copywriter and by 1910 had revolutionized the industry with her Woodbury soap ads. What she did was add 'the essential emotional appeal to the sales argument' and 'Instead of merely selling soap, the landmark ad also discussed the benefits of using the product, suggesting softness, sex appeal, and even romance.'[19] She wrote copy from a feminine point of view, with an eye to triggering feelings which modern audiences might classify as fear and guilt. Resor established that sex sells a lot of soap. As Sivulka concludes:

> Her words and visuals embraced women's hopes, fears, desires and dreams regardless of what they did for a living. She understood why women might prefer to buy soap over shortening, and so she presented provocative arguments for improving oneself and aspiring to the lifestyle of richer people.[20]

Palmolive would essentially follow Resor's approach, but they had other challenges. By 1921 they too would follow her theme of instilling sexual fears with the addition of the tag line 'keeping that schoolgirl complexion' alongside the Cleopatra images, usually in a bottom quadrant. But their soap lacked the sensory appeal of Woodbury's. As mentioned earlier, it was green and had an unusual fragrance. It was being peddled to grocers alongside BJ Johnson's Galvanic laundry soap and was not selling well as a mere cleaning agent.

In stepped Albert D. Lasker (whose biography is titled *The Man Who Sold America*).[21] Over his long career, Lasker got Warren G. Harding elected president and convinced women to use canned milk and canned meat, to smoke and to use Kotex. Unlike most admen of the day, he did not believe in jingles, outlandish claims or squeaky-clean Dutch towns, but instead believed in what he called 'salesmanship in print'. Like a good pitch man, he knew that with effective writing and clever illustration, he could demonstrate to the consumer 'the reason why' they should buy his goods. When BJ Johnson came looking for a new agency, Lasker put his best man on the job.

The company actually wanted to start a campaign for the Galvanic detergent (a very crowded market), but Claude Hopkins focused instead on Caleb Johnson's entry into the new vegetable oil-based soap market. It employed palm and olive oils to develop a soap mild enough for use on sensitive facial skin. One of the men at the meeting suggested that Cleopatra and Roman women had probably used those oils.[22] Claude Hopkins considered this to be one of his finest moments. He believed in 'scientific advertising' and was a staunch disciple of Lasker's 'reason why' approach. A year before the Woodbury ad, Hopkins had decided to market Palmolive in drug stores as a beauty treatment at the exorbitant price of 10¢ a bar. The copy repeatedly asserted that the reason that the green odd smelling soap enhanced beauty was due to the unique formulation of palm and olive oils. What made that written argument valid was the 'fact' that it was an ancient formula. The first ad appeared in May 1909 in the *Saturday Evening Post*.[23] At the same time, Hopkins launched a campaign in which he told drug store owners that he would be distributing coupons (later tokens) which could be redeemed at any store for a bar of Palmolive and the druggist would be reimbursed for the full dime, which meant they pocketed their discount. The advance orders more than paid for the full-page ad and the mailings.[24] It was such a success that by 1916 BJ Johnson changed the company name to Palmolive. Even after mergers with Peet and Colgate, the name and the soap are still around. The Depression and Second World War may have hurt Colgate-Palmolive, while an attempt to resurrect the Cleopatra connection did not fare well, but the early successes were remarkable.

Since the antiquity of the formula was the basis of the reason why the customer should buy it, the early ads focused on making this connection. In the spirit of the philosophy of 'salesmanship in print', a good deal of space was devoted to written copy. Many of the ads featured an 'authentic' hieroglyphic inscription and its translation which stood as proof that the formula for Palmolive soap was based on an ancient prescription. It read:

1. AS for her who desires beauty
2. She is wont to anoint her limbs with / oil of palm and / oil of olives.
3. There cause to flourish these / ointments like skin.
4. As for the oil of palm / and oil of olives, / there is not there like for revivifying, making / sound and purifying the skin.

Cleopatra was a natural extension of this concept, but 1913 seems to mark her first appearance in the ads. These ads all appeared in magazines targeted at women, such as the *Saturday Evening Post*, the *Ladies Home Journal*, the *Woman's Home Journal*, *Ladies' World* and *The Delineator*. Cleopatra did not appear in all of them, but all the ads invoked ancient Egypt as the source of the secret to beauty. Several that do feature the Queen have her wearing a metallic bra. The one depicted in Figure 3.2 predates the Theda Bara film (1917), appearing in *c*. 1916.

Most depictions of Cleopatra were in Helen Resor's style of 'atmospheric advertising'. Hopkins hired some of the leading illustrators of the day, but in contrast to the silent film queens, most were slender, white, young and non-threatening to male or female. Some of the depictions were indeed quite atmospheric, ghostly figures appearing as visions to the modern women channelling their own Cleopatras (see Fig. 3.1). There was certainly no slavish devotion to historical fidelity, as the campaign frequently used the tag '3000 Years and tonight'.

In the period from about 1919 to 1922, Cleopatra became the major spokesmodel for the brand. The costumes became quite daring, some with the metallic bras and/or a good deal of bare skin. A wide variety of styles were also employed, including Art Deco. Some of the top magazine illustrators were commissioned to provide the artwork and the ads have become quite collectible. Even with the variety of artistic styles and scenes, the ad copy remained consistently focused on the 'reason why' the consumer should use Palmolive: to enhance beauty. The reason it was supposed to work was the antiquity of the formula and the example of the ultimate spokesmodel, Cleopatra.

By 1921 the campaign began to adopt themes of sexual fears and peer emulation, already used by other advertisers. By 1922 the majority of Palmolive ads reflected Resor's approach. Cleopatra begins to be minimized, but she is still there, even if the artwork is recycled. An Egyptian scene would appear in a lower quarter, to reinforce the connection with the original message,

Figure 3.2 Palmolive ad 'Cleopatra's vision', c. 1916. From the author's collection.

and there is frequently a central female figure, though not often clearly exhibiting attributes of the Queen, but the intent was again to maintain the fundamental association. Cleopatra did not disappear entirely, remaining the focus of several very attractive ads, but the primary focus had definitely shifted.

This shift emphasized the fear and emulation themes and featured the tag line 'Keeping that schoolgirl complexion'. The reader was prompted to emulate both Cleopatra through the Orientalizing drawings in the margins and the soft-focus illustration of atmospheric women of indeterminable age. Looking at the range of these illustrations, one can establish a fairly clear picture of the iconography of female attractiveness in the 1920s.[25] While a modern audience might have trouble equating an adolescent complexion with mature beauty, it apparently struck a chord at the time.

The use of fear to motivate female consumers is relentless in this series of ads. Among the more aggressive ads were messages such as, 'The girl women envy and men admire'; 'Why fade at 30?'; 'Not a day older'; 'Will others he meets outrival you in natural charms?'; 'The business girl knows'; 'Better than jewels [...] that schoolgirl complexion'.

In his account of the Colgate-Palmolive company, Foster suggests that its history can be summed up in the phrase '169 years Overcoming Housewife Resistance through Advertising'.[26] But after 1929, the campaign dropped Egyptian and Cleopatra themes and references, perhaps due to the merger with Colgate in 1928–9. Palmolive had already merged with Peet in 1927 and a grand plan was underway to merge with Kraft, Hershey and others to put themselves on par with the industry giant Procter & Gamble.[27] The stock market crash and Second World War put an end to that period of expansion and probably accounts for the shift in advertising focus.

The Cleopatra theme was revived briefly during the Second World War with an ad that appeared in several different formats (see Fig. 3.3). The 1942 headline was 'Cleopatra had nothing on me!', but the footer says, 'Now more than ever [...] keep that schoolgirl complexion.' There is still the 'reason why' copy, but it is much reduced and includes a 'keep the home fires burning' message, with the girl in the arms of a soldier. The flipped Cabanel painting seems an odd choice for an illustration since Cleopatra is topless and the subject (cropped out) is her experimentation with poisons on slaves and prisoners. It was,

Figure 3.3 Palmolive ad 'Cleopatra Had Nothing on Me', 1942. From the author's collection.

however, in the public domain when original artwork would have been expensive and it does reflect the proliferation of bare arms and shoulders in the photographs. Just as with rubber and aluminum, wartime required recycling of ads as well. Since Lasker sold the Lord and Thomas agency to his executives in 1943, it is not surprising that we do not see the Cleopatra connection for several decades. The schoolgirl complexion line, however, was used into the 1940s and even appears in the 1960s. Colgate did attempt to market a successful French soap in 1984 in Canada, but it now features in all the marketing textbooks as a classic failure.[28] Cleopatra was not a major figure in pop culture in Canada or America in the mid-1980s, but most blame the overpricing and the recycling of French ads. It did not help that the market research for the Quebec roll-out was done in Toronto, as the textbooks gleefully point out.

As indicated by the brief survey at the beginning of this chapter, Cleopatra was hardly restricted to magazine ads for soap from 1909 to 1929. She appeared for all sorts of products in all periods, though such ads tend to be concentrated in periods of heightened interest in the Queen or in Egypt in general. There were intense Cleopatra eruptions surrounding the major films about her in 1934 and in 1963, many of them deliberate commercial tie-ins. The Palmolive ads, however, had a genealogy all their own. They began to appear before any of the silent films discussed earlier. Even the Palmolive metallic bra predates Theda Bara's snake bra, although I would conjecture that they were all suggested by the Haggard (1889) description cited above.[29] They definitely counted in the public's general knowledge of the Queen and her associations with beauty, elegance and luxury. But the images employed also distanced themselves from the nineteenth-century fear of the oriental *femme fatale* and avoided associations with fratricide, promiscuity and ignominious death.

Although there were several print works which assisted in this process, this protracted ad campaign seems to have helped formulate a revised image of Cleopatra in America. The nineteenth-century image had been of a dangerous, man-destroying Oriental outsider propagated by white Western males such as H. Rider Haggard, Victorien Sardou, Guazzoni's *Antonio e Cleopatra* and of course Theda Bara's vamp. A few years after the campaign, Claudette Colbert played Cleopatra as a childless flapper, very dependent on males and more passive than any other film Queen. I believe that DeMille's Queen and subsequent Cleopatras were shaped and defined as primarily tragic figures of loveliness and allure due to this attempt to make green stinky soap the ticket to beauty and that 'schoolgirl complexion'.

3.2 Cleopatra laughs

The worldwide production of films about classical antiquity peaked around 1912 and did not spike again until the heyday of the sword and sandal films of the 1950s and 1960s.[30] Between the iconic Theda Bara film (1917) and the equally beloved DeMille epic (1934), there were only around a dozen films about Cleopatra, all of them lost.[31] Due to the survival of five stills, only the oldest talkie (*Cleopatra*, 1928) yields many details. Wenzel quite reasonably concludes from a careful examination of these that it was derived from *Antony and Cleopatra* and portrays the Queen as the usual symbol for Oriental culture.[32] Based on the titles, actors and similar evidence, Wenzel also argues convincingly that most, if not all, of the other films from this period were comedies or parodies.[33] This would dovetail with the humanizing impact of the Palmolive ads in the interwar period and with the way writers of fact and fiction were going to treat her. She would remain a symbol of Orientalism, but would also gradually evolve in a way that more and more attracted the attention of female readers and writers, especially those influenced by larger movements such as the New Woman, Theosophy[34] and Modernism.

Over the last century, Cleopatra has always been well served by biographers, both the scholarly and the popularizing types.[35] Most are reasonably accurate and faithful to the ancient sources and to a contemporary scholarly consensus, but they tend to endorse only one possibility when there are multiple interpretations. A nineteenth-century example already mentioned is Jacob Abbott (1803–79) who was a teacher and pastor best known for his 'Rollo' children's books among his over 180 publications. His *Cleopatra* (1851) was part of an effort

> [...] aimed at young people. His target audience was age '15 to 25' and the Abbott brothers eventually produced a set of biographies that were critically acclaimed and widely read. Within a few years of their publication, the Abbott biographies became standard reference works of juvenile history and

were available in libraries throughout America. They were originally published as the 'Illustrated History' series but were republished many times during the next sixty years in various collections, entitled 'Famous Characters of History', 'Famous Queens of History' and others.[36]

Philip W. Sergeant (1872–1952) followed in Abbott's footsteps with *Cleopatra of Egypt: Antiquity's Queen of Romance* (1909). He wrote primarily about the game of chess but had branched out into biographies from all eras.[37] While this was his only apparent venture into classical antiquity, he seems to have been familiar with contemporary authorities and the principal ancient sources.[38] Sergeant's *Cleopatra* was part of the *Hutchinson's Library of Standard Lives* and was one of the seven volumes published by Doran in the USA,[39] but his influence on the popular imagination would pale in comparison to that of Arthur Edward Pearse Brome Weigall (1880–1934).

Although lacking a traditional academic background, Weigall was an Egyptologist having served as Inspector General of Antiquities and in other posts in Egypt until his 'breakdown' in 1914. The First World War forced him to change careers and he turned to the theatre, journalism and fiction.[40] The first edition of his biography of Cleopatra appeared in 1914, followed by biographies of Mark Antony, Akhnaton, Sapho (sic), Alexander and Nero as well as numerous books on Egyptian archaeology. Weigall's account of Cleopatra is fraught with errors of fact and interpretation and is not currently useful in factual research, but much of that is the fault of his sources, both contemporary and ancient.

But he did attempt to introduce some new elements to the discussion. He was one of the first and very few writers not to portray Cleopatra as a 'crowned courtesan'.[41] He vowed in his introduction to avoid anachronistic moral judgements: 'Fortunately, a biographer need not, as we so often must in regard to our contemporaries, make a clear distinction between good and bad, shunning the sinner that our intimates may not be contaminated.'[42] While no hagiographer, he did channel Plutarch's admiration and sympathy toward this Greek heroine. In doing so he produced a lively and readable narrative of what was already a pretty good story, but one which still reflects contemporary chauvinism. As an example of his account, I offer this paragraph which he has appended to Plutarch's compelling portrait of the Queen's interview with Octavian (Plut. *Ant.* 83):

> The picture of the distraught little queen, her dark hair tumbled over her face, her loose garment slipping from her shoulders, as she crouches at the feet of this cold unhealthy-looking man who stands somewhat awkwardly before her, is one which must distress the mind of the historian who has watched the course of Cleopatra's warfare against the representative of Rome. Yet in this scene we are able to discern her but stripped of the regal and formal accessories which have often caused her to appear more imposing and awe-inspiring than actually her character justified. She was essentially a woman, and in her condition of physical weakness, she acted precisely as any other overwrought member of her sex might have behaved under similar circumstances. Her wonderful pluck had almost deserted her and her persistence of purpose was lost in the wreck of all her hopes. We have often heard her described as a calculating woman, who lived her life in studied and callous voluptuousness and who died in unbending dignity; but, as I have tried to indicate in this volume, the queen's nature was essentially feminine – highly strung and liable to rapid changes from joy to despair. Keen, independent and fearless though she was, she was never a completely self-reliant woman and in circumstances such as those which are now being recorded, we obtain a view of her character, which shows her to have been capable of needing desperately the help and sympathy of others.[43]

Although hardly worthy of a dispassionate modern historian of antiquity, the passage illustrates Weigall's strengths as a storyteller and his impact on popular culture. His work has not escaped some serious criticism,[44] including that of the reviewer for *The Nation* (29 October 1914): 'It would be hard to find a book of serious intent in which "must have been", "might have been", "possibly", "probably" and other such symbols of lack of evidence are so persistently made the cornerstones of imposing structures of alleged certainty.'[45] One of the more curious examples of this was Weigall's thesis that Cleopatra 'must have' planted in Caesar's mind the idea of the Nile and Egypt as the path to the riches of India,[46] an idea which would find a home in several subsequent works of fiction.

Hughes-Hallett includes Weigall among those who infantilize Cleopatra, as the above passage well illustrates,[47] while Hoberman finds his narrative 'intensely patronizing in its treatment of women and power'.[48] At least he broke with the cynical interpretation followed by the French biographer Gaston Delayen: 'For this siren love would seem to have been nothing but a means to an end.'⁴⁹ Weigall was nevertheless very popular⁵⁰ and so widely read that a revised edition of the biography was called for in 1924 and also published in the USA. He was cited in other subsequent biographies and is one of only two English titles in Wertheimer's bibliography.⁵¹ Joyce Tyldesley, an Egyptian archaeologist, uses quotes from Weigall to open and close her own thoughtful biography of the Queen.⁵² His impact is even more evident when we consider the comments of two female writers of fictional accounts of Cleopatra from this period: Butts (1927) and Barrington (1927).

In the preface to her 1927 novel *The Laughing Queen*, British-Canadian author E. Barrington (a pen name for Lily Adams Beck, 1860–1931) acknowledged her debt to Weigall's 'delightful' book but offered her own as a counter argument: 'It takes much courage to differ with him, but I cannot agree with his estimate of her character in some important respects and of her relations with the two great Romans who were her lovers. This romance will show the manner in which I differ.'⁵³ It also shows the extent of his influence.

Mary Butts (1890–1937), an English Modernist not included in this study,⁵⁴ was even more specific in her references to Weigall. She even included what amounts to an in-line reference to his assessment of the influence of Fulvia on Antony.⁵⁵ In her afterword to her 1935 novel, after railing cleverly against Chaucer, Shakespeare, Shaw and Mahaffy, in fact in her final sentence, she voiced her debt to Weigall: 'Above all, he shows the Queen, taken out of her setting in a false Arabian Night and moving in a world completely intelligible to us, a world with a touch of Regency vitality to it; and in other respects only too like our own.'⁵⁶

It seems reasonable to credit Weigall and all those Palmolive ads with – at the very least – a renewed and evolving interest in the Queen which reveals conscious departures from Shakespeare, Shaw and Sardou. Before we consider the more innovative approaches of Barrington and Thomas, we should mention some more traditional but popular approaches.⁵⁷ Two works of humour featured Cleopatra in short sketches. In Don Marquis's charming *archy and mehitabel* (1927), the cat claims to have been Cleopatra in another incarnation.⁵⁸ As a chapter in *Famous Fimmales From Heestory witt Odder Ewents*, Milt Gross offered a conversation between Clipettra, Patolemy and Mock Hentony in a barely comprehensible Yiddish-inflected dialect which is oddly entertaining.⁵⁹

Henry Thomas Schnittkind (1888–1970), who wrote as Henry Thomas, emigrated from Lithuania, then part of the Russian Empire, and earned a PhD from Harvard in 1913. In addition to a career as an educator and translator, he published a series of 'Living Biographies', one of which included a chapter on Cleopatra.[60] He was a socialist and once listed his hobby as 'education of the masses'.[61] Although nearly invisible now, his novel has some claim to popularity. It did have a second printing and was included in a particularly cheesy paperback anthology of Cleopatra stories – complete with the requisite lurid cover – which included selections from Barrington, Mundy, Ludwig, Thomas, Ferval and Gauthier.[62]

Thomas's contribution, *Cleopatra's Private Diary* (1927), is a highly entertaining first-person account of her days in Rome in 46–44 BCE. There are frequent departures from fact for narrative purposes, such as the length of her stay, a friendship with Virgil, and Caesar acknowledging Caesarion. Such liberties are part of the nature of historical fiction as any student of reception studies must accept, but here they are justified because they advance a cohesive narrative. Thomas carries this license to a different level by inserting anachronistic elements which tend to reflect or address modern social issues. For example, Cleopatra rails against an intrusive and irresponsible 'Italian' press corps. Her 'diary' entries are gossipy and scandalous, although the reader is quite aware that there is a male voice behind her POV. Although the story focuses on her relationship with (or manipulation of) Caesar, there is a clear and conscious rejection of Shaw's version. The portrait of Cleopatra which emerges is of a very intelligent, beautiful and sexual young woman, but one who is promiscuous, amoral and murderous. It is probable that the Russian-born Thomas was influenced by the Pushkin/Gautier Cleopatra, along with an acute sense of humour and the absurd. Essentially, she is still a *femme fatale*, but a very amusing one. It is the only novel about Cleopatra which I could not put down.

E. Barrington (Lily Adams Beck, 1860–1931), author of *The Laughing Queen* (1929), was born in Ireland but wrote in British Columbia, Canada, under a number of pseudonyms. She did most of her writing in her sixties and was also a devotee of Theosophy and Eastern religions. Barrington is thought to be the first female fantasy writer from Canada. She used the Barrington pseudonym for her 'popular romances set in exotic locales'.[63]

We have already noted her use of Weigall, but the similarity of cover art (see Fig. 3.4) to some of the Palmolive ads which appeared in the same women's magazines which serialized her romances is striking. Like Talbot Mundy, Barrington followed Weigall's emphasis on India as an ultimate goal for Caesar and Cleopatra. At the very beginning of the novel, Cleopatra and Apollodorus conclude that Caesar's real aim is the vast wealth of India,[64] not a far-fetched notion for the daughter of Royal Navy Rear Admiral John Moresby. She even has Caesar proclaim that the Parthian campaign was 'the gate to India'.[65] Finally it is an Indian who brings Cleopatra a magical jewel which can poison or rejuvenate.[66] Every novelist feels the need to add a new bit of fiction to the Cleopatra legend and this bauble is quite cleverly employed. It does help to put into context the rather abrupt reference to India in the carpet scene in DeMille's *Cleopatra*, which so puzzles modern viewers and classicists. It could of course have come from Weigall or Mundy, but the Barrington connection becomes compelling when you note that a new (undated) printing of the novel features a title change to *Cleopatra: The Laughing Queen*, stills from the 1934 film used on all four cover pages and a new jacket featuring Claudette Colbert.

The Laughing Queen is primarily an exotic romance covering Cleopatra's life from the meeting with Caesar to her suicide with the Indian jewel.[67] As a final joke, she had an asp planted in a basket of figs. From the very first chapter she plots a sexual liaison with Caesar, but it is not consummated until page 68 and then in a single sentence. She does not shy from murder, manipulation and exploitation, but always with self-assurance and laughter. Her sexuality is seen through the eyes of others, infatuated lovers like Caesar and Antony, adoring retainers like Apollodorus and Charmion, and common people smitten by her theatrics and her enchanting voice. She seems to embody Barrington's ideal of a modern woman bolstered by her ambition and a theosophical understanding of her place in the world. And she does laugh.

3.3 *Femme fatale* to flapper

Popular culture of the interwar period in America had experienced a modest and varied interaction with the Cleopatra reception. There were several films (all lost), a long running ad campaign, several positive popular histories and interesting works of fiction – some of them in English translation. But it was a film – the earliest surviving Cleopatra talkie – that was to leave the greatest mark on the tradition: the 1934 *Cleopatra* directed by Cecil B. DeMille and starring Claudette Colbert.[68] This version has attracted critical attention since its premier and for varying reasons, such as: biographies of the cast and director; sexuality and censorship; marketing; product tie-ins; and set and costume design. Most significantly for my purpose, the film has also engaged the thoughts of several scholars of classical antiquity. Mary Hamer, Lucy Hughes-Hallett, Diana Wenzel, Martin Winkler and Maria Wyke each take a unique approach to the film and should be read in context.[69] My debt to each of them should be apparent, but no summary could do them justice here.

The Paramount Pictures release was produced and directed by DeMille from March to May of 1934 at a cost of $842,908.17. It premiered in New York in August of that year, eventually grossing $1,929,161.10.[70] Significantly the more rigorous Production Code only took effect on 1 July, a gap which the costume department and the director energetically exploited.[71] DeMille was very careful in casting the principals. Warren William as Caesar was well known for pushing boundaries as audacious and unscrupulous con men and hustlers,[72] while Henry Wilcoxon was a British newcomer who so impressed DeMille he borrowed him from another director;[73] but the film was constructed around its star, Claudette Colbert, who was enjoying the best year of her career.[74] She was *not* recruited to play 'The Wickedest Woman in History', as has been mistakenly asserted in some recent accounts.[75] That phrase was used in reference to the role of Poppaea, the wife of Nero, in *The Sign of the Cross* (1932).[76] DeMille himself tells the story: 'I stopped her one day on the Paramount lot and without any warning or explanation asked her, "Claudette, how would you like to play the wickedest woman in the world?" Claudette Colbert's beautiful big eyes opened wider. She said, "I'd love it."' The screen test with Fredric March only covered five words of the script before CB gave her the role.[77] Her role as Cleopatra was much larger, quite different and more sympathetic than what is suggested by the phrase 'the wickedest woman in the world'.

The plot covers most of Cleopatra's life, beginning with her desert exile at the hands of the evil Pothinus.[78] Her 'schoolmaster' Apollodorus tries to get her to focus, but she can only complain about missing breakfast. The next scene finds Caesar in Alexandria playing with a model siege engine (which will reappear in the final battle scene montage) when the laughing queen makes her entrance via the carpet. Caesar is charmed but not interested until Apollodorus prompts her to think of Egypt and to mention the treasures of India, further betraying the influence of Barrington or other interwar writers. It is possible that the admonition to 'Think of Egypt' was an allusion to a well circulated but probably apocryphal Edwardian quote attributed to Lady Hillingdon among others, advising wives with regard to unwelcome marital sex to 'lie back and think of England'.[79] If true, the allusion would certainly add to the rising tone of sexual tension. In this film, the phrase is always employed at moments when sexual and romantic impulses conflict with political considerations. DeMille frequently inserts similar sly anachronisms into this film, especially in the party at Calpurnia's. They retire to Cleopatra's chambers to further discuss India (and think about Egypt) where Pothinus lies in wait behind a curtain. When Caesar seems to lose interest and starts to leave, Cleopatra seizes a spear and handily dispatches Pothinus, setting the appropriate mood for seduction and a discussion of world domination. No doubt Caesar was attracted by her phallic penetration of the eunuch. This emphasis on grand political ambitions shows the unmistakable influence of the popularizing historian Oskar von Wertheimer (1931), which is meticulously and convincingly documented in Wenzel's commentary.[80] Alluded to partially in the following meeting with his staff but omitted from the narrative are the death of Pompey, her brother, his advisors, Caesarion and the entire Alexandrian war.

The scene shifts to Rome onto sets reused from *Sign of the Cross* (1932) and to a party at Calpurnia's where the guests gossip about Cleopatra and Caesar. One girl asks, 'Is she Black?' and the round of laughter is broken by a shift to tyrannicidal plotting. There follows the entrance of Mark Antony, displaying his arrogant masculinity with a pair of enormous dogs to announce the return of Caesar. The scene shifts to Caesar's entry, loosely and anachronistically portrayed as a triumph, with Cleopatra borne on a large litter. As the music changes to a more Oriental mode, she looks quite trepidatious.

Cleopatra's fears are justified in the next scenes where first the conspirators voice their opposition to Caesar's plans to establish an Oriental monarchy with Cleopatra as his Queen, followed by a lesson in Roman misogyny from Enobarbus and Antony. The rest of Caesar's story is basically in line with the traditions of Plutarch, Suetonius and Shakespeare except for the interweaving of Cleopatra's preparations and reactions. Her time in Rome has been compressed into a few days around the Ides of March, which is as unlikely as it is effective. In what is essentially a Homeric arming scene, Cleopatra girds her slender loins for battle with the Roman establishment and 'their fat wives' in a series of elegant tableaux celebrating her grace and beauty. Her first impulse is to rush to Caesar's side and only agrees to flee when Apollodorus reminds her once again to 'think of Egypt' and asserts that Caesar never loved her. The continuous Roman scenes end with Antony and Octavian united after the defeat of the tyrannicides and the decision to summon Cleopatra to Tarsus to face justice. The high-stakes conflict being set up is not attested in our sources but heightens the drama and the sexual tension of what follows. The masterful barge scene that follows is DeMille's greatest contribution to the Cleopatra tradition and will require an expanded discussion below, but I agree with Winkler that it is brilliant:

> But Cleopatra is a passionate woman who finds out that she has been caught in the very trap which she had set for Antony to manipulate him with sex and seductiveness. She falls for him as much as he falls for her.[81]

The scene returns to Rome long enough for Octavian to declare war. He calls Cleopatra a poisonous snake, reflecting Shakespeare's 'serpent of old Nile' label (*A&C* 1.5.25) and foreshadowing her death. Back in Alexandria the doomed couple lounge and drink in Oriental luxury. They are photographed through the strings of a harp and as the harpist moves her hand across them, she seems to stroke the reclining figure of the Queen.[82] When Cleopatra asks Antony why he does not seek another woman, he responds, 'Because you are another woman. New. Always new. Completely new.' It is DeMille's way of paraphrasing Shakespeare's 'Nor custom stale her infinite variety' (*A&C* 2.2.236–7). Henry Wilcoxon deserves credit for making it sound better than it reads.

The expected reversal begins when Herod arrives with a message from Octavian to kill Antony. He even warns Antony that he has done so! Apollodorus urges Cleopatra to comply 'for Egypt'. As per the traditions, she tests the poisons on condemned men but practically in front of Antony. She has poisoned flowers which she will dip in his wine, a gesture also made in the barge scene. When the letter arrives from Rome declaring war, Antony re-engages his latent masculinity. Octavian knocks the deadly chalice from his hand and confesses:

'I've seen a god come to life. I'm no longer a Queen, I'm a woman.' Perhaps this resonated better with a 1930s audience.

The battles to follow are presented in a montage featuring footage from *The Ten Commandments* (1923) interspersed with cutaway fights between the principals and lots of model ships and siege engines – including Caesar's toy. It has been criticized as a klutzy version of a naval battle fought with chariots, but I think that is unfair since the conflict was lengthy and was fought in various locations. As a montage with the shadowy Cleopatra looming over it, I find it effective. The death scenes are conventionally Plutarchan/Shakespearian and mirror the opening sequence, minus the naked slave girl.

In spite of the pervasive presence of echoes from throughout the Cleopatra reception, there is no literary adaptation at the heart of this film.[83] The guiding narrative clearly came from DeMille himself, who brought with him a vision of ancient Egypt and Rome honed by both *The Ten Commandments* (1923) and *The Sign of the Cross* (1932). While the screenwriters worked from various historical sources and English dramas as noted above, they were especially dependent on the admiring history by Wertheimer.[84] It should be noted that while the English title is *Cleopatra: A Royal Voluptuary*, in German it is *Kleopatra: Die genialste Frau des Altertums*, which translates as *the most highly gifted/ingenious woman of antiquity*. The scriptwriter Waldemar Young brought some background to the project, since he had worked on *The Sign of the Cross* in 1932 and had written *When Caesar Ran a Newspaper* in 1929, a short comedy about Cleopatra.[85] He surely applied those experiences to the 'historical materials' compiled by his colleague Bartlett Cormack. IMDB goes so far as to cite an uncredited writer ... Plutarch.[86] The imperfect fusion of diverse materials nonetheless emerged somewhat coherent because of the political thesis of Wertheimer, the vision of the director and the performance of the star. It may be terrible history, but it is a decent film. Wertheimer laid out his thesis quite bluntly:

> If we examine Cleopatra's political plans we find that down to the smallest detail they bore unflinching steadfastness of purpose. Her first thought had always been to secure the throne of Egypt, and from the very beginning of her career, and in times of the greatest danger, she had always been content with this task. But as soon as her throne was safe the most daring plans came to life in her brain and her imagination was ever busy conquering territories from east to west and west to east, whether in alliance with Caesar, or Antony,

or any other powerful Roman whom she could persuade to lend her his support.[87]

She did heed Apollodorus and think of Egypt. Some other less direct influences or inspirations warrant mention: the Theda Bara film of 1917, the Palmolive advertising campaign of the 1920s and the novel of E. Barrington of 1929.

DeMille may have been the last person to see the Theda Bara film. He viewed a copy on 15 February 1934, sent to him from the Fox storage facility in New Jersey. Three years later a fire destroyed the entire collection of nitrate films.[88] Based on the publicity stills alone I think it is safe to say that DeMille might have been influenced by the daring costumes, the pageantry and the elaborate Orientalizing sets.

The Palmolive ads discussed above ran into the late 1920s and could have influenced the costume designers. Numerous artists and illustrators were engaged to reinforce the message of beauty through soap. They helped to modernize Cleopatra's image and depict her as less of a *femme fatale* and more of a flapper whom the readers of women's magazines might wish to emulate. While the costumes were every bit as revealing as Bara's, they were more flowing and form fitting.

Figure 3.4 Comparison of the Barrington cover and the Palmolive ad. From the author's collection.

There is an odd marketing synergy between this film and Barrington's novel *The Laughing Queen*. There is no question of an adaptation, but there seem to be some deliberate influences. Weigall was not an obvious source for the screenwriters, but his obsession with India features prominently in the film. And Claudette does laugh heartily several times and display more than a little humour throughout the film. Most telling is the reprint of the book with the title changed to *Cleopatra: The Laughing Queen* and featuring screen shots from the movie on both end covers and at least one dust jacket with a photograph of Claudette Colbert in one of the more elaborate costumes from the scene of the death of Pothinus.[89] To close the circle, that costume closely resembles the earlier dustjacket depicted in the last chapter which is almost identical to one of the 1919 Palmolive ads shown here. Given the close attention to marketing and product endorsements which accompanied this film, coincidence can be ruled out.[90]

A lot of things were either omitted or merely alluded to in order to fit the 101-minute running time, but some of these deserve attention since they affected the characterization of Cleopatra. These would include the omission of the death of Pompey, her brother Ptolemy XIII and his other advisors, her sister Arsinoë, her other brother Ptolemy XIV and the entire Alexandrian war. Likewise, Cleopatra's relationship with Antony omits the 'Inimitable Livers' anecdotes, the Parthian campaigns, the Donations, his Alexandrian triumph and the reading of his will in Rome. The narrative of the film is thus sharply focused entirely on Cleopatra's relationships with two men, barely acknowledging the larger Ptolemaic and Roman contexts.

The most jarring omission is the complete absence of her children. In the silent films her childlessness was essential to the image of the vamp or *femme fatale*, but here it seems to appeal to the audience's dreams of female freedom.[91] As Mary Hamer concludes, 'It was a version of the feminine which [...] specifically denied the maternal, even by association. Elegant, self-possessed and able to stand up for herself, the screen persona of Claudette Colbert could be closely identified with the ideal companion and wife of the 1930's, but not, not on any account, with the mother.'[92] That identification was essential not only to the delineation of the screen character, but also to the meticulous marketing campaign and product identification, as discussed by both Hamer and Wyke.[93] While Colbert fully participated in these campaigns, it is interesting to note that she never again played such an overtly sexual character.[94]

The focus on India has already been mentioned and is not new to the Cleopatra reception. Since it was featured in several contemporary works, it is not surprising that it would have made it into this account. As the jewel in the crown of the British Empire, India could evoke the image of a wealthy area ripe for conquest, colonization and exploitation by the Romans. In the ancient world, wealth was primarily seen in terms of surplus food, not precious metals, gems or oil. Egypt was wealthy because it had the Nile, whose inundations allowed several crops per year, a bounty not enjoyed by most of the rest of the Mediterranean area. Even so, Roman expansionism was less motivated by economic factors than by ambitious leaders vying for social and political hegemony. That is much too complicated and subtle for a Hollywood epic. In this context, India served as convenient way for DeMille to provide Cleopatra with something that would get Caesar's attention, when her wardrobe was not enough. Regrettably it is now as silly, confusing and anachronistic as some of the 'howlers' she has to utter.

Cleopatra did not in fact stab Pothinus as he hid behind a curtain. Caesar had him executed later. He is not portrayed as a eunuch and his co-conspirators Theodotus and Achillas are not shown at all. In this film, this act changes Caesar's attitude toward the Queen both as a strong leader, a warrior queen and as a sexual partner. Later it adds plausibility to her capacity to poison Antony as well as the prisoners. At least she kills with some regret. Although quite inaccurate historically, this dramatic convenience is justifiable in light of the very extensive tradition of the 'Killer Kleopatra' within the general reception, as Hughes-Hallett has so ably documented.[95] The heyday of this depiction began to fade after The First World War, but is actually making a comeback especially in graphic novels as we shall see later in this study.

The single most significant contribution of this film to the Cleopatra reception has to be the barge scene and her visit to Antony at Tarsus. This episode had appeared in numerous earlier works of art and literature, but our sole source is Plutarch's description, probably based on an eyewitness account by someone like Quintus Dellius who had been sent to fetch her. It in turn inspired the speech by Enobarbus in Shakespeare. The Ptolemies had long enjoyed large and luxurious ships such as the *Thalamegos* of Ptolemy IV Philopator more than 200 years earlier. It is generally accepted that Cleopatra used such a 'houseboat' for her poorly documented trip up the Nile with Julius

Caesar and would have employed the same or a similar vessel for her trip up the Cydnus river to Tarsus.[96]

DeMille raised the *topos* to a new level of ostentatious display, orchestrated seduction and unfettered sexuality. In a letter to Agnes DeMille, whom he was trying to recruit as choreographer, he outlined his vision for the scenes:

> Cleopatra is here putting on a show deliberately, with the intention of so astonishing the tough, hard soldier Antony that he will have to remain long enough for her to get in her deadly work [...] This entire barge sequence should be the most seductive, erotic, beautiful, rhythmic, sensuous series of scenes ever shown.[97]

The success in achieving these goals has been expertly examined by several scholars whose efforts deserve perusal.[98] Hughes-Hallett concludes:

> The winking Cleopatra, consenting with one eye, denying with another, subverts all value, contradicts all certainty and invites her admirers to squander their all for a laugh. She is not a good woman, but she is something resembling a great one and the feast she offers is out of this world.[99]

This film deserves the attention it has received from film critics and social historians of all stripes and all of the carping from historical nitpickers who consistently ignore the fact that film is fiction and is entitled to construct its own reality. But my focus is on its place in the progression of the reception of Cleopatra in popular culture. This is characterized by building on earlier trends, transferring her image from an exotic luxury to an approachable amenity, smoothing the transition from vamp to flapper and inspiring even newer takes on her image to reflect the rapidly changing gender roles of the 1940s.

All of the product tie-ins associated with the release and distribution of the film helped to modernize or at least update the popular image of the Queen. Begun earlier with the Palmolive ad campaigns, the hair style, beauty and fashion products marketed with references to Ms Colbert and her role brought Cleopatra even closer to the popular imagination but on a more human level. This Queen complained about discomforts, laughed and seemed to enjoy life in between challenges and tragedies. Female audiences were encouraged to believe that they could be like her.

An important aspect of this approachability was to make her less of a threatening, man-eating vampire and more of a dazzling rich girl who could make towering and toxically virile figures melt in her embraces. The silent screen Cleopatras could look stunning and seductive, but the flapper-style dresses and abundant displays of flesh did not seem quite as dangerous. The funny and fun-loving queens of the novels of Thomas and Barrington could easily have worn the fashions of both the Palmolive ads and Claudette Colbert. She is still a dangerous foe with a potential for violence and murder, but she is a long way from Theda Bara.

Even more significant for the development of Cleopatra's reception during this period is the genre shift away from tragic romance to romantic epic. The twentieth-century reception began under the heavy influence of stage dramas, especially revivals of Shakespeare and Sardou which were the basis of some early silent films. In fiction, Mundy continued the Victorian pulp fiction tradition of H. Ryder Haggard, eschewing happy endings but aiding the transition to epic by emphasizing rollicking adventure. By the 1930s, the English novels of Lindsay and Butts had moved into more thoughtful and personal storytelling, with human characters caught in the tides of history. I conclude that the DeMille film was central to the realization of this transition.

The impact would not stop with the outbreak of the war in Europe. The 1940s would produce three novels and a significant, if unsuccessful, motion picture. But most astonishing is a rush of epic-style *pepla* or sword-and-sandal films of the 1950s and 1960s which filled the movie theatres of my youth until Lizpatra killed the genre. It was all, in my view, sparked by DeMille's *Cleopatra* of 1934 and its star, Claudette Colbert.

4

Thoroughly Modern Cleopatra

While there was a seventeen-year gap between the first two major films about Cleopatra and there would be another eleven until the next, the written receptions continued in the period between the world wars and even during the Second World War. The variety of approaches in both the popular culture versions and more literary aspirations, when combined with DeMille's epic film treatment, were going to help inspire the postwar receptions in print, comics and 'sword-and-sandal' films (aka pepla).

During the war years the principal English language contributions to the reception of Cleopatra came from Britain. The novels of Jack Lindsay,[1] Mary Butts[2] and Lord Berners[3] are some of the more interesting contributions, but since they were not American and do not appear to have had a wide circulation in the US at the time are not included in this study but do deserve a brief mention. Although well versed in the classics and ancient history herself, Butts sought Lindsay's advice and expertise and he was one of her greatest admirers. They ran in the same circles, sharing interests in William Blake, the ancient world and Marxist causes.[4] Jack Lindsay (1900–90) studied Greek and Latin at the University of Queensland in his native Australia and many of his 160-plus books were on the ancient world, including both fiction, non-fiction and several respected translations.[5] England in 1941 would not seem to be a conventional time to publish a satiric novel about Cleopatra, but little about (Gerald Hugh Tyrwhitt-Wilson) Lord Berners' life could be called normative.[6]

These trends are also reflected in the Palmolive ad from around 1942–3 mentioned earlier. It appeared in several different versions, but Figure 3.3 incorporates all of the elements I have seen. Perhaps it was a wartime revival to make up for the lack of new copy. The title 'Cleopatra had nothing on me!' is novel and more contemporary, but along the bottom they repeat the 1920s tag line with an addition: 'Now more than ever [...] keep that schoolgirl complexion.'[7] The middle panels recall the basics of the earlier campaign: that the source of Cleopatra's stunning beauty was the oils of the olive and the palm. The cropped and flipped Cabanal painting seems a bold choice with Cleopatra's breasts bare. At least they omitted the poisoned prisoners. The other registers update the message to the 1940s, with a young lady wearing red lipstick and a boyfriend in uniform. She is a modern, smiling, knowing Cleopatra and in many reflects the modern mid-century Cleopatra who is sexually aware and ready to engage in postwar changes.

4.1 *Caesar and Cleopatra* (1945)

Ordinarily one would not include any work of George Bernard Shaw in a study of American popular culture, but since *Caesar and Cleopatra* (1945) did appear as a major motion picture the *fin-de-siecle* play it recreates warrants inclusion at this point. Although this elite reception appeared in print in 1901 and was frequently produced for the American stage in the ensuing decades, it was not discussed along with Haggard and Sardou because the infantilized Queen-to-be did not seem to have made as much of an impression on the popular imagination.[8] Shaw always had a following among the intellectual elite and admirers of erudite snarkiness, but was usually considered alongside Shakespeare's *Antony and Cleopatra* which would have annoyed him to no end. A full colour film in 1945 was another matter.

The film was the product of director Gabriel Pascal, the only one Shaw would trust with his works. Shaw even added thirteen minutes of dialogue at Pascal's request. Filmed at great expense during the Second World War (including imported Egyptian sand) and beset by air raids, star illness and English weather, it was a critical and box-office failure, in spite of the breathlessly pious account of Marjorie Deans.[9] In fact, 'many in Britain found Pascal's wild expenditures in the midst of wartime austerity tasteless'.[10] According to *Variety*, the film lost $3,000,000[11] but was to date one of the most successful British films released in the USA in spite of postwar hostility in Hollywood.[12] In spite of being a rather slow moving and wordy display of Shavian philosophizing, advertising attempted to hype its 'lavish display' and rather spectacularly failed to live up to its own bullet points printed in the column. I would concur with the assessment of John R. Taylor that as a whole the film was 'over-designed and under-directed'.[13]

The acting on the other hand was quite good, although as Bean notes, 'Shaw's insistence that Cleopatra be acted according to his own vision, exactly as written, left Vivien no room for interpretation.'[14] Cleopatra was not the subject of either the play or the film, but Vivien Leigh's performance, costumes and looks heightened the Queen's presence. Since Pascal worshipped Shaw and every word he wrote, the characterization is true to the play. As Deans notes in her chapter on Leigh, '[Vivien Leigh] knew she could be that lovely, naïve, catlike creature – inquisitive and greedy and cruel, yet with such a noble capacity for passion and proudly loyal love that she ends by catching at one's heart.'[15] In other words, the character is meant to be ambiguous or even contradictory. As history, that is nonsense, but Shaw couldn't care less since his hero is Caesar who aims to mould this child into a female version of himself. As Hughes-Hallett notes:

> In Pascal's film Vivien Leigh does full justice to the childlike willfulness and naivety of Cleopatra's character as written by Shaw, but her performance is none the less unmistakably that of an adult, sexually knowing woman. Her pettishness, her silly prattle and her clinging ways are all forms of flirtation.[16]

In this way, Shaw had a profound effect on the reception of Cleopatra. Her image had already begun to morph from the turn-of-the-century vampire into a softer object of the male gaze and female aspirations in different forms in different works. Now it is possible to confront a single character contradicting herself in the same work. Not the recipe for a successful run at a postwar theatre.

4.2 Postwar novels

A radically different approach was taken in 1948 by John L. Balderston and Sybil Bolitho in an epistolary novel told largely from Cleopatra's point of view, with only the final section penned by Julius Caesar.[17] It is peppered with historical summaries and footnotes, primarily based on Tarn's idiosyncratic chapters in the *Cambridge Ancient History*, volume 10.[18] The result is a pompous, ponderous and rather boring philosophical recitation of arguments for a 'scheme of world union' based on Tarn's discredited vision of Alexander and Zeno of Citium. While it does offer a portrait of a very intelligent and articulate young Queen, deeply and playfully in love with an elderly cynic, she just comes off as a hopelessly romantic 'bluestocking'. However, the novel is not completely without original charm. Cleopatra not only meets Virgil and inspires his tale of Dido, but apparently he wrote the Fourth *Eclogue* about her son Caesarion! She does not care for Antony's behaviour and complains to Caesar about him. When he is shown the golden statue of Cleopatra, Antony remarks how the eyes of statues seem dead, a sentiment spoken by Caesar in the 1963 film. Perhaps the screenwriters had seen the script of the same name that the authors were pitching two years later.[19] Balderston had an extensive career as a scriptwriter, including *Gaslight* (1944), and would have been known in Hollywood. According to the summary in Hughes-Hallett, the script seems to follow a similar approach.[20] If so, it would have been an additional source for some of the odder elements of that flawed film, such as Cleopatra's muddled vision for the future.

Our other example was a genuinely popular and critical success, the 1948 epistolary novel by Thornton Wilder, *The Ides of March*.[21] He was no stranger to the ancient world and took a great interest in classical literature.[22] The acclaimed novella *The Woman of Andros*[23] was based on Terence's *Andria*, and he was proficient enough in Latin to do his own translations of Catullus in this novel. University of Wisconsin Classics Professor Paul MacKendrick gave *The Ides of March* an early and positive review in the *Classical Journal*.[24] Among the artists discussed here so far, only Jack Lindsay is Wilder's equal in terms of a familiarity with the ancient sources.

Like Lindsay, however, Wilder does not make Cleopatra the main character of his tale. That honour goes to Julius Caesar, so that Cleopatra's appearances serve primarily to characterize him. Still, we get a portrait of the Queen as she was received by America at the midpoint of the twentieth century.[25] Since the novel consists of letters and documents from several points of view, including Cleopatra's, Caesar's characterization unfolds gradually and frequently in a nonlinear and asynchronous fashion, much like that in the work of Mary Butts (1935).

Caesar is the focus and since she is a supporting character, Cleopatra only appears once in Book One, in the 'Commonplace Book' of Cornelius Nepos

(XII), representing the view of elite Roman society: 'the Queen of Egypt is coming to Rome, that's Cleopatra the witch'.[26] She is not mentioned again until the beginning of Book Two, where the majority of the Cleopatra exchanges occur, in an insulting letter (XXII) from Servilia to Pompeia, Caesar's wife, thoroughly trashing the Queen's adulterous character and dynastic motives. This is countered by Caesar in a letter (XXIII) to a fictitious confidante wherein he praises her intelligence and industry, followed by a less quoted assessment: 'And yet she is lying, intriguing, intemperate, indifferent to the essential well-being of her people, and a lighthearted murderess.'[27] This is followed by a section on how he has had to curtail her over-the-top plans for her entrance to and residence in Rome. Following that, Caesar reminisces about how he had taught Cleopatra to play the Egyptian and identify with Isis, betraying the influence of Shaw, as MacKendrick had noted.[28] Almost as an afterthought Caesar notes that he has forbidden her to bring Caesarion. We hear from the Queen herself in a memo (XXIV) to her ambassador in Rome to gather intelligence on Caesar's associates and to make sure her quarters are warm enough. The episode concludes with two letters between Pompeia and Clodia as they plot their interactions with the Queen (XXIV–XXV). This also allows the return to the Catullus/Clodia thread (XXVI–XXVI-B), another problematic romance. This introduces a rather icy exchange between Caesar and Cleopatra over her visit and the exclusion of Caesarion, but a later note indicates he is enjoying the give and take (XXX). In a clever allusion to Shakespeare, Caesar notes, 'I am charmed by this invariable variation.'[29] When Cleopatra is finally received publicly, we see her from multiple points of view. First, a maid of Pompeia, spying for Clodia, describes the astonishment at a fantastic gift, her simple appearance and gracious demeanour (XXXII). Nepos follows with a bare factual account (XXXIII) of the public welcome, but adds his wife's assessment of the Queen's appearance as 'decidedly plain', having cheeks so plump that they are condemned as 'jowls'.[30] In the next document (XXXIII-A), Cicero, offended that his gift is not a rare manuscript, mocks her appearance but has to admit, 'The prestige of her title, the magnificence of her dress, the effect of her two signal advantages – namely, her fine eyes and the beauty of her speaking voice – subdue the unwary.'[31] The strand is capped by a memo from Cleopatra with answers from Caesar (XXXIV). She pleads to see him but has to clarify some tedious protocol issues. He answers them with equal tedium, praises Antony's mistress and urges them to be friends and ends with arrangements for a secret rendezvous. The final strand of Book Two (XL–XLI-B) treats Cleopatra's reception and its aftermath. First, we get a positive view from Caesar's aunt, who contradicts disparaging accounts of Cleopatra's appearance and is charmed into an intimate conversation about children, a clever ploy to introduce the issue of Caesarion. The next letter (XLI) is an account by Cytheris, the mistress of Antony, who relates how she ended the affair at the party, because she has detected his unhealthy and unrequited passion for the Queen. As the reception turned into a drunken frat party, Antony attempted to force himself on Cleopatra when spotted by the narrator at Caesar's party. The Queen and the Dictator seem to make amends, but distractions lie ahead.

Book Three is devoted to the Bona Dea scandal which Wilder had consciously moved into his time frame for larger thematic purposes. The Cleopatra arc focuses on her unsuccessful attempts to take part in the secret ceremony. Of greater interest is letter XLVI, in which Caesar recounts his debates with Cleopatra about their divinity, noting, 'On that subject alone she is, perhaps, oriental.'[32] For Wilder, having Cleopatra vigorously assert her divinity is a means to characterize Caesar as rational and modern. Letters XLVIII and XLVIII-A are meant to show that distrust and guilt still remain from the incident with Antony at the party. Cleopatra uses her spy network to uncover the Bona Dea plot (LI) and warns Caesar (LV and LV-A) that P. Clodius was going to put on women's clothes to seduce Caesar's wife who was hosting the ceremony.

Book Four returns to the actual chronology leading up to the assassination. Most of the section focuses on the circulation of seditious chain letters (inspired by Italian resistance to Mussolini) urging Caesar's death. Wilder even has Cleopatra falsely accused of fomenting the movement (LX-C). She and Caesar are estranged, even though the cause is not evident to his Aunt Marcia (LXV). Cleopatra uses her acquired intelligence to try to warn Caesar, through Aunt Marcia, of a pending attempt on his life (LXVI), but is told that all is known (LXVI-A). They do not reconcile, and Wilder has Cleopatra leave Rome before Caesar's death. In a letter to the fictitious invalid friend on Capri (LXXI), he gives a valediction for the Queen, which places into sharp focus how much her image had changed over the previous forty years:

The great Queen of Egypt is returning to her country, having learned more about us than many who have spent a lifetime here. To what uses she will put that knowledge, to what uses she will put her ever-astonishing self it would be hard to say. There is a gulf between men and animals; I have always thought it to be narrower than many suppose. She possesses the rarest endowments of the animal and the rarest endowments of the human being; but of that quality which separates us from the swiftest horse, the proudest lion, and the shrewdest serpent she has no inkling: she knows not what to do with what she has. Too wise to be gratified by vanity; too strong to be content with ruling; too large for wife. With one greatness she is in perfect harmony and on that score I did her a great injustice. I should have permitted her to bring her children here. She does not know it yet to the full; she is that figure which all countries have elevated to the highest honor and awe: she is the mother as goddess. Hence those wonderful traits that I was so long in explaining to myself – her lack of malice, and her lack of that fretful unease to which we are so wearisomely accustomed in beautiful women.[33]

4.3 Pepla

The prevailing popular image of Cleopatra has generally focused on the best known of her film depictions featuring well known actresses such as Theda Bara, Claudette Colbert, Vivien Leigh and, as we shall see in the next chapter, Elizabeth Taylor. These were all heavily influenced by Shakespeare, Haggard, Sardou and Shaw, with a rare nod to Plutarch, and tend to reflect similar themes and preoccupations. We should not, however, neglect those postwar/pre-Lizpatra films which display remarkable independence from the usual receptions because they are partly responsible for the revival and perpetuation of the trends we see in the depiction of Cleopatra in mid-century America. Among those trends are the racialization, sexualization and vilification of Cleopatra and the emasculation of Mark Antony. As is the case with many other films of the sword-and-sandal or 'peplum' genre from this period, there is a consistently cavalier attitude toward historical or cultural accuracy. However, there is another common thread to these pepla. None of them are primarily about Antony and Cleopatra, or even attempt to tell their whole history. They are instead use a rather well-known narrative (with some less commonly told elements) as a backdrop to an original action adventure, love story, comic routine or even a moral treatise, focusing largely on the male characters.

The early 1950s saw an explosion of films about the ancient world, probably sparked by DeMille's *Samson and Delilah* (1949) and LeRoy's *Quo Vadis* (1951), as Jon Solomon suggests,[34] as well as postwar studio capacity in Italy, especially

Figure 4.1 Rhonda Fleming in *Serpent of the Nile* (1953). From the author's collection.

at Cinecitta. The year 1953 saw the release of *Salome*, *Slaves of Babylon* and our first example, *Serpent of the Nile*.[35] While the title is taken from Shakespeare, little more than the basic plot remains. This was a rare all-American, Columbia Pictures production, but a low budget one.[36] The sets are minimal and the same chariot appears in multiple armies, but the Technicolor was brilliant and Rhonda Fleming has the costumes to show it off. She is all Hollywood born and bred and the whole cast is American. The added-on storyline is a love triangle with an invented character who becomes the focus of the narrative. Lucilius, played by William Lundigan, starts as a soldier of Caesar in Alexandria, by the Battle of Philippi is a captain for Brutus, switches to Antony and finally sides with Octavian. It sounds outrageous, but actually mirrors the career of Q. Dellius, who was the agent and our likely source for the meeting of Antony and Cleopatra in Tarsus. Thus, Raymond Burr gets only third billing as Antony. Emphasizing the message of Cleopatra as a symbol of Oriental culture,[37] the barge scene (interiors only) is memorable for Julie Newmar's dance as the Gilded Girl: 'Voluptuous display for the purposeless, fleeting pleasure of it', as Hughes-Hallett notes.[38] Here the film reveals its departure from the stock portrayal. There is sexual attraction between Antony and Cleopatra, but his main interest and her principal lure is gold or, as it turns out, the illusion of Egyptian wealth. After an assassination attempt on Antony when they arrive in Alexandria, Lucilius learns that Cleopatra's wealth, as well as her love, is a sham and a shell. She actually loves Lucilius, but he cannot give her the power she had with Caesar. Meanwhile Antony becomes a pitiful drunk, hopelessly dependent on his 'Serpent' and wallowing in luxury. As he arranges for Lucilius' escape, which he knows will bring Octavian against him, he states that he has only had two friends: Lucilius and his sword. Throughout the film there has been a rather blatant 'McGuffin' style emphasis on phallic swords and daggers, culminating in Raymond Burr's pre-suicide dialogue with his little friend. The Romans are not quite fascists yet, but the leaders are depicted as power hungry and their brutality underscored by the frequent montages of gladiatorial and animal fights.[39]

Rhonda Fleming was accustomed to playing the 'bad girl'. Here she is a sexual predator and quite alluring for a 1950s film. Her tight-fitting outfits promise all but reveal little and while the sex is implicit and hypocritical, it is all talk. Like Julie Newmar's gilded girl, she is more image than reality and her interest in Mark Antony is more mercenary than amorous. Like many of the Cleopatras of this period, they want to 'have it both ways, morally and aesthetically. They are depraved and immoral, but likeable with it – considerably more amusing than the virtuous wives with whom they are contrasted.'[40] Fleming conveys some of the vampire from Theda Bara and the glamorous flapper sensuality of Claudette Colbert (including her bangs), but adds a political pragmatism and ruthlessness that will continue to play out in the coming decade. Since she is primarily there as one leg in a love triangle, her story recedes behinds that of Lucilius.

Two Nights with Cleopatra (1953) is our first Italian peplum in this selection.[41] It was a comic vehicle for Alberto Sordi and is dominated by his mugging monologues which, to be generous, do not translate well.[42] Most of Sophia Loren's screen time is spent as a prop in Cesarino's goofball scenes. It is a low budget affair, with exteriors filmed at the Museum of Roman Civilization in the EUR district. Sophia Loren has a dual role as the dark haired and serpentine Cleopatra and a body-double slave named Nisca. The latter is innocent, blonde and, according to Cleopatra, 'A bit too busty', the first of many references to Ms Loren's assets. According to Hatchuel, the split role allows the film to explore 'the ambivalence of the U.S. representations which have presented Cleopatra as the archetypal Oriental "other" woman, while denying her a dark skin and emphasizing her milky whiteness'.[43]

The film features a late element of Cleopatra's reception in which men are granted a night of passion with the Queen, knowing that death awaits them in the morning.[44] Pushkin (1835) and Gautier (1836) tell versions of this tradition, which only rarely appears in British or American receptions. The film also features Cleopatra's experimentation with poisons. Cesarino is the unwitting victim who meets and charms Nisca while Cleopatra slips away to see Mark Antony. Since this is a formulaic mistaken-identity bedroom farce, there are tokens, disguises and purloined poisons. Of course, Caesarino survives his second night with the real Cleopatra and rescues Nisca in a process that defies rational summary.

While this film is played for laughs, the 'real' Cleopatra is a much more sinister figure than the previous version. She is promiscuous, unfaithful to Antony and casually murderous. The scene is set shortly before Actium, but she takes little interest. Her rule is ruthless and she cares nothing for her people.

Antony's men despise him for his infatuation and lack of decisiveness. The Romans are barely mentioned, but the prominent use of the 'Roman' salute could only emphasize the identification with fascism.[45]

The next film, *The Story of Mankind* (1957), is a Hollywood fantasy about aliens judging a post-nuclear world.[46] Vincent Price as The Devil (addressed as 'Mr Scratch') and Ronald Coleman as the Spirit of Man argue the case against humanity and its moral fitness as a collective citizen of the universe. Listed as number 40 on Harry Medved's Fifty Worst Films,[47] it is a low budget series of clips and vignettes with 'has-been' actors. Virginia Mayo's Cleopatra gets four minutes, four episodes from her life and four changes of costumes. She is of course represented as one of the protégés of Mr Scratch and is the lead-in to Peter Lorre's Nero. Her film pedigree is underlined by a golden bra (Bara), her black bangs (Colbert) and her nickname, 'The Serpent of the Nile' (Fleming). But she is accorded none of the redeeming qualities of her predecessors. Her vices are illustrated by her poisoning of her brother, her greed by literally picking Caesar's purse, and her promiscuity and cowardice by her desertion of Antony and their separate suicides. Throughout the film, a sense of luxury is evoked by jewels, costumes and ostrich-feather fans. The emasculation of Antony is underscored when he repeats the phrase, 'I was the greatest Roman of them all.' He vows to kill Cleopatra, then turns the dagger on himself. Just as in a proper peplum, the focus is on the impact of female wickedness on the political potential of males. In each scene, Cleopatra is the instrument of the undoing of a male counterpart: her brother, Ptolemy XIII, Julius Caesar and Mark Antony. The formula is familiar Hollywood: a 'Love Boat' cruise to Hell. Splash the screen with vices and then moralize about it. In case you were wondering, the High Judge put us all on probation.

Meanwhile back in Italy, Cinecitta was working on *The Legions of Cleopatra* (1959).[48] It is not a well-known film, since 20th Century Fox bought it for $1 million and shelved it while Lizpatra was in production. It is set, apparently, after the Battle of Actium while Augusto (accompanied by Ovid!) is advancing on Alexandria. As Jon Solomon notes, it is 'a cinematic comic book containing brutal ruffians, sleazy or sassy girls. and over bold heroes, each cut from the thinnest cardboard'.[49] Cottafavi is highly regarded by the French, the cinematography and the writing are good and some of the actors – Georges Marchal as Mark Antony and Ettore Manni as Curridius (he was Marc Antony in *Due Notti*) – do the genre proud. But it is a peplum about Curridius's effort to get his old friend Mark Antony to give in to Augustus, in the course of which he meets a tavern dancer named Berenice who is Cleopatra in disguise. We do not actually see her as Cleopatra until forty minutes into the movie, because this is a 'guy' film with Augustus as a fascist, Mark Antony as an idealistic freedom fighter, gladiators, sadistic gladiator trainers, evil priests, torture chambers and plucky slaves, all getting more screen time than the title character. Plutarch does tell us that Mark Antony and Cleopatra did wander the streets of Alexandria in disguise, although he seems to have overlooked her driving a ten-horse chariot to meet Augustus wearing a Theda Bara snake bra motif woven on her gown. To dispel doubts about her cinematic genealogy, Curridius calls her a *vipera* – a Serpent of the Nile.

The Argentine Linda Crystal makes a lovely Cleopatra, but is even more lithesome as the dancer Berenice, ironically the name of the Queen's historical elder, executed sister. She is also much nicer, making the abrupt bipolar switch to beast rather unconvincing as well as unsympathetic. When she is Cleopatra, she is as murderous and manipulative as the previous two versions, provoking Curridius to call her a *belva* – a beast or monster. This is one of the more disappointing Cleopatras in that she appears in a rather decent, well-made film, but does not get to be the star of her own story. Hatchuel finds redeeming qualities:

> [T]he story of the historical protagonists is viewed through the defamiliarizing gaze of the fictive characters, and the Cleopatra figure is openly revealed as double – playing two characters that represent her multiple facets and cast doubt on her true motives and feelings.[50]

Cleopatra is not even in the next film in spite of its title, *Cleopatra's Daughter* (1960).[51] This was filmed as a story of New Kingdom Egypt and Assyria, originally called the *Tomb of the Kings*, with little connection to our Queen other than a tenuous thematic relationship.[52] In the non-Italian dubbed versions, it was given a new scrolling intro and a few references which transformed it to Ptolemaic times and changes the heroine Shila, played by Debra Paget, into Cleopatra's offspring. It was a not-too-subtle attempt to capitalize on the upcoming epic.

Our next example, *A Queen for Caesar* (1962) could not be more different.[53] The French sex kitten actress Pascale Petit (twenty-four at the time) plays an eighteen-year-old Cleopatra after the death of her father Ptolemy Auletes and up to the point when she emerges from the carpet at Caesar's feet.[54] Apparently in the European version she was nude for this scene and perhaps for the bath scene, but not in my dubbed DVD version, a wretched pan and scan job. It is actually a movie about Cleopatra and one which at least starts from Plutarch. Petit is charming, sexy and her character well played in a story of palace intrigue and seduction. All the usual suspects are present except for the eunuch Pothinus, who would have been somewhat less susceptible to her charms. While the allure is clearly physical, Cleopatra is most effective with the spoken word, perhaps reflecting Plutarch's remark about her lovely voice. As is to be expected in a peplum, the narrative departs from history at several points – Achillas is on her side, Apollodorus is with the Romans and Pompey attempts to bed her – but it does end up where most narratives would start. Aside from being charming, amusing and actually entertaining, this is perhaps the most positive and sympathetic portrait of Cleopatra on film. She is certainly manipulative, ambitious and sexual, but she shrinks from murder and ardently defends herself from unwelcome attentions – until of course she sees Gordon Scott as Caesar.

Released the same year (two weeks later) as Lizpatra, *Toto and Cleopatra* (14 August 1963)[55] is a fast-paced vehicle for Totó, 'Il Principe della risata', a Neapolitan comic genius who can be described as a Buster Keaton, simultaneously channelling the Marx Brothers, the Three Stooges and Abbott and Costello. The tragedy of Antony and Cleopatra once again provides a backdrop for a madcap Plautine comedy featuring doubles and double-crosses. Fulvia enlists Antony's double to foil the marriage to Octavia and sends the crooked slave dealer Totonno to Egypt to muck things up. The real Mark Antony is thoroughly eclipsed by the roguish double and eventually gets the boot. The ending is too absurd and hilarious to reveal, and the rapid fire, often anachronistic, jokes are hard to keep straight. For example, Antony does a parody of a Mussolini balcony speech, while Octavian is clearly a fascist too. And yet actual events are used as plot points: the Donations of Alexandria, their wedding, Antony's Alexandrine triumph and Caesarion.

Other elements of the tradition referenced include Cleopatra's expertise with poison, her portrayal as Aphrodite at Tarsus (she is brought in on a clam shell) and her famous nose with which she conducts a dialogue through her mirror. Although the mode is always comic, Cleopatra is depicted as hypersexual, exploitative and lethal. That is probably why I like her, or more precisely, her portrayal by Magalí Noel, better known from her several turns in Fellini movies, especially as Fortunata in the *Satyricon* (1969). Noel's Queen looks more like my vision of a cinematic Cleopatra, sensual but not a vamp, striking but not an ideal of beauty and able to hold her own in rapid-fire dialogue. And she has that Ptolemaic nose! Just after the mirror scene, she and Toto compare *nasoni*! And when it bites her, the snake dies. If only Ms Noel had been cast in that other movie being filmed in Italy at the same time.

I conclude with a nod to *The Son of Cleopatra* (1965), although she is not in it and it is correctly omitted by Wenzel (2005). Lizpatra had effectively killed the genre of the peplum the year before and many of the cast and crew would move on to its artistic offspring, the Spaghetti Western. This is the story of Caesarion who has become a freedom fighter battling the fascist Augustus in his attempt to expand his empire in Africa. Cleopatra can still be the backdrop for a novel plot, even when she is dead and her big movie has tanked at the box office.

Although none of these are great films, they were surprisingly successful and, taken on their own terms, entertaining enough. They also remind us that Cleopatra was a regular presence in popular culture during this ten-year run. The result was a popular image of Cleopatra as white, sexually aggressive if not predatory, unsympathetic if not evil, who unmanned a good Roman only to be ground under the jack sandals of paleo-fascists. Every now and then a screenwriter might accidentally read some Plutarch, Pascal or Pushkin, but Lizpatra was very much both a product and a processor of pop cultural and sword-and-sandal cinematic traditions.

4.4 Pulps

The following novels published between 1950 and the debut of the Taylor/Burton film in 1963 reflect similar trends as the pepla, but with a lot more emphasis on sex. Only *A Queen for Caesar* (1962) featured Cleopatra as the central character and few of the following mostly pulp novels actually foreground the Queen and her traditional story. Instead, they focus on minor or fictional characters and their own intersecting storylines. Although of little merit as literature, they do illustrate the contemporary image of Cleopatra with emphasis on her sex life.

We mentioned the earliest, Barnard (1950), in a previous chapter because as an anthology it included two excerpts from Thomas (1927). It also included five from Barrington (1929), two from Mundy (1929), two from Ludwig (1937), one from Ferval (1924) and the entire novella of Gauthier (1838), *One of Cleopatra's Nights*. As the cover announces, the collection features the sensual nature of the Queen, but the inclusion of Gauthier revels in her predatory sexuality in the tradition of the Sophia Loren comedy (1953), Aurelius Victor and Alexander Pushkin (1835), bringing to mid-century America the questionable tradition that Cleopatra had sex with slaves or guards and murdered them the next morning.

Gerson (1956) was a very prolific writer of mostly historical fiction including three other titles which appear to have dealt with the ancient world. The competently written tale covers the period from Caesar's departure from Alexandria to his death. The author's ignorance of Roman history and culture detracts from the narrative, but it at least follows what little we know of Cleopatra's movements at this time. She is barely afforded more space than Octavius, even having him meet her in Alexandria. Gerson's description of Cleopatra and her clothing led me to think he was describing Claudette Colbert or Vivien Leigh (22). Invented and anachronistic characters – Aunt Julia long dead – clutter the story and there is not enough sex to interest anyone, but at least Cleopatra drives the narrative.

That is not the case for Matthews (1958), where the story of Antony and Cleopatra is just a backdrop for a ludicrous and poorly researched Talbot Mundy imitation featuring Paullus Didius, a gladiator turned Roman general, and his love interest, Berenice, a former handmaiden of Cleopatra. Since he eventually switches his allegiance to Octavian, Paullus might be loosely based on Q. Dellius. Cleopatra has been reduced to a framing device for a mediocre pulp adventure. Even her death is just a setting for the heroic rescue of the beloved.

In contrast, Warner (1960) is a well-researched and carefully written account by a trained classicist and veteran translator. It is a first-person novel about Julius Caesar written as a sequel to his successful *The Young Caesar* (1959).

Warner adheres closely to the ancient sources, especially Caesar's own writings, which makes it not nearly as much fun to read as the more speculative first volume. Cleopatra becomes just a minor supporting character. Their affair is presented as a casual fling, although she does come off rather well as a sensible and pragmatic girl. 'Certainly I was and am greatly charmed by her. She is a woman of immense energy and ambition, extremely intelligent, daring and ruthless.'[56] That is as sexy as it gets.

Hornblow (1961) is a Landmark book targeted at children or young adults. In fact, there have always been a surprising number of books on Cleopatra aimed at young people. Although part of a history series, it has been novelized beyond unadorned facts and furnished with imagined dialogue. The eunuch Mardian has been transformed into a faithful dwarf, for example. Cleopatra's relationships have been sanitized and children just arrive. It does, however, give a fairly complete and faithful summary of her whole life. The hands of Weigall and Wertheimer are quite evident. This very popular series does underscore that Cleopatra and the basic outline of her life was not completely lost to the turmoil of the 1960s.

That was a period of great social and political unrest in America, impacting attitudes toward power, race and gender. One of the hallmarks of the decade was the so-called Sexual Revolution. Changing standards affecting birth control, women's liberation and sexually explicit literature were shaping the 'baby boomer' generation's assumptions. Gardner (1962) is graphically explicit in its love scenes as well as on the lurid cover with half a snake bra. Two examples will suffice. The Pushkin/Gauthier theme of the costly one night with the Queen is featured.[57] When this Cleopatra arrives at Caesar's feet, she emerges naked from the carpet.[58] Even so she is not the porn star. That belongs to fictional characters Conon, another ex-gladiator, and his true love, Berenice, a handmaiden of the Queen. It is pulp fiction with more explicit sex.

We can save the trashiest for last. Vickery (1962) bears no connection to the events of Cleopatra's life except for some names and locations, but these probably saved it from being considered utterly without any redeeming social importance. This smut is mostly about the sexual adventures of a German war captive, and the author displays a cavalier ignorance of all aspects of Roman history and culture. Cleopatra is depicted as having had an affair with Caesar while in Gaul! Like Gardner, Vickery's book was probably marketed to cash in on the growing hype about Lizpatra, then in production hell while its stars projected sexual fantasies of their own.

4.5 Comic and graphic novels prior to Lizpatra[59]

Prior to the 1960s there was a mixed reception of Cleopatra in comic books. The oldest graphic depiction I have been able to find underscores the close association with film, in that it is little more than a three-page synopsis of the 1946 film *Caesar and Cleopatra*, starring Vivien Leigh.[60] On the other hand, the premier issue of *Ideal: A Classical Comic* is one of the longest treatments and also shows the influence of this film.[61] The headdress of a slave resembles that worn by Ftatateeta in the 1946 film, while Cleopatra and several of the Romans resemble their counterparts in the 1934 *Cleopatra* of Claudette Colbert. As in the Colbert film, there are no children. It tells the whole story of the historical Cleopatra but contains so many historical inaccuracies and inventions that it is difficult to detect a single historical or even literary source. Some are complete fabrications. For example, in a curious role reversal, Octavian attempts to seduce Cleopatra and then is duped into delivering the asp in a bouquet of flowers. On the other hand, there are several obscure real events and characters (e.g., Serapion and Dellius) which suggests some familiarity with Plutarch or at least a popular biography. Although the writers are not constrained by facts, they do stick to a consistent interpretation of Cleopatra's story familiar in the English-speaking world from the Renaissance and Restoration dramatists. The splash page conveys the theme: 'All for the love of a woman!' Compare the title of John Dryden's 1677 Antony and Cleopatra play, *All for Love*. In the tradition of earlier American films and advertising, Cleopatra is shown as white, a Queen at the mercy of a series of powerful men and a great beauty, sensuous but not overtly sexual.

This apparent public familiarity with the basic story of Cleopatra[62] is also reflected in three comics from the 1950s which feature science fiction/fantasy plot lines. Time travel adventures would be a frequent device in later comics and the earliest example stars Batman and Robin.[63] They notice a bat signal on an Egyptian frieze and arrange to travel back in time – using hypnosis – to Egypt to investigate. In the process they save Cleopatra from multiple

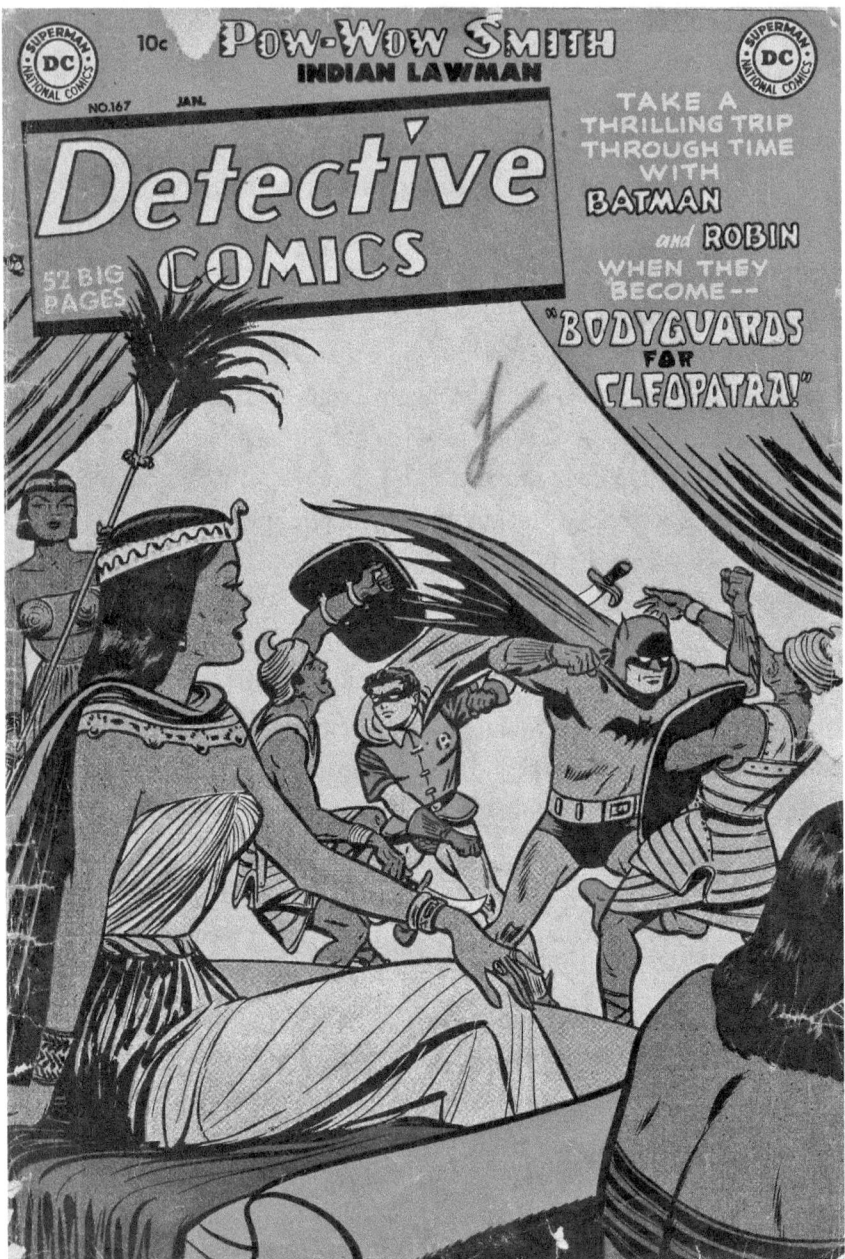

Figure 4.2 Cover of *Detective Comics* 167 (1951). From the author's collection.

assassination attempts, all involving iconic physical elements of the Cleopatra reception: the barge, a snake and a large cat. All of these could have come from exposure to the 1912 *Marcantonio e Cleopatra* and the 1917 (Theda Bara) and 1934 *Cleopatra*, but the hair and clothing point to the 1934 Claudette Colbert version. This makes it all the more odd that there are no Romans in this story, but perhaps they would have complicated the plot, a typical Batman police procedural with enough sexual tension to evoke a celibate 'GULP' from the caped crusader.[64] None of the critical events of Cleopatra's actual life are present. She is totally dependent upon the men around her for protection, especially Batman, whom she declares she will marry. Although she is inexplicably dark skinned on the cover (obviously by a different artist), Cleopatra is white, beautiful and sensuous in her metal bra.[65] In the same way she was used in cosmetic advertising earlier, this Cleopatra has been separated from her own narrative and has become just another stunning beauty smitten with a disinterested superhero.

The other two examples have relatively brief Cleopatra appearances which also avoid most of her traditional narrative. In the first, the Time Conductor is stranded briefly in 1955 in a wax museum. Napoleon and Columbus venture out to determine which is more famous, while Cleopatra stays to adjust the make-up on her statue.[66] In the second, we return to a wax museum, where Cleopatra comes to life in a room devoted to the most beautiful women in history. The wax Cleopatra is actually an actress posing for pictures to promote an upcoming movie – contemporary films include *The Serpent of the Nile* (1953) and *Two Nights with Cleopatra* (1954) – and is actually part of an ironic hoax engineered by a phony psychic.[67]

Most of the comics in this group show some influence of filmed versions of Cleopatra. In all of the examples to this point there has been a uniform presentation of Cleopatra's race, gender role and sexuality. With the exception of the Batman cover, she is depicted as white, although her Egyptianizing clothing does evoke an Oriental otherness. She may be a Queen, but she is defined and controlled by the males around her. She is uniformly depicted as beautiful, even sensuous and alluring, but there are no overt expressions of her sexuality, not surprising given the standards of the time. The curious fact that she is never depicted as a mother can best be attributed to the impact of the 1934 Colbert film, where none of her four progeny are mentioned.

4.6 Television pre-Lizpatra

A final example of the influence of the media frenzy about the coming film is an episode of the *Dick Van Dyke Show* from 1962, titled 'Somebody has to play Cleopatra'. That of course falls to Mary Tyler Moore.[68] At first, she does a calypso song and dance for the musical version of Cleopatra, but the rest of the plot is about how the actor playing Antony stirs jealousy and conflict among three couples, clearly inspired by the drama unfolding on the set in Italy. Lizpatra awaits.

4.7 Cartoons pre-Lizpatra

The cartoons follow a similar pattern to comics. They tend to try to insert Cleopatra into their narrative of established characters and ongoing plot lines through some tried and true techniques such as time travel, impersonation and revivification or reincarnation.

The earliest example I know of is a time-travel plot, from one of my own youthful favourites, the *Rocky and Bullwinkle Show* episode titled 'Peabody's Improbable History'.[69] In this version, Mr Peabody has Sherman set the Wabac machine to visit Cleopatra. Although it aired in late 1963, it was probably drawn well before the release of Lizpatra. Nevertheless, the episode appears inspired by some of the hype which accompanied its drawn-out filming. It is focused on Cleopatra's seduction of Julius Caesar and his defeat of her brother Ptolemy XIII. Voiced by June Foray, Cleopatra quickly beguiled 'Julie Honey'. Her Egyptianized clothing and hairdo, the eye make-up and the sanitized seduction clearly reflect what was public knowledge about the coming film, but the 'Wilson, Keppel and Betty'-style[70] sand dancing poses, the vestigial snake bra from Theda Bara and the atrocious puns are all Jay Ward originals. As in many contemporary versions, Cleopatra is defined by the men to whom she attaches herself. She has to use feminine charms to find a champion to fight her brother and has to be rescued by a dog – twice. Even her feminine mystique is undermined by her voice, stick figure and Pascal worthy nose.

5

Lizpatra[1] and Its Aftermath

By any measurement conceivable – financial, artistic, critical – the 1963 *Cleopatra*[2] was a failure. And yet it and its hapless star Elizabeth Taylor are so tightly linked to Cleopatra in the popular imagination that many students are sometimes astounded to learn that there have been others. For example, when I Googled 'Cleopatra' on 26 April 2020 there were seventeen pictures of Elizabeth Taylor before any other actress who had played the Queen. It is therefore not surprising that this film should have had an enormous impact on the popular culture image of the Queen. It is also not surprising, given the scandals, controversies and losses associated with it, that it has probably done more harm to Cleopatra's image than any other work of fiction since Aurelius Victor.

5.1 Mankiewicz (1963) aka Lizpatra

The chaos surrounding the making of the film, the tawdry affair and reckless lifestyle of Taylor and Burton, followed by the disastrous editing of the final product has been well chronicled by several scholars. In her chapter on the film, Cyrino[3] is very comprehensive and detailed and a good place to start, as would be the less scholarly but quite engaging AMC Documentary, *The Film that Changed Hollywood*.[4] Solomon sums up the consensus quite succinctly: 'In the final analysis, Cleopatra is a mighty and a mighty choppy spectacle, with serious flaws and magnificent moments.'[5]

Rather than revisit discussions of the problems of the production, the antics of the stars and the process which butchered the different releases,[6] let us focus instead on the existing product, especially the influence of past receptions, the conscious and unconscious changes to the image and finally what enduring elements the film added to the tradition.

Figure 5.1 Detail of ad for *Cleopatra* (Mankiewicz 1963). From the author's collection.

The entire project was reportedly an attempt to remake the Theda Bara film,[7] although no copy existed at the time. The influence of Weigall (1924) and his followers is apparent in the emphasis on Cleopatra's concerns with politics and imperialism. This thesis had been expounded in a 1957 'novelistic biography'[8] used by Mankiewicz.[9] The result is a film Cleopatra who is 'more intelligent and cultivated' than any other heretofore.[10] The images of the laughing Queen, the proto-flapper and the calmly elegant soap spokesperson have been superseded. She is more Rhonda Fleming than Claudette Colbert, except that Ms Fleming actually acted when in front of the camera.

Regrettably, one part of the tradition was respected without question. Cleopatra is white and very beautiful. Francesca Royster has examined in brilliant detail how what she calls the 'White Grotesque' has permeated this and other Cleopatra depictions.[11] Race had always been on the fringes of the Cleopatra reception. Even in the DeMille version (in the party scene), one of the young women asks, 'Is she Black?' With the 1963 film there is a new dimension. 'When the historical Cleopatra becomes Liz Taylor-in-*Cleopatra*, Cleopatra's race nation and even class are conflated with Taylor's performance and biography.'[12] Much of the later racial dialogue about the Queen is prompted and sometimes focused on Lizpatra rather than on Cleopatra VII Philopator.

The final general tradition adhered to in this film is what Sarah Hatchuel has recently termed the 'Cleopatra/Caesar Intertext'.[13] Basically she asks the question, 'Is William Shakespeare's *Antony and Cleopatra* a sequel to the earlier *Julius Caesar*?'[14] Hatchuel demonstrates how many filmmakers have believed so and have conflated the two plots, much to the horror of Bard scholars. 'In the films that conflate the plots [...] the heroic status of the queen elevates her from the start. The spectators follow her from early adulthood to death and see her as the only fixed, immovable character in the story.'[15] The conflation is confirmed by the addition of a scene in both the 1934 and 1963 films in which Cleopatra meets Caesar in Rome and celebrates the occasion with a procession that was never a part of the tradition. Hatchuel notes:

> Just as Caesar visits the Egyptian world at the beginning of each Cleopatra film, the Egyptian queen visits the Roman world when Caesar is about to be killed: Caesar narratively invades the world of *Antony and Cleopatra* and, in turn, Cleopatra intrudes into the world of *Julius Caesar*.[16]

Among other scenes and images from past receptions, there are the snakes and snake jewellery, anachronistic chariots, bath scenes, beautiful handmaidens, barges sailing up the Cydnus,[17] luxurious banquets, repressed and submissive Roman wives, impressionistic battle scenes or montages, poison testing and missing children. And a little sex. Most of the Plutarchan and Shakespearian supporting characters are there, with a few minor augmentations and cultural adjustments, especially in the cases of the smitten Apollodorus, the practical polymath Sosigenes and the loyal Rufio. Unfortunately, the last, well played by Martin Landau, lost most of his scenes in the editing frenzy, along with Richard Burton's.

I can credit the film with several contributions to the Queen's reception, including elements of self-parody, Isaic mysticism and magic, motherhood and of course, as Solomon pointed out, glorious spectacle. The DeMille film had been a visual delight, but none of the pepla or Pascal's Shaw had fully utilized modern technology to so dazzle an audience. The use of Todd AO, the Alex North music and the gorgeous if hilariously inaccurate sets and costumes outdid all its predecessors. You can almost forget that the story is largely incoherent while counting Ms Taylor's costume changes.

Lucy Hughes-Hallett was an early critic to note with approval the elements of self-parody in the film, which she characterizes with the phrase 'Cleopatra Winks':[18]

Such camp-Cleopatras, presenting their cleavages, their hordes of jeweled slaves, their grossly over-gilded palaces and their salacious reputations with a knowing wink, are doubly subversive. They promise forbidden pleasures, and they refuse to solemnize those pleasures by treating them as dangerous sins.

As we shall see in the next chapters, it will become increasing rare to find authors and artists who can take the Queen seriously, much less respectfully. For that I can never forgive this film.

The 1963 film puts heavy emphasis on Cleopatra's identification with Isis and her devotion to her cult. Although this is perhaps historically accurate, we have no way of knowing whether she believed it quite so literally. In other fictional works, authors going back to Haggard have run the gamut and portrayed all degrees of devotion and belief, but Lizpatra brought it firmly into the film genre. Not only does Cleopatra claim to *be* Isis, but she also uses magic during Caesar's death scene – and reportedly in some of the deleted scenes. As we shall repeatedly see, magic, sorcery and the occult will assume a prominent position in the reception from here on, especially in comics, fantasy tales and books about her children.

Cleopatra as a mother seems to have been problematic throughout her reception. Although mentioned in *Antony and Cleopatra*, the children are not depicted.[19] Indeed, her childlessness seems rooted in American film traditions.[20] She has no children in the DeMille film. It was therefore quite a departure for Lizpatra not only to devote much attention to the conception, birth, nurturing and murder of Caesarion, but to make Cleopatra's role as a mother central to her character and even to her decision to die. It was perhaps too much to ask for some screen time for Antony's three children, but Lizpatra is going to make it harder to ignore them.

Cultural memories of this film will resonate throughout the rest of the 1960s and 1970s, but mostly in the form of parody and mockery. Some of it was motivated by reactions to the scandalous behaviour of the stars or the disastrous critical and financial fallout, but much of it will be aimed at the cinematic shortcomings evident to any disgruntled viewer. Even as a fifteen-year-old forced to pay an outrageous premium ($.75) at the Air Force Base theatre, I was not impressed. My Junior High Latin book was more exciting. The backlash did not take long.

5.2 Historical fiction after Lizpatra

While the 1970s did not show much interest in Cleopatra, writers of multiple works of historical fiction did not pass up a ready-made plot. They all stick close to the established narrative and commendably keep her as the leading lady of her own life story, but none were able to resist the annoying anachronisms and superfluous made-up characters. Only Cowlin 1970 eschews the first-person approach but is the least engaging and intimate. Bostock 1977 on the other hand offers up not only a first-person title and narrative, but a lengthy one, generously sprinkled with rather graphic sex scenes. At the time it qualified as a 'bestseller' and won a minor award. Rofheart 1976 is the most readable and seems more sensitive to women's issues. With all of them, the impression lingers that Cleopatra was just another name in the list of potential subjects for the next book and not a vehicle for a meaningful exploration of the human condition.

5.3 Historical fiction for children and young adults

Writers of historical fiction for young people faced the same issues. Leighton 1969 covers Cleopatra's whole life in the third person, derived mostly from Weigall. Although not an American writer, Naomi Mitchison's publication of 1972 is worth mentioning since it is well written and a delight to read. Much of her other work is in the genre of historical fiction and more reflective of British rather than American culture, but is enjoying a burst of renewed interest. This story, however, is told in converging threads in different time periods, demanding an engaged reader. Mitchison is as interested in the offspring of slaves and courtiers as in the royals and is quite explicit in her treatment of sexuality. Herself a free-love Fabian socialist, Mitchison applied a multicultural and feminist lens to these tumultuous times. Her true children's book from the next year is one of the best of the genre, celebrating the courageous curiosity of a young princess.[21]

5.4 Science fiction

The received Cleopatra is going to enjoy a long association with science fiction and fantasy. As we have seen, comics, graphic novels and cartoons had already tapped into her story. The prose masters would not be far behind. One of the earlier examples, if not the earliest, also carried the imprimatur of one of the masters of the genre. Anderson 1977 does not actually feature the Queen. Rather, he created a planet named after her in a solar system which he invented and endowed with very specific properties carefully detailed in the introduction. His premise is that since mythological names have been used up, the Caesarian System has nomenclature derived from first-century BCE Roman history, or more likely from the *Dramatis Personae* of Shakespeare.[22] He then asked three other writers to join him in writing stories about its colonization and history. He hints at his choice of names in his own chapter when he opens with 'Regardless, the planet was beautiful'[23] and when his courageous female protagonist muses, 'Wryness twitched her mouth upward. *We named you better than we knew, Cleopatra. Lovely but – hm – capricious*.'[24] The other authors are not as specific, but clearly had the same image in mind.

5.5 Comedy

Humorous takes on the 1963 film were not limited to comic books. Jose Jimenez (Bill Dana)[25] and others put out comedy albums, but they focused more on the Liz and Dick scandal than on the film. Andy Griffith[26] and Mel Brooks (with Carl Reiner from 1960)[27] recorded their routines which did not focus as much on the film.

Probably the best-known parody was the near contemporary episode of the British 'camp' Carry On comedy series, *Carry On Cleo* in 1964.[28] It was actually shot on the abandoned London sets of Lizpatra using some of the same rented costumes. While a favourite of many classicists, this very clever spoof had little impact on American popular culture due to the disastrous failure of Lizpatra. Much of the very British humour is still lost on most contemporaries, since it reflects such different traditions, knowledge of antiquity and disdain for the excesses of the American epic film, as has been so carefully and intelligently documented by Nicholas Cull.[29] As he notes, *Carry On Cleo* and similar Roman-based comedies 'tells us little about Rome but much about Britain in the 1960's, its cultural needs and obsessions'.[30] More recently, Hatchuel has focused on the more serious underlying issues of imperialism, class and gender reflected in the humour and intertextual dialogue.[31]

5.6 Comics

The changes in the Cleopatra reception in comics which appeared during the 1960s and 1970s also reflect the impact of the 1963 *Cleopatra*. The speculation and hype about the film began as early as the beginning of the decade and generated an unprecedented amount of publicity for the production.[32] In the years following Lizpatra's release, several comic books capitalized on the public's familiarity with the story and their obsession with the scandals and cost over-runs.[33] Given the massive publicity and commentary which both issues generated at the time, this is hardly surprising, but some of this negative feeling was transferred to the historical Cleopatra. In spite of Plutarch's and Shakespeare's fairly sympathetic versions, the Augustan propaganda and nineteenth-century European fears of Orientalism and the 'New Woman' had insured that there would always be a negative thread in the Cleopatra tradition. Some of the comics from later in the decade also reflect the social and political upheavals which characterized the 1960s. Of the twenty-one examples from this decade, eleven involve some kind of time travel, seven are humorous, ten employ a direct reference to a movie about Cleopatra, one is based on a Victorian novel and one is hardcore pornography.

Among the humorous efforts, most are based on a single joke related to the film. For example, *Mad Magazine* featured a spoof of an ad for the movie which concentrated on the Taylor–Burton affair and the massive expenses incurred in the production.[34] The *Archie* series weighed in with Veronica posing with her 'Cleopatra Hair-Do' on two covers.[35] *Herbie* had two encounters with Cleopatra, the first in 1963 when the Devil tries to lure him to the dark side with an acting role opposite a 'Miss Baylor' who quickly forsakes a 'Richard Merton'.[36] Herbie, in 'The Fat Fury', later meets the 'real' Cleopatra when his father watches Lizpatra in the cinema and lusts to meet her while Mom is away.[37] Herbie misconstrues his request, time travels and brings back a Cleo who is ugly, obese and wild for Dad. This is the first time (in comics) we meet a counter-Cleopatra who does not live up to expectations of beauty and romance. There is also the time travel adventure of Bob Hope[38] and the mummy tale of Jerry Lewis.[39]

These all pale in comparison to one of the best comic depictions, an entry in the long-running *Asterix* series.[40] Unfortunately, this effort falls outside of the scope of this study since it is neither a product of the American reception of Cleopatra, nor does it appear to have had much influence on subsequent American comics. Indeed, it is indirectly critical of the shallower American efforts, as the creators display their superior knowledge of her narrative. In addition to the spoof of the Lizpatra movie ad and trailer on the cover, there are several other clear references to the film, including temper tantrums (5), the set design for Alexandria (11), the Sphinx-mobile (27), dancing girls (43) and an allusion to Liz's frequent costume changes (44). As with all the titles in the *Asterix* series, there is very close attention paid to historical and cultural detail, even when it is adapted for comic effect. For example, the statement of Pascal[41] about the size of her nose becomes a running gag, extending even to a two-page joke on the nose of the Sphinx (21–2). Equally amusing are the comic takes on Plutarch's reference to Cleopatra's ability to speak Egyptian (6) and Pliny's anecdote about drinking a dissolved pearl (11). These are details better known to a French or European audience. This Cleopatra is appropriately young and attractive but is represented as Egyptian and not overly sexual. She is manipulative and proud of her station, but she is clearly dependent on men for political support and validation.[42]

Historical accuracy does not fare as well in action hero comics, but several are almost as clever and creative as the *Asterix* issue. Most seem to have used the increasing popular awareness of Cleopatra to provide a storyline, plot device or establishing frame for a conventional heroic tale often involving time travel, mummies and romance. The earliest of this group features both a time travel hoax and 'actual' time travel, when Lana Lang poses as a fifteen-year-old Cleopatra until Superboy calls her bluff by taking her 'home' to meet the real one.[43] The premise for the plot – that Cleopatra is beautiful, fascinating and irresistible – reflects the studio hype about the star search. The next also involves time travel, this time to the future, when enemies of the Fly attempt to ruin him by bringing 'Cleopatra the Second' from 2262, complete with heavy Lizpatra eyeshadow.[44] As one would expect from Stan Lee, his *Iron Man* episode is quite original.[45] The story is framed by a reporter asking the playboy Stark if he could have 'made an impression' on Cleopatra, first as he arrives in Egypt and finally at the premier of a Lizpatra-style movie, 'The Loves of Cleopatra'. In between he unearths a tomb, time travels and defeats Romans and Hatap, a resurrected rival. Cleopatra is a violet-eyed beauty but reduced to the role of damsel in distress. This 1963 comic is perhaps the earliest to introduce horror movie style mummies into the Cleopatra narrative, a fusion of Egyptian movie motifs which will continue to the present day. This is a very vain and petty Cleopatra and quite different from Stan Lee's second treatment of a tragic Cleopatra. Dr. Strange encountered a bewitched and mute young woman and sets out by time travel to identify her and free her from another magician's spell. He sends her back to Mark Antony, 'back to the destiny that awaits you!'[46] Jimmie Olson is almost the victim of a time travel hoax involving a movie set which he ascribes to a movie called 'The Queen of the Nile', although he also mentions having seen Elizabeth Taylor in 'Cleopatra'.[47]

Cleopatra is linked with Helen of Troy and Marie Antoinette as icons of irresistible beauty when Superman, befuddled by red kryptonite, proposes to Lois Lane.[48] The *Wonder Woman* episode, continuing the fusion of Cleopatra romances with mummy-style horror plots, follows the movie theme in a story of espionage and sabotage surrounding an over-budget Cleopatra film.[49] In a long *Spiderman* story, actors make cameo appearances as Antony and Cleopatra in one frame which establishes the fake 'Paragon Studios' as an epic film factory, indicating that she has already become a sign for extravagant movie making.[50] Finally we encounter another sinister 'mummy' story in which Cleopatra has been reanimated as part of a convoluted plot to ruin Lana Lang's father and Suberboy.[51] Named Cleop-Ahmadi, she immediately seduces both Clark Kent and Superboy to take her to the costume ball dressed as Cleopatra. She is portrayed as beautiful but also as wearing unique perfume and having a musical voice, both aspects attributed to her in ancient sources. This increased interest in at least some aspects of the historical Cleopatra are used to even greater effect in the following examples from the same decade.

Rip Hunter, the Time Master, encounters Cleopatra twice in 1964. The first effort is a complex twenty-five-page story which betrays evidence of actual historical research and a reading of Plutarch.[52] The careful weaving of fact, fiction and humour make this one of the best Cleopatra comics. Cleopatra is beautiful and intelligent, scheming and manipulative, but still needs men to keep her in power. After crash landing, Rip aids the damsel in distress and then is lured into further interference by her charms and a charm. When that amulet is snatched by his crew, Rip sides with Ptolemy to restore the course of history. He gets her back into Caesar's graces by giving her two frames alone with him. I especially like the final frame when the underappreciated Bonnie says, in a paraphrase of Plutarch, 'HMPH! ... I still don't think Cleopatra's all THAT beautiful!' This same flawed Cleopatra returns in another long-story issue in which she is supposed to be part of a beauty contest rigged to be won by an actress playing Marie Antoinette – 'Liz Traymore', an obvious allusion to Elizabeth Taylor. Rip is engaged to bring forward Helen of Troy, Cleopatra, Theodora, Scheherazade and accidentally Marie, a milliner's apprentice from the eighteenth century who will, of course, be the winner.[53] This is a more comic Cleopatra who, after greeting the crew (including 'little Bonnie') and showing much skin and many tears, gets Antony to let her go. Even though the story is set shortly before or after their defeat at the Battle of Actium, a beauty contest seems more important. There follow several witty cat fights with the other contestants and Cleopatra even tries to seduce Justinian.

While this was hardly a positive image of Cleopatra, toward the end of the decade and into the 1970s things would take an even darker turn. Lizpatra kindled sexual fantasies for the author of a hard-core pornographic comic[54] which circulated underground until it was reprinted in 1991, minus one panel which can be construed as child pornography.[55] The text, unlike the graphic artwork, runs surprisingly close to the historical account. This is an early example of sexually specific material which will include an X-rated film, *Notorious Cleopatra* (1970), and an anime film, *Kureopatora* (1970), released in the USA in 1973 as *Cleopatra, Queen of Sex* and billed as 'The first X-rated animated film'.[56]

My final example from the period does not show any direct references to Lizpatra, but does continue the trend of showing a darker side to the Egyptian Queen. *Classics Illustrated* made its first foray into antiquity with Bulwer-Lytton's 'Last Days of Pompeii', so it was not out of character for them to anoint H. Rider Haggard as one of the world's greatest authors.[57] Sir Henry Rider Haggard (1856–1925) wrote fifty-five novels including *She* and *King Solomon's Mines*, but his lesser 1889 effort, *Cleopatra, being an Account of the Fall and Vengeance of Harmachis, The Royal Egyptian, as Set Forth by His Own Hand*, presented a pulp fiction vision of Cleopatra as an overtly sexual and manipulative villainess, told through the eyes of a mortal enemy and victim. These foreshadow the darker and more dangerous comic book Cleopatras of the 1990s.

There are only two Cleopatra comics in the next twenty years, but they too mark a transition to a very different Queen. The villainous side of Cleopatra, or at least her Sceptres, emerges in a very strange story tied to the Bicentennial celebrations.[58] An English exchange student named Lilibet Winsor (an allusion to the childhood nickname of Queen Elizabeth II)[59] views Cleopatra's sceptre (actually a Crook) which comes to life and possesses her. Since it forces everyone – except for Supergirl and Batgirl – to obey her, she almost becomes Queen Cleopatra of the Potomac. This Cleopatra is a controlling tyrant, but it is all about girl power. She intended to rule on her own and could only be defeated by a blonde and a redhead working together. The second incarnation does show clear references to Shakespeare, but with a lot of skin and blood.[60] This story explains that the alien Vampirella was once Cleopatra who was turned into a vampire by her brother Ptolemy and that her suicide was to facilitate her reincarnation on the planet Drakulon. This interweaving of a time travel/horror tale, Vampirella's occupation as an itinerant stripper and Shakespearean plot points is not seamless, but it is very clever, sensual and dark. We will return to this vampire theme in a later chapter.

5.7 Manga and anime

But in the meantime, there is an offering from Japan from the God of Comics himself – Osama Tezuka. The minimal movement of Japanese anime originated in budgetary constraints but has evolved into a sophisticated art form backed by psychologically insightful storytelling, clever dialogue and a rich tapestry of cultural references. *Astro Boy* started in 1955 under the original Japanese name which means 'Mighty Atom'.[61] The original black-and-white anime aired in the US from 1963 to 1965.[62] The print or manga version came out in 1969 and two colour versions of the anime have appeared since then.[63] In this story a mad scientist named Baribari or Rasburton has created a robot to impersonate Cleopatra in order to inspire a conspiracy to restore the Egyptian Empire and conquer the world. But he needs an artefact which had belonged to the real Cleopatra to complete the plot. This has somehow ended up in Japan and is placed in Astro Boy's chest for protection. He has Cleopatra's heart! Rasburton (Rasputin + Richard Burton?) sends his robot, complete with rabbit ears for control, to get it. When Cleopatra encounters a robot with a heart and a compassion for humanity, she changes and has to be sent back to the shop, but alas she, like Astro Boy, now longs for a father figure – and world peace. After Astro Boy smashes a few things and breaks her command connection, robo-Cleo brings down the temple on herself and her creator with one request – 'Let me call you "papa".'[64]

There are clear references to Lizpatra as an inspiration. When the Heart appears, the professor gives the back story and calls her the most beautiful woman in the world, part of the Lizpatra film hype in the 1960s, but also misquotes Pascal on the next page.[65] Later the Egyptian Brotherhood shout 'Long live Queen Cleopatra. Long live Elizabeth Taylor.'[66] Clearly the movie was influential in the 'What if she were a robot?' phase of the creative process, but the rest was a product of Tezuka's fertile imagination and established Astro Boy themes. But as in other receptions, this Cleopatra is still reliant on her beauty and on males to guide her, control her and rescue her. But at least we see flashes of a woman who has her own values and dreams, and in the end, she

Figure 5.2 Robot Cleopatra, *Astro Boy* manga (Tezuka 1969). From the author's collection.

acts on them as she destroys herself to save the world. Tesuka clearly saw that there was more to the real Cleopatra and would return to tell her story again.

The *Speed Racer* episode 'The Race against Time' is also anime which was and still is quite popular on US television but cannot match the artistry or the intelligence of Tezuka. This is also an impersonation plot. Go Mifune or Speed Racer (the M on his helmet is for Mifune motors which makes the Mach 5 racer) meets an archaeologist, appropriately named Digger O. Bone, who seeks help for his daughter Calcia. She has been hit on the head and thinks she is Cleopatra, whose tomb she has found. Her evil assistant Splint Femur is using her to steal the treasure. Speed and his pals are able to foil the plot mostly by driving very fast through the desert and into the Nile until Calcia regains her memory and her pith helmet. The opulence and Calcia's appearance clearly show the influence of Lizpatra on this rather thin storyline. This is not a particularly admirable Cleopatra. She is manipulated by men and largely ornamental. When she does act as the Queen, she is autocratic, cruel and vindictive. Her idea of mercy is to enslave our heroes.

Osamu Tezuka treated the Cleopatra legend twice, but the feature-length *Kureopatora* (1970)[67] is derived from both historical events and various fictional elements of her reception. It was a theatrical release from Tezuka's *animerama* or adult film period.[68]

Tezuka himself is a fascinating figure as a leader in the development of manga or comics in postwar Japan, as a pioneer in Japanese animation – anime – and as an imaginative genius. The range of his work is vast, but particularly impressive is his knowledge and understanding of Western literature and popular culture, especially the depth of his familiarity with the traditions about Cleopatra. He was highly educated and well read in Western or non-Japanese culture both high and low and this interest lasted throughout his life.[69] Tezuka treated Cleopatra in *Astro Boy* and *Kureopatora*, but he also interpreted Dostoyevski, Mussorsky, European painting, vampire tales, Sinbad and friends, Beethoven and the Bible.[70] He was attracted to other elements of classical antiquity as evidenced by the *Phoenix* series[71] and a long-form manga called *Apollo's Song*.[72]

For several years, Tezuka had been branching out from children's comics. Combining this with his growing passion for animation, it led him (in a risky move) to take on adult-targeted films which he dubbed Animerama. To this end he formed Mushi Productions, requiring an expensive plant and payroll. It did not pan out and was almost bankrupt when the first of three efforts, *1001 Nights*, appeared. To offset the cost over-runs and lacklustre box office returns, *Kureopatora* was released. Neither *1001 Nights* or *Kureopatora* were actually financial or critical flops, but the return on investment was not enough to stem a massive defection of talented animators. By the third film, the company was doomed and Tezuka had resigned. An English-dubbed version (now missing) was issued in 1972, but in an ill-advised effort to raise some cash, the studio sold the US rights to Xanadu Productions, which decided to market it as pornography. They retitled it *Cleopatra: Queen of Sex* and advertised it with an XXX rating. It had not been submitted to the MPAA and most doubt that it would have received even an X rating. This was thought to be a ploy to cash in on the forthcoming animated *Fritz the Cat*, which traded heavily on its rating in ads. This tactic did not work, as the film, while quite erotic, was hardly pornographic even by 1970s standards. It quickly faded from the scene when word got out that it was no *Deep Throat*. It did fare slightly better in Germany as *Cleopatra und die tollen Roemer*, but they cut twenty-eight minutes of the sci-fi and the non-sex scenes. Mushi Pro did release a third version, *Belladonna of Sadness*, but Tezuka had no hand in it.

Cleopatra: Queen of Sex begins in the future with an effort to thwart an alien attack by the 'Pasateli' which is known only as the 'Cleopatra Plan'.[73] To crack it, three agents are sent back in time to occupy the bodies of close associates of the Queen: a slave of Caesar, a princess and a pet leopard (a nod to Orientalism). The scene shifts to Caesar invading Egypt amidst graphic slaughter, rape and pillage. Caesar, who is green, actually molests and abducts the daughter of an official. The images seem to evoke either the Rape of Nanking or postwar Japan, or perhaps both. Before the future spies arrive, a plot is already afoot to kill Caesar. Apollodora suggests that only Cleopatra can do it. While this Cleopatra is quite ugly, she possesses a mighty weapon – the Cleopatra Grip. Apollodora arranges for her to be magically beautified and sexualized and ready for the assassination. Pascal's dictum is actually applied. Her nose is changed, and with it, history. In the meantime, the agents arrive from the future and will play their parts. Cleopatra is delivered to Caesar in a sack, but instead of killing him, she falls in love. The ensuing sex is minimalist and abstract and vintage Tezuka. There is a subplot involving two of the alien agents, but eventually the film returns to a Caesar and Cleopatra story including the birth of Caesarion, a visit to Rome and a triumphal parade on a Ferrari. The parade continues the anachronisms with a marvellous history of Western art as a parody of the Lizpatra entry parade. Calpurnia, Octavian and Mark Antony appear as well as a gladiatorial match complete with flyswatters, pistols and Astro Boy. When Calpurnia proves that Caesar loves her, Cleopatra turns to Brutus to convince him to kill Caesar. The Shakespearean assassination of Caesar is played out as a Kabuki drama. Cleopatra returns to Egypt, seduces Mark Anthony at Tarsus and eventually emasculates him. She and the women of Egypt ensure that his troops are as unfit for battle as he. Although she engineered his defeat, Cleopatra mourns the death of Antony and yearns to return to the ugly powerless woman she once was. The space aliens take her to a 'Temple of Death' where she is cornered by Octavian, who turns out to be gay. Cleopatra is bitten by a snake. The aliens return and appear to report that the 'Cleopatra Plan' involves beautiful women leading astray all of Earth's leaders, and is almost complete.

As is the case with many of Tezuka's works, there are frequent gags, mostly visual. Stock characters such as Mustachio and Astro Boy pop up. Tezuka likes to mix time periods and cultures – such as placing Caesar on Mount Rushmore – and he evokes modern events like the Rape of Nanking and the occupation of Japan in his non-historical representation of the Roman 'invasion' of Egypt. The sci-fi plot is basically a parody of *Invasion of the Body Snatchers* including pods. Some of the anachronisms are extended, such as turning Caesar's triumph into a survey of Western art, the gladiator games into a TV special and Caesar's death into a Kabuki play. Even Power, a Tezuka authority, is stumped by some of the contemporary pop culture references.[74] I rather liked the homage to the *Time Machine* and the eye patch on the prow decorations of the quinquereme at Actium.

Although at its core a straightforward romantic tragedy, *Cleopatra: Queen of Sex* is punctuated by very abstract animated scenes worthy of an 'art house' experimental film like his *Tales of the Street Corner* (1962), *Male* (1962) or *Pictures at an Exhibition* (1966).[75] Violence gets diverse treatments, but the two-colour fight between the blue Romans and the red Egyptians is gorgeously gory. Viewers are puzzled that Caesar is green, but of the principals only Ionius (an alien), Anthony and Cleopatra are normative. I would note that Caesar is the colour of the numerous statues of himself in the Rome scenes, as is the Dictator poster in *Tales of the Street Corner* (1962) and Anthony after being poisoned. Octavian on the other hand is blue. Cleopatra going into and out of the tiny sack (no carpet!) is a fantasy check amidst momentary realism. Two of the sex scenes are rendered as abstraction: headless line figures writhe to music when she beds Caesar (but neglects to kill him) and mirror drawings merge and separate when she and Apollodora have lesbian sex. The bath sex scene is literally steamy, but more cinematically erotic. None of them approach the level of pornography associated with an X rating, even by 1970s standards. Crude and graphic comments abound if the translations are accurate, especially in the Spanish and German versions I have seen.

While character motivations and personalities have undergone considerable alteration, the narrative adheres very closely to the traditional story arc and even reveals more than a passing familiarity with Plutarch. The influence of Shakespeare and Lizpatra are blatant, but there are also French and Russian influences as well. Cleopatra's beauty and sexuality are upfront, but Tezuka seems to have noted Plutarch's remark that her beauty was not extraordinary and has her transformed via magic cosmetology. I see in this scene an echo of his 'Cosmetic Surgeon' in *Pictures at an Exhibition* (1966). Among the standard events, Tezuka also includes two which are rarely seen in British and American reception. The first derives only from Aurelius Victor and claims that Cleopatra would sleep with random men and have them killed in the morning. Pushkin, Gauthier and Sophia Loren expanded on this. The other event has no ancient source I can find and that is the so called 'Cleopatra Grip'. The Cleopatra Grip (aka Pompoir or Wallis Simpson) is a sexual manoeuvre requiring some highly developed Kegel (pelvic floor) muscles. Cleopatra's unique ability in this region is the basis for Apollodora's plan to use her as an assassin. This plan requires that Cleopatra be made as sexy as possible in order for her to gain access to Caesar. After the sight gag, it is not mentioned again, but it is an established element of the Cleopatra tradition. A dubious element from her reception hence becomes an essential plot point in Tezuka's version.

Of course, the differences are more revealing about the agenda of any reception. The bookended sci-fi plot and the three alien characters are not all that intrusive. The elaborate makeover is a novel addition but could reflect Pascal's thoughts about Cleopatra's nose. Homophobia is inserted by the change from Apollodorus, loyal servant, to Apollodora, the lesbian puppet master/sexual partner to Cleopatra, and making Octavian gay to thwart her attempt to seduce him. The torrid love affair is now with Caesar and extends beyond the second half of the film. Caesar's true love for Calpurnia motivates Cleopatra to lure Brutus into the assassins' plot.

The most jarring alteration is in the character and depiction of Antony. Antony is still seduced by Cleopatra, her barge and her lovely entourage, but he is whiny, ineffectual, sexually inadequate, produces no children and is poisoned by Team Cleopatra-Apollodora. At least he is still a drunk! He can't perform when she gets him in bed, until she convinces him, with two bananas, that size does not matter. Cleopatra seems fond of Antony but goes through with the plan to poison him. It does, however, motivate her split with Apollodora and her attempt to seduce Octavian. In light of the recent scholarship on Antony, we might see the depiction as prescient.[76] Libia is left to scream at the Romans, through the storm from the top of the tomb, to go home, just before she is transported.

Kureopatora had minimal impact on American popular culture at the time since it had a limited release and was marketed with a fake XXX rating. It did, however, have an influence on the depiction of Cleopatra in pornographic films.

5.8 Pornographic films

As noted above, once fanned by Lizpatra the erotic aspects of Cleopatra's reception had received the expected renewed attention in the fiction of Bostock 1977, in the graphic novels of Diggs 1977 and in the anime of Tezuka 1970. She also began to appear in pornographic films about this time.[77] One of the earliest is *The Notorious Cleopatra* (1970)[78] issued the same year as *Kureopatora*. This is one of the earliest films to portray Cleopatra as Black and hypersexual, even for the genre. As Hatchuel notes, the film takes a slightly different turn:

> Like the traditional *Cleopatra* films, *The Notorious Cleopatra* has the powerful woman punished for her sexual activity and her foreign status. But contrary to the 'Classical' versions, it displays its agenda more openly, without any mediation, revealing the political, racial and gender issues posed by the Egyptian queen in a more forward, though quite unrefined, way.[79]

Two other similar sex films appeared in the early 1980s: *Irresistible* (1982)[80] and *The Erotic Dreams of Cleopatra* (1983).[81] Both draw on the ancient propaganda sources for their material. *Irresistible* draws on Aurelius Victor's charge of death as a price for her favours in the short time-travel episode featuring the Queen.

5.9 Musical theatre

Perhaps the best known if least successful musical comedy version is *Her First Roman*, which had only seventeen performances in 1968.[82] It is also quite remarkable for featuring a Black actress as Cleopatra and because no review remarked on that fact. I have not seen the script, but the cast album is available (surprisingly good) along with a detailed plot summary in the liner notes.[83] Leslie Uggams still features it on her website.[84] Based on Shaw's *Caesar and Cleopatra*, it too was a 'comedy' and was intended to capitalize on the success of *My Fair Lady* (1964), but Drake sacrificed almost all of Shaw's witty satiric dialogue for the love story and the songs.[85] Due to some criticism in the previews, massive script and music changes were implemented, without the knowledge of the director, according to Uggams.[86] It did not help that both Clive Barnes and Walter Kerr panned it savagely.[87] *Her First Roman* probably came too soon after Lizpatra to have had a chance, but the consensus seems to be that it was a bad concept, badly executed by all but the valiant stars.[88]

5.10 Television

Also falling into the category of humour was the PBS talk show *Meeting of the Minds*, hosted by Steve Allen and featuring 'guests' who were historical figures, including Cleopatra in the first two shows,[89] as portrayed by Jayne Meadows. As Allen has noted:

> The idea is that every syllable will be part of an actual quotation. The degree of the exact quotation varies from character to character. In the case of some people who played important roles in the drama of history, of course, there is no record of anything they ever said or wrote. Two examples that come to

mind are Cleopatra and Attila the Hun. Nevertheless, they were both fascinating characters for our show. And there's nothing difficult in creating dialog for them. You bring factual information into conversational form – and commit no offense in doing so.[90]

Despite its admirable attempts at historicity, the seriousness is tempered (or undermined) by the ultra glamourous appearance of the Queen and her witty responses to other characters.[91] It is nevertheless entertaining to watch a reception of Cleopatra retell facts of her actual life.

The reception of Cleopatra underwent a drastic change after the disappointing Lizpatra of 1963. She had been a man-eating vamp and femme fatale in the late nineteenth century in French drama (Sardou), English pulp fiction (Haggard) and Italian and American silent film (Theda Bara). That image had been tempered by a softer and more romantic Cleopatra in the Palmolive advertising (1918–45), given some remarkably sympathetic treatment in several novels and tempered further in the Claudette Colbert and the Vivien Leigh films. The pepla Queens from Rhonda Fleming to Elizabeth Taylor only slightly hardened the edges, while at the same time according her more respect for her political acumen and leadership. I credit the disastrous Lizpatra with triggering a shift back to the *fin-de-siècle* Cleopatra, back to the *femme fatale*. Throughout the 1960s and 1970s we have watched her become an object of humour and parody and witnessed an increasing re-focus on her alleged sexual excesses. The only positive portrayals in this period were by non-Americans: Mitchison and oddly enough Tezuka.

6

Eighties' Ladies

After the Lizpatra effect began to fade in the early 1970s, there were fewer and fewer receptions of Cleopatra in American popular culture, only one (Tezuka 1970) worthy of serious interest and none which enjoyed noteworthy financial success. On the other hand, while the second half of 1980s would offer only four additions to the tradition, three of them would set Cleopatra's reception off in new directions in poetry and fine art, in science fiction and in fantasy horror.

6.1 *Maxie* – Glenn Close[1]

Our first example is actually a revival of the kinder, gentler Queen of the 1920s and 1930s who is simultaneously comical and sensual. *Maxie* (1985) was a light comedy clearly designed to exploit the impressive range of Glenn Close.[2] The film required her to play a dual role: Jan, a mousy and repressed church secretary who unintentionally starts channelling the spirit of a 1920s flapper; and Maxie, the very spirit of that silent film actress who died on the way to a breakout screen test. The husband Nick summons Maxie's spirit after they rent her old apartment, discover her lipstick graffiti behind the old wallpaper and learn about her from her former song and dance partner. Since Nick is an ardent lover of silent film, he arranges to watch her only existing scene.[3] Once Maxie has been summoned to her old apartment, she takes over Jan's body with comically predictable results. The climax of the film features the fulfilment of her dream of a screen test in the role of Cleopatra, complete with several verbal and visual allusions to the most famous films about the Egyptian Queen, including the 1917 *Cleopatra* starring Theda Bara and her equally famous snake bra.

Figure 6.1 Screen shot of Glenn Close as Cleopatra in *Maxie* (Aaron 1985).

Possession was a theme dear to writer Jack Finney, whose book *Marion's Wall* inspired this script.[4] Best known for *The Bodysnatchers* which was made into films four times, Finney was also fascinated with time travel and time bending – a topic he visited in two novels.[5] *Marion's Wall* touched on both of these themes and explored Finney's passion for the silent era of Hollywood. Nick, the principal character here, is drawn to Marion's connection with the era and with his own father (they had been lovers) and is himself possessed by Rudolph Valentino once they get to Hollywood. It is a charming tale, but with a radically different ending to Marion's nude audition and a climax which involves the discovery and tragic destruction of the entire AFI Lost 100 Silent films. There is no mention of or allusion to Cleopatra in the novel.

To have included Cleopatra in a 1970s book on silent film would not have been remarkable, but Finney was clearly not the source for the decision to have Maxie audition for a role as the Egyptian Queen. It was not an obvious choice, as there was relatively little American pop culture interest in Cleopatra during the 1980s. Between 1973 and 1978 the Cleopatra Jones–Wong–Schwartz trend had made its mark as Francesca Royster has cleverly analysed.[6] There was no shortage of pornographic Cleopatras, including a recent one variously titled as *The Erotic Dreams of Cleopatra* (1983).[7] Cleopatra had also appeared on several TV shows mostly based on reactions to Lizpatra – as *The Patty Duke Show* did in 1963– or in brief allusions in episodes of *MASH* (1972–86) or *The Love Boat* (1977–86). Dr Pepper television ads featuring Judy Tenuta (occasionally as Cleopatra) aired as late as 1989.[8] Clearly *Maxie* was not part of a general revival in the long reception of Cleopatra.

The nude audition scene was not feasible in 1985. The most likely inspiration for the switch to a Cleopatra scene was from other films. The 1917 Theda Bara *Cleopatra* was lost by this time, but interest in it and its many stills was piqued in 1963. The pre-code 1934 Claudette Colbert version was clearly the source for several images of the costume. The impact of the images from the 1963 Elizabeth Taylor version and the ballyhoo surrounding the search for a star are clearly reflected. None of these three films were on the popular culture radar in 1985, but the screenwriter clearly knew of them and had access to copies and/or still images. Both Taylor and Colbert are mentioned by name in the press scene immediately following the audition.

After several comical attempts, Maxie finally lands a screen test in Hollywood for the Cleopatra movie. Since Maxie is currently angry with Nick, Jan is forced to go through with the test as herself. She hobbles onto the sound stage in platform shoes and full Cleopatra regalia including a cloak, vulture headdress complete with the uraeus, large pectoral-style necklace, wrist bracelets and a bikini top with an elaborate jewelled snake embroidered on it. There is a good deal of glitter on her chest and arms, but it is clear from her posture and demeanour that it is Jan and not Maxie. She is greeted by the director who attempts to introduce her to Harry Hamlin, playing himself in the part of Mark Antony, and to prep her for the scene, but she turns to Nick and pleads to leave because she does not want to 'throw up on Harry Hamlin'. However, he forces her to carry on, with disastrous results. Jan is petrified and has to read the lines off cribbed notes taped on her bracelet. The angry director stops the action, but Nick literally pushes her back on. This time she slips to the bottom of the pillow-strewn bed, but swoons dead away when Harry kisses her. Everyone is ready to throw in the towel as Nick revives her, when in sultry tones she says, 'Who's the good-looking guy in the skirt?' and we know that Maxie is back in Jan's body.

The transformation is rapid and complete. Maxie rips off the bracelets and necklace and asks for another take. No one seems interested. She fastens the cloak at her shoulder, concealing the snake bra, and starts the scene again, with a deeper, sexier voice and so much feeling that everyone on the set leaps back to action, including an obviously smitten leading man. Jan has disappeared, along with all of the body glitter and the pile of pillows. This time there is real emotion and obvious sexual chemistry as Maxie does the same lines and more. The props and gimmicks that were meant to recall earlier sexualized Cleopatra's – the bra, the bed, the glitter – weren't necessary. This Cleopatra exudes all of those things on her own. Earlier film Cleopatras were evoked only to show that a true vamp does not need them. This passage loosely follows a scene from the 1963 *Cleopatra* (near the end of the first half), when her political ambitions for an equal partner ignite the sexual chemistry with Mark Antony.

What were the sources of some of the images, costumes and characterizations? First of all, Close is wearing a bra with a snake motif. This is clearly an homage to the famous snake bra worn by Theda Bara in the 1917 *Cleopatra* film. There is a marked disconnect between the overt sexuality and sensuality of the costume – note the glitter on her skin – and Jan's timid awkwardness. She is outfitted with the one of the most enduring icons of Cleopatra's sensuality, but she is still Jan the church secretary.

Most of the movies employ a vulture headdress and uraeus, but this one seems very close to the one worn by Claudette Colbert in the *Cleopatra* of 1934. Even for a pre-code film, Colbert's costumes were quite daring. When the spirit of Maxie reappears and suddenly becomes so self-confident and comfortable with her sexuality and her authority, she is reflecting *this* Cleopatra. She is so confident in her sensuality and desirability that she sheds the ostentatious jewellery and covers the iconic snake bra with her cape.

The glitter and the added element of political power which emerges as a covered-up Maxie repeats Jan's lines seems to me also to evoke the 1963 *Cleopatra* or Lizpatra. The scene evokes this comparison by the position of Cleopatra and Mark Antony on the bed, inspired by the billboard ad from Lizpatra, the one which was done before Rex Harrison's lawyers had him inserted. In 1985 it was still fashionable to make fun of these images. That comic element could also have been derived from the British spoof *Carry On Cleo* (1964), starring Amanda Barrie. The prominence of the bed in both films points to a deliberate choice. The shift from the humiliating humour at Jan's expense to the sexual tension and manipulation in the second take is the climax of the film.

Central to the book and alluded to in the film, however, was an intense search for an actress to pull off the scene in question. That was perhaps enough to remind the writers of the well hyped search for a Cleopatra in the 1960s. That would have led them to the Taylor and Barrie camp Cleopatras and the superbly sensual Colbert version. Since the Theda Bara film had been lost for about thirty years and silent films were not back in vogue, it might have come to the attention of the costume designers through the plot points and through the uncredited use of Carol Lombard's image from *The Campus Vamp* (1928) to represent Maxie's only screen time. Theda Bara was after all the quintessential vamp, earning that title in *A Fool There Was* (1914).

Maxie's snake-style bra deserves some mention. The premise of the costuming and the opening of the scene is that to embody a powerful queen who can also attract an alpha male with her sensuality, one needs all of the headdresses, armlets, necklaces, glitter and most of all a snake-emblazoned bra frequently associated with a stage or movie Cleopatra. But a true vamp or *femme fatale* can shed most of that and even cover up completely, but still show everyone in the room that she is the one who deserves their complete attention. In the end, the director, producer, Harry Hamlin and even a young Leeza Gibbons and *Entertainment Tonight* are convinced they have found an authentic Cleopatra for their rather peculiar reception of the Queen. Maybe that is why they revived her reception in this period of Cleopatra neglect – as a statement that only the spirit of an uninhibited flapper untainted by Hollywood's decline from its silent purity could possibly capture the essence of a strong, politically astute and sexually self-confident figment of their imagination.

6.2 Barbara Chase-Riboud

Barbara Chase-Riboud, an African-American artist, poet and novelist, was raised and educated in Philadelphia and now divides her time between Paris and Rome.[9] Her long-time fascination with Cleopatra VII of Egypt has resulted in six large-scale sculptures, several mixed media wall pieces, three books of poetry and several allusions in her novels. The result is not only a very personal reception of Cleopatra, but also an intelligent and informed contribution to the ongoing receptions and discussions of Cleopatra's race, gender and sexuality. At first glance, Chase-Riboud would not seem to belong in a discussion about American popular culture, especially since Shaw was marginalized earlier. I have included her out of a sincere admiration of her work and her efforts to communicate her visions as proudly as possible through her popular novels and her commitment to public art, especially in the form of her *Africa Rising* memorial at the African Burial[10] and her proposal for a Memorial to the Middle Passage slave trade.[11] She certainly reflected Black American culture as she confronted European and Egyptian traditions, using Cleopatra to channel many of those experiences in her sculpture, poetry and novels. The heroine of her most recent novel also 'has a thing about Cleopatra'.[12]

Chase-Riboud's talent was recognized early on by her parents and mentors. One of her prints was purchased by the Museum of Modern Art before she was out of high school. Between a BFA from Temple in 1957 and an MFA from Yale in 1960, she received a John Hays Whitney grant to study at the American Academy in Rome. While there she was immersed in Greek and Roman art and history. As a result of a dare at a Christmas party, she left for a trip to Egypt. It was a formative event: 'For someone exposed only to the Greco-Roman tradition, it was a revelation. I suddenly saw how insular the Western World was vis-a-vis the non-white, non-Christian world.'[13]

After her marriage to photojournalist Marc Riboud, Chase-Riboud lived in Paris and travelled widely. She made her mark first as a sculptor, with her breakthrough marked by the acclaim and criticism of her *Malcolm X*[14] and *Zanzibar*[15] series in the 1970s. These pieces, the subject of a recent book,[16] also illustrate her signature technique involving wax moulded with a blowtorch, the lost wax bronze casting and the silk, hemp and/or wool draped to hide a steel or wooden armature. Artistically they show her debt to Bernini's sense of movement and the mixing of contradictory elements. Thematically they also demonstrate her growing concern for Black issues and especially for the Atlantic slave trade. 'Why Did We Leave Zanzibar?', the first poem in her first book, both illustrates her anguish over the African Diaspora and contains her earliest published allusion to the Cleopatra legend.[17] After her marriage to Sergio Tosi and the opening of an atelier in Rome, the influence of Egypt and the classical world merge in 'Isis' from 1995[18] and in the homage to the Winged Victory of Samothrace in the 1994 public monument *Africa Rising* at the African Burial Ground near Wall Street in New York City.[19]

The critically successful 1974 book of poems (edited by Toni Morrison), *From Memphis & Peking*, reflects what Chase-Riboud is most passionate about: Egypt, China, a hunger for her own history,[20] her focus on Black issues in general and the slave trade in particular,[21] and confronting her own sexuality. Barbara Chase-Riboud is a passionate woman. Many of the poems are autobiographical and are also very visual, arranged in pyramids, triangles and zigzags almost like 'Concrete Poetry' at times.[22] Other poems create visual impact through short, even single-word lines and the use of parallel or alternating columns. As she is frequently quoted, 'First of all, writing isn't my second choice. Writing is a parallel vocation.'[23] Her second book of poetry, *Portrait of a Nude Woman as Cleopatra* (1987), which I will discuss shortly, received the Carl Sandburg Prize for Poetry in 1988. A third volume has recently appeared which contains new poems and reprints the contents of both earlier volumes.[24]

Chase-Riboud is perhaps best known for her five published novels and the controversies she seemed to stir up with each one. With the exception of the *Echo of Lions*,[25] which concerns the *Amistad* incident, her novels tend to focus on 'seemingly powerless women' whom she sees 'as powerful because they survived violence, depredation, disdain and contempt in life because their names have emerged from the darkness of the past to become part of human history'.²⁶ Theses women are Sally Hemmings, the quadroon mistress of Thomas Jefferson;²⁷ the white slave who becomes the queen mother of the Ottoman Empire;²⁸ Harriet Hemmings, Sally's daughter;²⁹ Sarah Baartman;³⁰ and 'The Hottentot Venus', whom Chase-Riboud also evoked in the *Africa Rising* monument.³¹ Most recent is *The Great Mrs. Elias: A Novel*,³² which features a heroine who, according to the author, 'has this thing about Cleopatra'.³³ It joins four other novels which feature '"invisible" women of color'³⁴ who find themselves caught between the values and traditions of their homeland and the imposition of all that is white, Christian and European. The image of Cleopatra is central to this novel and its main character:

> She believed herself to be the reincarnation of Queen Cleopatra: her raw femaleness, her approachability, her maternal instincts, her woman warrior exterior were all overshadowed by the one thing she had built her life around: her sex – in all its power and imperialness.³⁵

The young Bessie learns all she can about Cleopatra and seeks to emulate her.³⁶

These references abate around the midpoint of the novel until late in the story when she (now Hannah) faces ruin: 'In Hannah's mind she was Greater New York's Cleopatra, barricaded in her gilded palace, staving off the encroaching Roman army after the defection of her lover.'³⁷ Hannah found the strength to prevail against racism and misogyny through her lifelong heroine and role model: 'She was Cleopatra against the Marc Antonys of the world.'³⁸ In many ways, Chase-Riboud has shared Hannah Elias's (or Bessie Davis's) obsession with Cleopatra throughout her notable literary and artistic career. This is especially pronounced in the poetry and sculpture in which she demonstrated her own 'thing about Cleopatra'.

I have discussed Chase-Riboud's Cleopatra sculpture elsewhere.³⁹ When she saw her husband's photographs of the recently excavated Han dynasty sarcophagi of Liu Sheng and Dou Wan made of jade plaques wired together with gold,⁴⁰ she applied the technique to her Cleopatra sculpture series.⁴¹ This began in 1973 with the *Cape*, which is made up of 3,500 multicoloured bronze squares of different sizes engraved with thirteen different designs and a length of braided hemp. The 200cm-high piece 'appears to rest softly on the ground' and might reflect Plutarch's description of Cleopatra's arrival in Tarsus.⁴²

Figure 6.2 *Cleopatra's Door*, Barbara Chase-Riboud, 1984. Author's photograph.

Cleopatra's Door was completed in 1984.⁴³ This large work, 11 feet high, is constructed of the same plaques linked as a kind of shawl and draped over an oak armature, which she uncharacteristically celebrates rather than conceals. Instead of fabric, we find the bronze treated as textile and the structural oak providing the organic element, emphasizing the allusions to both Cleopatra's power and her sexuality.

Energy seems to pulse from the solid *Chair* (1994),⁴⁴ a seat of power, but also in most stories of her end, the site of her demise. While in Rome, Chase-Riboud came under the influence of many and diverse artists, but the Baroque in general and Bernini in particular added exuberant emotion to her abstractions. She has frequently expressed her admiration for another African American who also worked in Rome and who shared her fascination with Cleopatra – Edmonia Lewis, to whom *Cleopatra's Chair* is a clear homage.⁴⁵ Selz and others have noted Chase-Riboud's admiration for Edmonia Lewis: 'The queen is dying with a sense of pride.'⁴⁶ In the words of Scott Trafton, Lewis's Cleopatra is 'a racially ambiguous, sexually transgressive, powerful yet tragic figure, with an African past and an American future, who seems exhausted to death'.⁴⁷ That could apply to all three women. There is fabric on the back, but otherwise it is an empty chair, like Bernini's unoccupied *Cathedra Pietri*.⁴⁸ When I think of all the thrones, especially empty ones in Cleopatra movies, this becomes all the more powerful a symbol of her power and her powerlessness.

Cleopatra's Bed (1997) clearly pays homage not only to the Rembrandt drawing which inspired 'Portrait' and the frequent references in the poem, but also to its prominence in Western depictions of her narrative. Chase-Riboud seems to bring this series full circle back to the seductive opulence of the *Cape* by not only including fabric, but having the mattress and the braided piece at the rear made of silk. This piece evokes Cleopatra's sexuality, but also her display of luxury and power that lured Antony.⁴⁹ She has also informed me that she has completed a sculpture of *Cleopatra's Wedding Dress* as well as the *Staircase*, which I have not seen and which might conclude the series.⁵⁰

In the midst of this four-decade-long multimedia focus on the Egyptian queen, Chase-Riboud wrote *Portrait of a Nude Woman as Cleopatra* in 1987. It is appropriate that this collection of fifty-seven sonnets in different voices should have been inspired by a work of art, a drawing by Rembrandt.[51] What struck Chase-Riboud at the time was that she saw a Cleopatra who was just a nude woman sitting on a bed (a sculpture subject) with none of the attributes from her long reception: 'Not one of the famous romantic elements of the historical Cleopatra was evident, but she was more real than any Cleopatra I had ever seen.'[52] This is a very personal portrait of Cleopatra. She depicts her as shaven headed, never calls her beautiful or Black, but frequently refers to her as African.[53] Chase-Riboud calls the work a 'Melologue', which she defines as a recitation with musical accompaniment. The musical origin of the work is reflected in a cantata which Andy Vores created from the poems in 1990,[54] and the jazz opera *Portrait of a Nude Woman as Cleopatra* by composer Leslie Burrs, with Lisa Edwards-Burrs of Virginia State University singing the role of Cleopatra. *Portrait* is a fascinating piece, although the surrealistic and anachronistic portions are quite challenging for literal-minded classicists. It is based largely on Plutarch (including quotes from the 1579 North translation) and is largely, but not entirely, free from the influence of English drama and American film. In my previous article in *New Voices*,[55] I only discussed some passages which departed from the Plutarchan narrative, particularly those dependent on Pushkin (Sonnet 26) and Chaucer (Sonnet 53). As Chase-Riboud said in an interview:

> The genesis of my interest in Cleopatra is based on my fascination with POWER as wielded by women throughout the ages. The concept of women ruling the earth and shaping society in immutable ways continues to be a revolutionary idea even though it has been a fact for eons. The exceptional woman – a woman of legendary status – is the essence of what Cleopatra is. She is an icon for modern women.[56]

Structurally the poem is free verse in fifty-seven stanzas, almost operatic in dialogue between Anthony (20) and Cleopatra (31), with occasional monologues, letters or duets (5), except for the very last sonnet, when 'Plutarch' gets the final word, likening Cleopatra to a comet predicted by Eratosthenes. Like that prediction, this Cleopatra is no more historical or 'real' than most of her receptions, including Pushkin's and Chaucer's bizarre contributions. Chase-Riboud is interested in portraying Cleopatra's raw emotions, unabashed sexuality and volcanic emotions, that is as a Nude Woman. Chase-Riboud divides the poem into nine sections introduced by a quote from Plutarch and given a date from 41 to 30 BCE. The dates 41, 33 and 30 BCE are used twice and do not strictly conform to the events described or referenced. The beginnings of the quotes each follow their order in Plutarch's Life of Antony, but Chase-Riboud occasionally mixes in related passages out of chronological order. As I read the poem, in each section Chase-Riboud is reacting to the situation in Plutarch in the way she thinks *her* Cleopatra and Antony would react. It is refreshing how few anachronisms and modernisms there are, which I attribute to Chase-Riboud's exposure to classical and Egyptian art, history and culture. The second and eighth sections have thirteen sonnets and the fourth has eight, corresponding to the emotional peaks of Cleopatra and Antony's initial infatuation, their reunion after the Parthian disaster and their post-Actium death spiral.

The first section (Sonnets 1–5) is dated 41 BCE and begins with Plutarch *Ant* 25.2 when Anthony orders Cleopatra to meet him in Tarsus. The first and second sonnets, although fraught with sexually charged language, do not mention Antony but allude to Cleopatra's Egyptian connections and a 'monument' which both foreshadows her end and recalls her recent love. The second sonnet is constructed in the shape of a pyramid and filled with images of Egypt and Africa, ending with the line: 'which might be as beautiful if Caesar were in Africa'. The third sonnet, which reflects the overall poem, is a bridge between Caesar and Antony and worth quoting in its entirety:

> I shall be Venus Genetrix and greet
> With chaste lips this Dionysus I first saw at fourteen.
> I shall trap his quintessent heart and waltz it around
> My own Gods quivering in unmarked graves.
> For so long as one dank breath escapes from Karnak,
> So long as one brace of bones, churns like rolling dice,
> Away from Delphi's oracle, so long as one
> Handful of red earth crumbles under the
> Saturnine & Equatorial sun of Ethiopia's Pharaohs
> I refuse to be eclipsed by Caesar's shadow & Caesar's sex,
> For, so long as Egypt rests its shaven head
> On my Cleopatrian breasts,
> Caesar's manhood curled loosely in my hand,
> Rome, don't cross me.

Sonnet 4 lays out Cleopatra's plan to seduce Anthony: 'Caesar knew me when I was but a young thing. / You discover me filtered through finesse, men, and years.' Chase-Riboud's Cleopatra was as promiscuous as Augustan propaganda depicted her. In the fifth sonnet we first hear from Anthony who is quite leery: 'You are a dangerous woman.'

The second section is also dated to 41 BCE and begins with Plut *Ant* 28.1 when Anthony abandons all and goes to Alexandria. He is hopelessly in love when he sings, 'My blood sings through your tuned flesh' in the first of thirteen sonnets. Cleopatra in Sonnet 7 might not be in love yet, but she is in lust for this 'Male, mysterious / Beyond your sex.' Their ardour and infatuation with each other's bodies escalate to two frankly orgasmic duets in Sonnets 14 and 18, but interspersed with dark feelings on both their parts – Cleopatra in Sonnet 9: 'The Darkness and the Void'; and Anthony in Sonnet 10: 'My darkness covers all your light.' Chase-Riboud places this episode in a Plutarchan context when she refers to the *Amimetobioi* – the 'Inimitable Livers' – but does not translate the term. The last sonnet of this section, number 18, is prophetic:

> Tonight let us at least not lie to each other
> That this or anything is more than life can make it
> Or more than we can bear
> For who knows but we will not lie here again
> But you will leave me an empty house.

The third section of only four Sonnets (19–22) is introduced by Plut *Ant* 30–1, which references the death of Fulvia and Anthony's betrothal to Octavia. It begins and ends with duets full of regrets – Sonnet 19: 'And so we stand quits and quivering / Two fools, / In love without faith'; and Sonnet 22: '"How cruel you are," you said / But you turned your back / When you said it.' But between these duets is a two-sonnet (20–21) brief (and unfortunately erroneous) history lesson for Antony: 'But beware, beloved, Ptolemy women engender violence, / Command money, men and manumission. / Cleopatra revels in infanticide, regicide and patricide.' While not entirely historical, the point is made, and much better than having Elizabeth Taylor shred the bedding.

In the next several sections the chronology becomes blurred, non-specific and sometimes just wrong, but the subject is a relationship and not history. The fourth section (Sonnets 23–30) dated to 36 BCE reflects Plut *Ant* 35.5–36.2 and

Anthony's Parthian debacle, their reunion and even the Donations of Alexandria. Cleopatra starts out angry and resentful (Sonnet 23), while Antony is still besotted (Sonnet 24) until they reunite in a lusty duet (Sonnet 25). In Sonnet 26, Cleopatra exacts a price for their love and alludes to the charge repeated by Pushkin (1835) and Gauthier (1838): 'You're not the only man to pay for my Egyptian Nights.' But the doomed nature of their liaison is alluded to in each of the remaining sonnets as Antony says in Sonnet 29, 'The drunken rumors of real life unsettle our bodies.'

The history becomes quite discombobulated in the next three short sections dated to 31, 31 and 30 BCE respectively and introduced by a pastiche of out-of-sequence quotes from Plutarch – first *Ant* 60, 62 and 76; 66.7–8; then 71 and 67– mixing events from before, during and after Actium. Chase-Riboud is perhaps viewing the event as one would view one of her very abstract sculptures. You see the whole before you can form its parts into a narrative. Therefore, the first of this series (Sonnet 31) begins with Cleopatra's flight. The next section (Sonnets 35–38) is mostly an exchange of letters looking to a grim outcome. In Sonnet 38, Antony says, 'A doomed man, I sit on death's row / And dream of *Synapothanoumenoi*'s last meal', an allusion to the 'those dying together' club in Plutarch. The last of these sections (Sonnets 39–41) are laments for loves and ships lost, as with Cleopatra's words in Sonnet 39: 'The flower that once has blown forever dies.'

The penultimate section is as long as the second (Sonnets 42–56) and begins with Plut *Ant* 74, the beginning of their end. It is not a narrative or even description of their deaths, but a testament to their love and to the forces which destroyed it and them. Some of those forces are their own passionate natures and self-destructive characters. Sonnet 49 sums it up: 'If we part, you will leave with half of me, / Or I with half of you, and nothing will kill / The pain of dismembering.' Finally, in Sonnet 56, Cleopatra turns into a comet, which sets up the last section, Sonnet 57 ('Like Gods, they coupled to form a new race, / Destined to love more than we ever loved') framed by Plut *Ant* 86 as an Epilogue.

Barbara Chase-Riboud has had a long-term and productive obsession with Cleopatra which she has expressed in all the media she has mastered in her long career as an artist, poet, novelist and admirer of the ancient world. In doing so she has helped to forge a stronger connection between American popular culture and the reception of the Queen.

6.3 Science fiction and fantasy

There will be a veritable explosion of interest in the Queen among writers of science fiction, fantasy and magical reality and related genres in the twenty-first century and it was starting to build in the late 1980s. Unlike the purer sci-fi of Anderson 1977 a decade earlier, *Byzantium's Crown* (1987) is alternate history laced with magic and sorcery.[57] The premise of the story is that Antony and Cleopatra won the Battle of Actium and moved the capital of their empire to Byzantium. A thousand years later, the last of their line struggles for power in a culture derived from a fusion of Greco-Roman and Egyptian elements. It is a cleverly constructed society highly dependent on Isaic magic and an engaging if derivative plot. Cleopatra is only incidental to the story, but she is invoked when the royal siblings wrap their victim – a half-brother – in a carpet.[58]

Cleopatra makes a brief appearance in the time travel TV series *Voyagers!* (1982)[59] when the heroes rescue her after Caesar's assassination only to lose her in 1927 New York. She likes modern amenities and is in no mood to go back, especially when Lucky Luciano promises to introduce her to Calvin Coolidge if she will help prevent Babe Ruth from getting his sixtieth homer. She is depicted (by Andrea Marcovicci) as a gold-digging, beautiful bimbo who pawns everything but her snake bracelet and launches herself enthusiastically into the lifestyle of a prohibition era flapper (à la Colbert). When things go sour, Cleopatra sees the light and has the Voyagers return her to Rome and a smitten Mark Antony.

6.4 Anne Rice, *The Mummy* (1989)

In twentieth-century America, Cleopatra appeared in numerous comic books, cartoons, novels and films, with most of them reflecting Lizpatra. At the end of the century, however, a much darker version of the Egyptian Queen began to emerge, influenced, I believe, by Anne Rice's novel *The Mummy* and the subsequent graphic version.[60] Rice in turn seems to have launched several decades of immoral immortals, be they mummies, vampires or Witchblade wielders. The reception of Cleopatra has taken many strange turns over the centuries, but this one is quite remarkable.

The Mummy was originally conceived as a script bible for a film project. When that went awry, Rice turned it into a trade paperback which sold well. Along with *The Witching Hour* (1990), it marked a detour from vampire novels into Gothic romance. But according to Roberts, mummies witches and spirits share concerns with vampirism: the living-dead relationship, immortality and its physiological consequences.[61] Critics have not taken this relatively light-hearted romance as seriously as some of Rice's other novels, but most 'were amused by its campy use of the mummy genre'.[62] It was quickly followed by a twelve-volume graphic version, which tracks the novel quite closely, except for the explicit sex. Annerice.com provides a plot summary:[63]

> An archaeologist has just unearthed the find of his career, the tomb of Ramses II. The door to the tomb is lettered with a curse, the mummy of the king who claimed to be immortal lies shriveled inside. The archaeologist dies and the treasures are shipped to his daughter Julie in England, who finds that the mummy comes to life as a perfect man. Julie grows to love him and introduces him to modern life, including the museums that purport to reconstruct his time. He becomes disturbed and disgusted with the modern portrayal of his beloved Cleopatra. Ramses and Julie, her ex-fiancé and his father Elliott in tow, travel to Egypt. There, Ramses is further upset by the tourist flavor given to his ancient civilization. In one of the museums, he recognizes an 'unknown' mummified woman as his beloved Cleopatra. One night, he returns with the immortality elixir and raises her from the dead. But Cleopatra is not restored to her beautiful body or mind. She is a horrid monster, a walking corpse of rotting flesh and a disoriented mind that kills without mercy. Ramses abandons her, leaving her to Elliott, not realizing that he too is in peril. All in the party partake of the elixir, with Cleopatra and Ramses in the shadows.[64]

Rice herself acknowledges her debts to Arthur Conan Doyle's classic tale of a resurrected mummy (1892) and to H. Rider Haggard's *She* (1886). But also, from the same period we have Haggard's *Cleopatra* (1889), a novel and Sardou's play (1890), both of which influenced the early silent films starring Helen Gardner (1912) and Theda Bara (1917). Bara was the sixteenth actress to play the Queen on the screen, but she brought to the role her image as the vamp, itself drawn from the Kipling poem 'The Vampire'. Rice is clearly working within the British Gothic tradition.[65]

Several other popular versions of Cleopatra as a vampire appeared around the time the novel was written. They seem to reflect the Boris Karloff 'Mummy' films in general, but the Wonder Woman and Superboy comics are specifically linked to the Lizpatra film of 1963. *Vampirella*, on the other hand, is a highly original reimagining of the story. It was revisited in *Vampirella* 38 and in the unfortunate *Steampunk* version of 2014. I find no proof that Rice was aware of these, but in any event, hers was not the first Cleopatra mummy on the scene.

Rice has clearly researched Cleopatra, especially Plutarch, by having Ramses rail against his mistakes and calumnies. She is scrupulous about dates and about Cleopatra's relations with Caesar and Antony. The Queen is portrayed as Greek and Ptolemaic and a competent steward of Egypt and its heritage, though Rice seems to have followed Haggard's *fin-de-siecle* violent and sexually predatory character. I believe she signals this debt when she has a character announce her with the words, 'it is She',[66] an allusion to one of Haggard's most successful heroines. Rice repeats several ancient errors, including her beauty (which she was not), her promiscuousness and her testing of poisons. The author also calls her Cleopatra VI, which betrays either bad editing or the use of an inferior source.

Of more interest are some items Rice added to the reception. From Doyle's racist assumptions about all Egyptians,[67] she uses Cleopatra as the monster of the formula, with extreme passions for sex and murder[68]. While the elixir has a similar effect on Ramses' libido, he exercises more control. This association of Cleopatra with mummies, magic and the occult and overt sexuality is not an innovation by Rice but has had a significant impact on receptions of Cleopatra since its publication due to her high profile within popular culture. Since it also appeared as a graphic novel series, it seems to have inspired some others such as Jim Silke's *Bettie Page* (1999–2000), Avery's 2003–4 *Cursed* series and Daniel's 2010–13 *Tony and Cleo* series. In addition to these comics there have also been several novels focusing on magic, Isis worship and the supernatural featuring either Cleopatra or her daughter Selene. These feature as much sex, violence and romance as the comics, and will be discussed in more detail later.

Usually, a paradigm shift in modern Cleopatra reception has been triggered by a major film. Since there were no popular films to provide a stimulus for the remarkable burst of interest in Cleopatra in the last three decades, the most likely candidate is Anne Rice's *The Mummy*, especially since its popularity was extended when it was issued as a serialized graphic novel over the next three years. The portrayal of Cleopatra reflects thoughtful research and a great familiarity with both the historical and pop-cultural traditions. Rice also recently penned a sequel along with her son, Christopher.[69]

7

The Fantasy Queen of the Nineties

7.1 Traditional historical fiction

As a powerful female with a tragic romantic history in a dangerously exotic setting, Cleopatra held a natural attraction for the more prolific writers of historical fiction of every stripe and nationality, from Haggard (1889) to Rofheart (1976) thus far in this survey.[1] Each writer brought a different point of view to her story and, since they were generally good storytellers and effective users of contemporary diction and concerns, they have consistently added greatly to the body of the Cleopatra reception. It was rather odd that not until the end of the last millennium that interest in a work of traditional historical fiction devoted exclusively to her entire life would emerge.

Allan Massie specialized in biographical novels on four male Romans, and Cleopatra is featured as a supporting character in two of these – *Augustus*[2] and *Antony*.[3] Since the former is a first-person narrative, it is not surprising to find a negative and even vitriolic portrait of the Queen. He gives two major appraisals of her.[4] The first one sums up by saying that 'she was depraved, but not evil; my enemy, but, in her own right, justified'.[5] The second novel is quite entertaining, since it is ostensibly by Antony's fictional homosexual secretary Critias, who interweaves Antony's dictation with his own bitchy observations as in his colourful account of Cleopatra's arrival in Tarsus.[6] Although both versions display careful research and attention to the ancient sources, especially Plutarch, the Queen is not presented in a very flattering light and does not even get many pages. A sample:

> I can think of at least two dozen women whose favours Antony enjoyed over the years (or the other way round if you like), and if I was asked to rank them in beauty, there's no doubt that Cleopatra would be placed in the lower half of the league table. In a certain light she could even appear ugly, and no one

could deny that her chin was out of proportion. You could see that in old age (if she attained that condition) it would hook around and approach the tip of her nose. Then, being small and neat-limbed in youth, but as fond of eating and drinking as my lord himself, she was already inclined to be fat. Moreover, in the mornings, when she had a hangover, she looked more than her age, even then; it can't have been a pretty sight to wake up next to her.[7]

Colin Falconer (2000) on the other hand, who wrote many historical novels and crime fiction under various pen names, made Cleopatra the centre of his effort. As had many other writers, he used minor Plutarchan characters to aid with the backstories and exposition, in this case Apollodorus, the eunuch Mardian and the physician Olympus. It is on the whole a well written tale, full of local colour and a little sex, but not carefully edited. Too much of the dialogue is more anachronistically modern than usual and occasionally details of ancient material culture are not quite accurate. These rarely, however, detract from Falconer's ability to entertain and inform the general reader about the historical Queen.

In a much better and earlier effort, Margaret George (1997) wrote a massive and detailed account of Cleopatra's entire life and her every inner thought. George is a very prolific writer in this genre and has penned several other novels centred in the ancient world.[8] The first-person narrative is quite well researched, as the Author's Note indicates.[9] While one might take issue with some of the choices which she makes, none of the positions that George has taken on critical questions are entirely indefensible as she has made very careful use of both ancient and modern sources. She does not omit anything and the result is the longest single-volume work of fiction in my Cleopatra collection. She joins Thomas (1927), Balderston (1948) and Bostock (1977) in letting Cleopatra speak entirely for herself, although the physician Olympos (one of Plutarch's named sources) provides the final scroll. Regrettably, the TV miniseries[10] based on her book omitted much and altered crucial facts rather clumsily.

7.2 Film and TV

This *Cleopatra* (1999) was a four-hour TV miniseries produced by Hallmark and shown on ABC over two nights in May of 1999. The star was Leonor

Figure 7.1 Screen shot of Leonor Varela, *Cleopatra* (Roddam 1999).

Varela, an unknown model and inexperienced actress whose vaguely multi-racial appearance was apparently deemed an asset. Timothy Dalton was well cast as Caesar, but rarely rises to the occasion. Billy Zane was a terrible Antony and the scriptwriters seem to have run out of room in the second half of the film for George's expansive and thoughtful treatment. Varela is completely overshadowed by the artwork, her slaves and even her sister Arsinoë, which is probably why she is strangled a decade too early. The portrayal of Cleopatra is generally positive and not far from George's in broad detail: she is intelligent, competent but brutal as well as ambitious, very sexual but not promiscuous. Unfortunately, the acting and the writing did not live up to the sets and costumes. I am not alone in disliking it.[11]

The next year saw Elisa Moolecherry as a delightful sixteen-year-old Cleopatra in the *Royal Diaries* series intended for younger audiences.[12] She too is multi-ethnic (East Indian and Canadian) and is convinced she got the part by 'looking Egyptian'.[13] The script is closely based on a young adult novel which was part of Scholastic's *Royal Diaries* series.[14] Like George (1997), it is written in the first person, with all the attendant anachronistic attitudes. Since very little is known about Cleopatra's youth, Gregory can be creative, although she includes more than thirty pages of historical material. She has Cleopatra accompany her father to Rome, for example, where she gets to know Mark Antony. Since the series is about exotic foreign royalty it is not surprising that the Oriental theme gets featured:

> Arrow, my sweet old leopard, has jumped onto my bed, purring loudly. Her front paws are as big as my hands, and she is now licking those paws to wash her long, silvery whiskers. [...] But woe to intruders: A leopard hides in the shadows of our palace walls.[15]

While this is basically an after-school morality play about living in dangerous times, it does rather effectively underscore the dilemma of a young woman caught between worlds and cultures, especially when she complains (to Mark Antony here) about having to wear those weird Roman clothes. Both the book and the TV episode came highly recommended by my advisory panel of preternaturally opinionated pre-teens, all scions of faculty colleagues.

Figure 7.2 Screen shot of Elisa Moolecherry as Cleopatra (Bradshaw 2000).

7.3 Science fiction and fantasy

None of these more or less reality-based works of historical fiction seemed to have had much of an impact on Cleopatra's reception at the end of the twentieth century. But the 1990s did also see the growth of fantasy tales featuring the Queen as the focus of works from the genres of horror, science fiction, alternative history, magic and superhero stories. These were not bolts from the blue. There were elements of horror in the mummy tale of Melies (1899), magic and the supernatural in Haggard (1889) and the occult in Mankiewicz (1963) and Tezuka (1970). But, as outlined in the previous chapter, the most influential development in this realm came with the gothic novel of Rice (1989) and its subsequent serialized graphic version. Cleopatra fully entered the world of fantasy fiction in the 1990s and what follows is a survey of a diverse collection of works of several science fiction/fantasy genres whose only common denominator is the presence of some fantastical version of Cleopatra.

Cleopatra only makes a brief cameo in *Highway to Hell* (1991) – a 'B' horror comedy film – but is worth noting because it has recently been accorded cult status. Chad Lowe is on a quest to retrieve his girlfriend, kidnapped to be a bride of Satan. The film is a gold mine of classical allusions and imitations, but I am not aware of a major study of it by a student of classical reception. One of the attractions is the frequent cameos by rock stars, comedians and the entire Stiller clan. Amy Stiller appears as Cleopatra in a night club named Hoffas on the outskirts of Hell City.[16] Along with Adolf Hitler (Gilbert Gottfried) and Attila the Hun (Ben Stiller), she appears to be a resident of Hell. She tells Hitler, who is ranting about his 'mistaken identity', 'Would you just get over it and get therapy like I did.' The camera then pans to the next table with reservation cards for several notorious living moral criminals ... and Jerry Lewis. His is written in French.[17] The appearance of an evil Cleopatra in 1991 illustrates the contemporary but gradual shift back to the nineteenth-century bad girl.

The 1993 *Animaniacs* episode, 'Home on De-Nile', is based on Lizpatra, but gives her an even more negative twist.[18] This is a slick Warner Brothers animation with a paper-thin plot. The cat and dog, Rita and Runt, are looking for Sonny Bono's house in Palm Springs and they accidentally time travel to Egypt where they encounter Cleopatra who just happens to be looking for the perfect cat. Rita, voiced by Bernadette Peters, is of course deemed ideal and she accompanies Cleopatra and Antony on a Sphinx-like vehicle to the temple. Only the dim-witted dog realizes that she is meant as a sacrifice and rescues her at the last minute. It is amusing and the songs are good. It is clearly based on Lizpatra since there is an internal credit, a Sphinxmobile and Cleopatra's appearance. Antony even has a Welsh accent and sings 'Who's afraid of . . .'. It is hard to see how these thirty-year-old references might have resonated with young children or even their parents. The writers seemed to have assumed that the mere presence of the Queen meant only trouble for the protagonists. The depiction of a casually murderous Cleopatra is also indicative of the shift in her image.

Cleopatra also appears in two episodes of the television series *Xena: Warrior Princess*. In 1997 she is played by a seductive Gina Torres, bath scene and all.[19] (Torres would also appear in *Cleopatra 2525*, but not in the title role.) For the plot of 'King of the Assassins', her race was irrelevant and her role minimal. The comic plot is quite thin and focuses on a minor character and his twin brother. When she is onscreen, this Cleopatra exudes sexuality as well as confident power, even though her life is in imminent danger. She is out of Egypt recruiting an army to fight her brother and radiates strength and confidence. The bath scene is replete with sexual double entendres as she negotiates with Autolycus for an alliance with his fictional client and ends the dialogue with the exclamation 'Kinky!' – quite appropriate in the Xenaverse. At the end, Cleopatra invites Xena, who has appeared to save the day, to visit her in Egypt. Torres was apparently not available when that came to pass two seasons later. A possible contemporary inspiration for this and other Black Cleopatras is quite likely the 1991 Michael Jackson music video *Do you remember the time?*[20] which portrays a Black Pharaonic Egypt ruled by Eddie Murphy and Iman. Black Cleopatras had already been alluded to or portrayed in several works discussed earlier.[21] The costumes for Cleopatra certainly resemble some of those worn by the dancers in the video.

When the episode 'Antony and Cleopatra' appeared in 2000, a white actress, Josephine Dawson, played the Queen, perhaps because the script called for Xena to pose as Cleopatra who is murdered during the credits.[22] Fortunately, the Xenaverse can handle such anomalies. The real Cleopatra is bathing in milk while her advisors provide the exposition to let us know that Caesar is dead, that Antony is yet to fight the assassins and that Octavius is a threat. Then she receives a scroll with a concealed poisonous snake which kills her. Before she expires, she instructs a trusted handmaiden to get the scroll to Xena, who accepts the mission and has herself delivered to Antony in a carpet wearing only golden chains. For the rest of the episode, we do not have a Cleopatra, but Xena pretending to be the Queen. This meta-Cleopatra is of course beautiful, very sexual and deeply engaged in the military and political tides of her kingdom and the known world. Xena falls for Antony in cringeworthy fashion, Octavius becomes idealistic and Brutus gets played. They stole their title from

Shakespeare, eliminated the principals and their tragedies and reduced it all to Xena in a blood-soaked gown in an unlikely Egyptian rainstorm. It is a travesty, not particularly entertaining and in many ways an appropriate ending for the twentieth-century reception of Cleopatra.

7.4 Prose fantasy fiction

Penelope Lively (*Cleopatra's Sister*, 1993) is a very prolific, popular and award-winning British author.[23] Since she grew up in Cairo, she has frequently used Egypt as a setting for her novels. This is an example of speculative fiction or alternative history in that it assumes that Berenice, Cleopatra's older sister, escaped execution by their father and fled to the fictional country of Callimbia between Egypt and Libya, roughly ancient Cyrenaica. The first half of the book interweaves the lives of Howard and Lucy and Callimbia, in which they have become stranded. The country is given a plausible history from 57 BCE to the present, complete with links to contemporary events, movements and fictional quotes from Herodotus, Plutarch, Ibn Hawqal and others. A constant element is the mention of the monumental statue of Berenice in the square of Marsopolis, the capital. Since this is actually worth reading, I will not spoil the experience by detailing how the lives of Howard and Lucy evolved and coincided in this speculative locale. Cleopatra has no role, but she is essential to the macro and micro premise of this 'what if?' story.

State of Change (1994)[24] is part of an extensive and carefully coordinated series of novels, *Dr Who: The Missing Adventures*, which were written to fill gaps between events in the television shows.[25] You do not have to be a die-hard Dr. Who fan, although that is the target audience. A passing knowledge of the series is sufficient since this author weaves in the science fiction backstories unobtrusively along with the actual history of Cleopatra and her children. The novel also belongs to alternative history in that due to the interference of an evil Time Lady – Rani – Antony and Cleopatra gain powerful modern technology, win the Battle of Actium and pass the new dominion to their children Caesarion, Alexander Helios and Cleopatra Selene who are ruling as a triumvirate in the dramatic date of 10 BCE. The author displays an impressive knowledge of Ptolemaic and Roman culture and even Latin and quite cleverly patches in some of the weapons and technology acquired. The sixth Doctor and his current sidekick Peri were caught up in the time slip when they stop in Egypt to watch the real Cleopatra cruise the Nile right before she leaves for Tarsus to meet Antony. She serves the plot mainly to explain the character and motivation of her daughter. The main character is Ptolemy Caesar or Caesarion, who emerges as the courageous and competent leader he might actually have become.[26]

As her own rather good translation of Horace's Cleopatra Ode (1.37) printed at the opening of *Throne of Isis* (1994) indicates, Judith Tarr has an extensive background in Latin and classics. In addition, several works from her expansive bibliography are also based in the ancient world. Her contribution[27] is well researched in every aspect. The narrative begins shortly after the death of Caesar and continues to after Cleopatra's death, because the focus is on a fictional character, Dione, a Priestess of Isis, and her lover, the Roman Augur Lucius Servilius. Their story is structured around and interweaved with Antony and Cleopatra's, resulting in an engaging tale.

In addition, Tarr adds two innovations to the reception of Cleopatra which will recur frequently. The first is the movement away from the prevailing notion that Cleopatra was an extraordinary beauty, as prevailed in Lizpatra and most earlier receptions. This tendency was accelerated by the backlash against Lizpatra, especially in comics, and had already been manifested several times such as in the anime of Tezuka (1970) and in the monumental study by Lucy Hughes-Hallett.[28] Since Tarr actually cites her book,[29] Hughes-Hallett (1990) may have been the source of this shift in works of fiction and I suspect that this massive and authoritative study has influenced many more receptions. As we shall see, some authors such as Colleen McCullough[30] went so far as to call Cleopatra ugly.

The worship of Isis and the inclusion of Isiac symbolism was not new to the Cleopatra reception. Acts of magic do influence the action, especially in Haggard (1889) and Mankiewicz (1963), but as we shall see, they will become more and more dominant into the twenty-first century and firmly attached to the Cleopatra narrative. Tarr would appear to have been a pioneer in the sub-genre, if not the actual founder. The magic is practised by the two invented characters to allow Antony and Cleopatra to remain closer to the 'historical' figures. Tarr manages to keep the magic and the magicians organic to the story and not as clumsy intrusions into reality.

7.5 Graphic novels

Kurt Busiek's *Astro City* (1995–2019) does begin in 1995, but I will discuss it with its twenty-first century contemporaries. *The Phantom* episode does not feature Cleopatra at all, but the robbery of her tomb in 1798, where she had secreted treasure for her son Caesarion.[31] Phantom's ancestor finds the tomb and her mummy but escapes with only the mummified asp which killed her. Originally published from 1996–8, the recollections of Sheba, a mummified cat, include her role in Cleopatra's flight at the Battle of Actium.[32] Sabrina's adventure with Cleopatra is precipitated by magically induced time travel to facilitate a homework assignment, a motif doubtless borrowed from *Bill and Ted's Excellent Adventure* (1988).[33] Cleopatra likes 1997 and zaps Sabrina back to Egypt along with her cat. When she recovers and returns with Mark Antony, she still has to convince Cleopatra to want to return. Being an *Archie* comic, there is no sex and Cleopatra is for the most part a type-cast clone of the petulant, manipulative and vain Veronica.

Bettie Page was a pin-up model who, as far as I can determine, never posed as Cleopatra. Dave Stevens decided to make her a comic book action hero and one of her adventures involves time travel and an encounter with a very sinister Cleopatra who happens to be a Bettie double.[34] Written and drawn by Jim Silke, it is a delightfully campy and sexy version of her encounter with Caesar, which displays an impressive familiarity not only with her real story, but also with conventions of the tradition. Needless to say, Bettie is placed in mortal danger (mummies, crocodiles, vultures), loses her bra frequently, has sex with Caesar and battles Cleopatra before leaving history unchanged. In the process, we see Theda Bara's snake bra, Claudette Colbert's vulture headdress, a tribute to a Cabanel painting, reference to poison experiments, asps, a lusty carpet scene, barges, the Sphinx scene from *Caesar and Cleopatra* of 1946, a procession and a bath scene. In addition, Jim Silke has also marketed several prints, a cigarette lighter and an action figure, one of my most prized possessions.

The mummy theme reappears in a *Xena: Warrior Princess* comic.[35] In this episode, Cleopatra is portrayed as dark-skinned and the blonde Gabrielle attempts to take her place. Although a Queen, Cleopatra learns lessons from Xena on how to be a warrior as well, saving herself without the help of Autolycus. Although she is beautiful and dressed above the waist in little more than a metal bra, she is more sensual than sexual in this story, set immediately before she meets Caesar. When Cleopatra appears again with Xena, she is merely a station in a longer quest to rescue a pregnant girl.[36] This Cleopatra is not only white, but her role as a Macedonian outsider and an agent of Roman domination is a plot point. She is depicted as stunningly beautiful and even more voluptuous than Xena and Gabrielle, complete with barge and bath scenes. Her sexuality is implied but obvious and, although the story is set after Julius Caesar, she has no child. She is an independent powerful female ruler who is not shy about being ruthless, assertive and alluring. As Gabrielle notes, after Xena meets Cleopatra, 'Oh, assertive women always get bad press. They probably say the same thing about you. In fact, they do. And what's more, they're right.'[37]

In many ways the 1990s reception of Cleopatra mirrors that of the 1890s. Haggard and Sardou would recognize the paradigm and some of their own contributions. Although the *femme fatale* had frequently given way to a more human and humane Queen, beginning in the 1920s and enduring into the 1960s, the long hiatus invoked by Lizpatra was revived in large part by the reappearance of the monstrous and destructive side of Cleopatra. The kinder, gentler side of Cleopatra featured in the Palmolive ads and the performance of Colbert seemed to be about to rewrite the negative traditions of the *fatale monstrum* or the vamp, but those never truly disappeared from the narrative. As a result, the Cleopatra tradition has taken on a confusing and contradictory landscape which is capable of embracing the realistic and the fantastical, the competent ruler versus the impassioned vampire, the realistic female monarch and the magical monstrosity.

8

The Twenty-first-Century 'Authentic' Cleopatras

8.1 Sources for the increased interest in Cleopatra

The current century (and millennium) has witnessed a surge of interest in Cleopatra, at a scale not seen in almost 100 years. There have been a half dozen feature-length films and TV series, two dozen works of prose fiction, several graphic novels and video games (a new form of mass media) and who knows how many toys and gadgets I have not even seen – yet. In the twentieth century, such episodes of increased interest were centred on the release of a major Cleopatra film such as those in 1917, 1934 and 1963. In this case we should look to several other experiences for the source of this eruption, since the 1999 Hallmark miniseries had no direct impact. A devastating recession unfortunately killed the building interest in any new film.[1] We need to look instead to art and artefacts, horror novels and comics and a film which never even portrays our Queen. Three key events were the 2001 British Museum Exhibition 'Cleopatra of Egypt: From History to Myth',[2] the publication of Anne Rice's novel *The Mummy* in 1989,[3] and the release of the first major film set in antiquity since the 1960s, *Gladiator* (2000). It is quite possible that we will soon see several major films on Cleopatra.[4] The recent publication of several scholarly and popular non-fiction accounts seems to me to be more the result than the cause of this interest.

The British Museum exhibit on Cleopatra travelled to the Field Museum in Chicago and sparked a good deal of interest in the art world beyond just the elite consumer. There were numerous news stories and documentaries of varying quality and more importantly an increased presence on the internet. Anecdotally, I noticed an increase in items related to Cleopatra on my frequent Ebay searches during this period. I do not think it a coincidence that there were so many high-quality non-fiction accounts of the Queen in the first decade of this century.⁵ Some of these provided material for the various receptions we will encounter below, but they appear to me to be the results of heightened interest rather than causes of such interest.

In an earlier chapter, I have credited Anne Rice (1989) with much of the renewed interest in Cleopatra among fiction writers, who readily took note that one of their most successful peers had found a rich source of inspiration outside of the standard historical fiction format. Rice opened up new genres such as horror and fantasy as arenas for the Cleopatra reception. Of even greater import was the publication of the story in a graphic novel format, which meant the tale would come to the attention of the writers and consumers of this non-elite and more popular branch of classical reception in print, animation and most recently electronic gaming.

My third factor, *Gladiator* (2000), might seem off the mark since Cleopatra is not in it and indeed is set two centuries after her death. The previous major films about antiquity were from the 1960s, including *The Fall of the Roman Empire* (1964),⁶ which covers some of the same events.⁷ Just as Rice's novel had done for other genres, the blockbuster-level success of this film opened the way for many other popular treatments of antiquity, especially Roman historical tales. While this did not result in very many film treatments of Cleopatra, it did show that there was a market for other media in this area, especially novels, comics and video games.

Since there is such a wealth of material from this period, I will treat them generically, concentrating in this chapter on the more or less authentic, 'historical' or realistic works. While they may take great liberties with the known facts and greater liberties with less well documented parts of her life, they at least obey most of the laws of physics. The next chapter will be devoted to the realms of magic, fantasy, horror and science fiction, where even those laws go by the wayside. For good or ill, the majority of current Cleopatra receptions seem headed toward the far side of reality.

8.2 Miniseries and films

There has actually been only one feature-length theatrical release on Cleopatra so far this millennium and it would not actually meet my criteria for inclusion here. *Asterix et Obelix: Mission Cleopatre*[8] was not dubbed in English or even released in the USA on DVD until quite recently. As a very well made and clever reception, it is worth noting if only for the highly sexualized and humorous portrayal of the Queen by Monica Bellucci. It is part of a very rich reception of Cleopatra in France from this century which includes, among many fine examples, an episode from the comedy series *Peplum*,[9] featuring her 'successor' Cleopatra IX, and the large scale live musical spectacular *Cleopatre: La Derniere Reine d'Egypte*.[10] Television miniseries took up the mantle (but regrettably not the snake bra) and included Cleopatra as a supporting character in the stories of Julius Caesar[11] and Augustus.[12] While the Italian starlets Samuela Sardo and Anna Vale are lovely and sensual, they hardly tell much of Cleopatra's complex story in what are expanded cameos. That changed drastically when the BBC and HBO entered the fray.

Cleopatra's appearance in *Rome* (2005, episode 8, 'Caesarion') came as quite a shock for many viewers. She is small, thin and has short spiky hair. While the remarkably accomplished British stage actress Lindsey Marshal is by no means unattractive, what appears on the screen is no beauty. Her drug use, her

Figure 8.1 Screen shot of Lindsey Marshal in HBO's *Rome*, episode 8 (Heller 2005).

sexuality and her calculated plans to seduce Caesar in order to save herself shocked the audience as much as her petulance, self-absorption and violence, but what we see is not a complete departure from earlier traditions or even from the historical figure.[13]

We first encounter Cleopatra when assassins arrive from Alexandria. She is chained to a bed and in an opium stupor. After Charmion slaps her conscious, she receives the notice of her death sentence and is reciting an Egyptian prayer when Pullo and Vorenus come to her rescue. In a high shrill voice, she alternately insults and clings to her loyal but caustic slave, Charmion. The next morning, we see her in the same chamber smoking her opium pipe and hissing like a snake. Charmion chides her for being too weak to give it up and Cleopatra orders it thrown out, allowing the viewers to see that she has been in a massive slave-borne litter escorted by her rescuers. Next, as Charmion assists in her detoxification, Cleopatra declares her intent to survive by seducing Caesar and having his baby. Charmion devises a plan to get her pregnant by one of the Romans and orders Vorenus into the chamber. In the comic scene that follows, Charmion appears to be translating. The semi-celibate Vorenus is appalled by the blatant proposal but aroused by her open sexuality. After a shrill protest, he retreats and orders Pullo into the chamber. Pullo, of course, obliges. Subsequently they smuggle Cleopatra and Charmion into Alexandria in a bag rather than a carpet. When the bag is opened before Caesar, Cleopatra gasps for air and immediately attends to the grit coating her sweat-soaked and only partially detoxed body. It is not attractive. Even Vorenus rolls his eyes. But then she realizes who is there and instantly becomes the seductress, striking an alluring pose that mimicks Claudette Colbert in her carpet scene. Immediately, Cleopatra reappears transformed into the royal Ptolemaic princess, dressed and wigged as the other minions of the court. She terrifies her brother and condemns his advisors to death. It is worth noting that she speaks to everyone in the third person, except for her equals, her husband/brother and Caesar. Next, she and Caesar engage in verbal fencing, climaxing in her proclamation that, unlike her brother, she realizes that she is Caesar's client and slave. Sex follows and the episode ends with Caesar's presentation of Caesarion to the troops and his presumed real father, Pullo.

There are a number of ways in which the 'Caesarion' episode is consistent with the historical Cleopatra. Most of the events and characters depicted are to be found in either Caesar or Plutarch,[14] though the compression of the storyline required some omissions. For example, Cleopatra does not appear in Rome as we know she did.[15] Also, the loyal carpet-carrying Apollodorus is replaced by Vorenus. Screenwriters almost never read Plutarch, but in the audio commentary the director Steven Shill refers to him in his comments on the 'Carpet Scene' and actually follows the biographer in having Cleopatra brought in in a sack rather than a carpet.[16] And Shill notes that Plutarch had written that she was not particularly beautiful. What enchanted Caesar here was not her beauty, but her clever audacity.

There are several other areas where I find the episode refreshingly authentic. Care is taken to characterize the vast gulf between the court and the Bedouin-like people of Alexandria. The makers also went to considerable lengths to create a visual court which is a fusion of Macedonian and Egyptian elements, so bizarre that it appears alien and grotesque even to the Romans. None of the cosmetic face-painting or costumes are authentic to the period, but the producers deliberately tried to depict the Ptolemaic court as neither Greek, Roman nor classical Egyptian, but something different, decadent and dangerous. Since we know she spoke many languages, Cleopatra is depicted as speaking Egyptian and later not fully understanding Latin. Charmion appears to be translating as she explains what is expected. Cleopatra is correctly depicted as very young, with no attempt to portray her as a great beauty. Her vicious and ruthless assaults on her brother and his counsellors are well established. She was in fact responsible for the death and/or banishment of all of her siblings and their supporters.

The writers clearly had William Shakespeare's *Antony and Cleopatra* in mind since Mark Antony frames her appearances. The influence of Shakespeare can also be seen in her drug use: for example, Act 1, Scene 5, Lines 4ff.: 'Give me to drink mandragora [...] that I might sleep out this great gap of time my Antony is away.' Other Shakespearian allusions may be clever inside stage jokes. When Charmion is trying to detox Cleopatra, Lindsey Marshal hisses like a snake and Kathryn Hunter remarks that she will turn green if she does not cooperate. I take this as a humorous allusion to *Antony and Cleopatra* (1.5.73–4) when she recalls her time with Caesar: 'My salad days, When I was green in judgment: cold in blood, To say as I said then!' The snake-hissing could be an allusion to Act 1, Scene 5, Line 25ff.: 'Where's my serpent of old

Nile? (For so he calls me).' My last example may account for the high-pitched voice used by the diminutive and androgynous actress in the opening scenes: 'Some squeaking Cleopatra boy my greatness / I'th' posture of a whore' (5.2).

In the same way we can see the influence of G. B. Shaw's *Caesar and Cleopatra*.[17] The character of Charmion was never part of the Caesar narrative, but here she seems to be playing a role similar to the fiercely protective and sarcastically manipulative nurse known as Ftatateeta in Shaw's play. Charmion also follows the lead of Shaw's Caesar who requires her to give up the opium pipe and cease to be weak. 'Weak, am I?' After this, the thin and squeaky voice deepens and steely determination replaces the frightened drug addict. Both versions, as well as Gabriel Pascal's 1945 film adaptation emphasize Cleopatra's transition from girl to Queen. Ftatateeta's elaborate wig and heavy make-up from Pascal's film appear to have influenced the imaginative headdresses and face paintings worn by women in the Alexandrian court.

Claudette Colbert in *Cleopatra* (1934) also sets out to seduce Caesar and when her charms cannot distract him from playing with his miniature war machines, she catches his attention with the 'gold of India'. Likewise, Marshal's Cleopatra bluntly addresses Caesar's financial needs. In the *Serpent of the Nile* (1953), we see a reptilian Rhonda Fleming portray her as a murderous manipulator of a loutish Antony. The snake imagery used for *Rome*'s Cleopatra may have been influenced by this very negative look at the Queen. The oriental vamp reappeared the next year in an Alberto Sordi comedy, where Sophia Loren plays a dual role as the deadly Queen and her innocent body double in *Two Nights with Cleopatra*. This was done in the Orientalist tradition as represented by Theophile Gautier's lurid tale, *One of Cleopatra's Nights* (1838), which repeats the slander of Aurelius Victor that she would sleep with slaves only to kill them in the morning. Although Pullo, who previously got the impression that 'She wants me', survives his night with Cleopatra, the scenes presuppose her willingness to have sex with inferiors, as it adds yet another 'Forrest Gump' moment to the storyline. Pullo is implicitly portrayed as the father of Caesarion.

It is quite clear from the DVD audio commentary by director Stephen Shill that they wanted this Cleopatra to be visually different from the most familiar cinematic version, the 1963 Taylor-Burton *Cleopatra*. But still there are several deliberate allusions. After her rescue, Cleopatra is carried in an elaborate, luxurious and ostentatious conveyance which recalls the barges and the Sphinxmobile in the 1963 film. When they first meet, Liz rummages among maps on a table and criticizes Caesar's strategy. Marshal does almost the same thing as she establishes her usefulness, but her aim is more seductive. Although she does not appear as often in full regalia, Marshal wears outrageous wigs and elaborate make-up, as did Liz. Finally, as Rex Harrison did, Ciaran Hinds's Caesar acknowledges the child to his men, including an enthusiastic Pullo.

Almost at the end of Shakespeare's *Antony and Cleopatra* (c. 1607), the tragic Queen expresses her fears (5.2.214–21):

> Saucy lictors / Will catch at us like strumpets, and scald rhymers / Ballad us out o' tune. The quick comedians / Extemporally will stage us, and present / Our Alexandrian revels; Antony / Shall be brought drunken forth, and I shall see / Some squeaking Cleopatra boy my greatness / I' the posture of a whore.

This metatheatrical prophecy is revisited in the second (2007) season of HBO–BBC's *Rome*,[18] as it begins and concludes with Antony's orgiastic excesses and a shrill Cleopatra's twin attempts to prostitute herself for survival. The Cleopatra scenes are indeed heavily indebted to Shakespeare's play but, as Jonathan Stamp and Bruno Heller note in the DVD commentary to the last episode, they do try to find 'a new way into something familiar'.[19]

Cleopatra appears in the second season in episodes 14, 20, 21 and 22, which also bear witness to similar influences and offer their own novel depictions. Unlike many of her cinematic receptions, however, in *Rome*, Cleopatra only appears in the context of her relations with Antony. Her own complex backstory and her monarchical competencies are largely ignored, but this is not her story: it is the story of Octavian's defeat of Antony.

There is considerable continuity between the two seasons of the series. Since Stephen Shill directed both episode 8 and episode 21 ('Deus Impeditio Esuritori Nullus'), there is close similarity in the Alexandrian sets, the unnerving costume and wig designs for the Ptolemaic court and in the performances of Lyndsey Marshal as Cleopatra and Kathryn Hunter as Charmian. And of course, Pullo appears to rescue his son, Caesarion/Aeneas. Cleopatra has not changed much. She still uses drugs, still wears daring outfits and is quite comfortable with her sexuality, which she still uses to her advantage. This dark, vicious and vain Cleopatra is still a shock to many who were accustomed to the gentler, more romanticized versions of the 1920s Palmolive ads, Claudette Colbert in the 1934 *Cleopatra* and Elizabeth Taylor in the 1963 *Cleopatra*. But there has always been a dangerous side in the reception of the Queen, in Victorian novels, in more recent comics and in films such as *Serpent of the Nile* (1953) or *Two Nights with Cleopatra* (1953). She had been trending in that direction throughout the 1990s. This dark and dangerous twenty-first-century Cleopatra shares more with a nineteenth-century European reception than the kinder, gentler twentieth-century American version.

It is not surprising that this largely British production would draw heavily from Shakespeare for much of what is familiar, but it is worth noting some themes which appear in more than one episode. References to how 'changeable' Antony is, Cleopatra's mercurial moods and the imaginary theatre the besotted pair substitute for reality owe much to the Elizabethan tragedy. As attested in the DVD commentary, the creators paid close attention to Plutarchan accounts of their personal excesses and deaths in Alexandria, while only alluding to the military losses in Parthia and Actium and to the political bombshells such as their marriage and the Donations of Alexandria. It is also quite evident that they were aware of aspects of previous filmed versions of the story. The metal bra Cleopatra wears in the hunting scene in the palace is clearly an homage to the snake bra tradition begun by Theda Bara in *Cleopatra* (1917), continued in the Palmolive ads and echoed numerous times in American popular culture.[20] From the Claudette Colbert 1934 film, we can see her smouldering sensuality, Antony's growing effeminacy and the prominent thrones in the death scene. From the Liz Taylor 1963 version, we have Antony's single combat challenge, the effect that Cleopatra's entrance has on the women of Rome and even the reuse of curtains found at in the storerooms in Cinecittá. And finally, there is the impact that a series of stunning beauties in daring costumes have had on the sexualization of Cleopatra. The writers, producers, directors, consultants (especially Jonathan Stamp) and even the actors seem well informed about the historical Queen as well as the ancient, Elizabethan and contemporary receptions.

Since relationships, especially dysfunctional ones, are a major motif of the series, it is not remarkable that Antony and Cleopatra are treated more as a couple than as individuals. Cleopatra will only appear when her story directly affects that of a principal Roman figure, whether he be Caesar, Antony or

Octavian. Even in effigy on a cart in Octavian's triumphal parade (episode 22), she is literally bound to Antony. Cleopatra's bond to Antony is precariously financial when they first meet in the second season. In episode 14 ('Son of Hades'), she is in Rome and their dialogue implies that she has just arrived. The precise chronology of her visit (or visits) to Rome are unclear, but since the setting is a little more than a month after the death of Caesar, the historical scenario is possible.[21] This is drama, however, so her presence in this episode is essential to later plot developments and conflicts with Atia and Octavian in particular. Since her visit to Rome had not been included in season one, the first mention of Cleopatra comes when Antony describes her to a suspicious Atia as 'a dark skinny little thing who talks too much'. This in itself is a clever allusion to Plutarch's assessment of her unremarkable looks (*Life of Antony* 27.3), although the author never claims that she was ugly. Marshall's Cleopatra is confident, self-assured and handsome, but hardly stunning.

When she meets with Antony, Cleopatra is not wearing the elaborate Ptolemaic clothing, headdress or make-up from Alexandria, just a simple Greek-style dress with an Ankh precariously balanced in her cleavage. He notes that she has changed: it is a nice touch for Antony to allude to their first meeting when he was with Gabinius in Egypt (Plutarch, *Life of Antony* 3) and for Cleopatra to fail to remember him. Her interview with Antony about grain pricing is terse but formal and conducted almost entirely by their alter ego servants, Charmian and Posca. It is an impersonal negotiation, although Antony is obviously intrigued by this powerful woman. He is put off by her mention of Caesar as her husband and remarks prophetically, 'A Roman consul with an Egyptian wife. Wouldn't do, you know.' When she brings up Caesarion, the tone sours even more and the possibility that she might prostitute herself for what she wants is explored almost clinically. She refers to his 'changeability' for the first time.[22]

The Shakespearean themes have been established with this scene. Although it did not go well, Cleopatra keeps her composure. As the camera follows her walking away from her meeting with Antony, looking like a very conventional Hellenistic woman, the shot gives a very clear impression of the impact she has had on the males of Rome: the togate elders step aside as she passes by. She only flinches when she sees the actual father of her child, Pullo, waiting to catch Antony. Continuing this framing device, Cleopatra goes to dinner at

Atia's. Prior to this, Antony had given Atia an edited version of their encounter in which he played down the Queen's appearance and demeanour. But this time she is dressed in the 'Alexandrian' mode introduced in season one. She makes a grand entrance to the dinner where she has the same powerful effect on the assembled men and women that Liz Taylor's moving Sphinx had in the 1963 film. 'Just as you described her,' says Atia sarcastically: 'Quite the little mouse.' The montage of the dinner emphasizes Cleopatra's sensuality and attraction along with the growing interest and fascination of Antony. She immediately antagonizes Atia by implying that Antony had described her as 'nice'. To make matters even more tense, she introduces her son as the son of Caesar to the mother of Caesar's heir. In the course of the dinner, Atia shoots murderous looks, but not nearly as murderous as the ones Octavian has for a four-year-old Caesarion. As Cleopatra proffers friendship, Atia whispers to her the prophetic line: 'Die screaming you pig-spawn trollop.' The Egyptian entourage, her revealing and exotic costumes and especially her sensuous attention to food and drink foreshadow the 'Inimitable Livers' of episode 21.

Cleopatra does not appear again until the end of episode 20 ('A Necessary Fiction') when Antony has finally gone to the East to take up his provinces and armies. It is roughly 41 BCE when Antony arrives at the court of Alexandria in full military kit, only to find the official throne room, later to be the place of his death, a child's playroom. To the side appears Cleopatra, backlit in a transparent gown of Coan silk.[23] Antony is sweating profusely from the Egyptian heat as his male gaze scans the essentially nude and coolheaded Queen. The only dialogue they share are two words: 'Antony!' ... 'Cleopatra!' In this brief but compelling exchange, another doomed couple is formed, with the whole barge scene from Tarsus condensed into two words, two gazes, two fates sealed.

In pronouncing the title of the tragedy, the Shakespearean section of the series begins in earnest. By the next episode (episode 21, 'Deus Impeditio Esuritori Nullus'), as noted in the DVD commentary by Purefoy, they have cut out the courtship and they are shown in full debauch shortly before the 'Donations of Alexandria'. The episode progresses to the revelation of Antony's will and the declaration of war against Cleopatra, rough dated 35–31 BCE. The campaigns in Parthia and Armenia are assumed but not mentioned, perhaps because they seemed to belong to a tale of Antony alone, not of them as a couple. Almost casually, but with the effect of emphasizing their partnership, *Rome* presents the fruits of their union, the twins Alexander Helios and Cleopatra Selene, although the youngest son, Ptolemy Philadelphus, is omitted.

At the beginning of the episode, they are 'hunting' a hapless slave dressed as a stag in front of a delegation of mortified Roman Senators (Plutarch, *Life of Antony* 71.7). According to the DVD commentaries, actors Purefoy and Marshal had apparently discussed their roles at length and had decided to play them as soul mates in a genuinely passionate but destructively abusive relationship. They felt that Antony and Cleopatra would have used any drug available, routinely abused alcohol and continuously sought satisfaction for their appetites for sex, power and food (Plutarch, *Life of Antony* 71.4), especially foods that were, in Purefoy's words, 'wet, moist, and sexy'. Plutarch himself makes a connection between drugs and the relationship of Antony and Cleopatra (*Life of Antony* 37.4). Director Shill wanted the scenes to be packed with visual information about their excesses and their sadness, but also their profound attachment to one another (Plutarch, *Life of Antony* 53). In his visual appearance, Antony has become softer, effeminate in dress and make-up and dissipated enough to shock the Roman emissary.[24] The snake tattoo on his chest foreshadows the end of their affair. The deer-hunting scene brings out the cruel and violent side of Cleopatra and the shocking effect of the scene gives credence to the Augustan propaganda summarized by the Newsreader at the end of the episode.

Cleopatra tries her best to egg Antony on to war. As she did in episode 14, she calls him 'changeable'. The only thing that forces his hand is the sudden appearance of Atia and Octavia sent to procure more grain. Although this event is not attested in the historical sources, it is not entirely fictional either, being based on the actual grain shortage of 39 BCE, on his wife's attempt in 35 BCE to bring Antony supplies and troops, on Cleopatra's subsequent jealous reaction and Octavia's useful public humiliation. In a pivotal scene set in the now double throne room equipped with a giant bed/couch, the full range of Cleopatra's moods is on display: passionate lover, petulant wife and arrogant autocrat are all artfully woven into one believable character. She even reveals the beginnings of doubt as to her choice of champions. In one drug-addled and remarkable exchange, Antony accuses Cleopatra of wanting 'to play the queen' in front of Octavia. Enraged, she says, 'I am the queen.' This may reflect the fantasy theatre that the Shakespearean protagonists construct for themselves. It builds as their dispute over how to handle the delegation goes from affection to passionate grappling to shouting and crashing pottery. The true source of Cleopatra's anger is her realization that Antony is not willing to humiliate or kill his former lover and doubts both his love and his will to win. The embassy fails, but mother and daughter secure even more when Antony shamefully sends them away, along with desperate stowaway Posca carrying a copy of Antony's incriminating will.

Episode 22 ('De Patre Vostro') ties up the several storylines of the series, including the ones most relevant to this study: the ring begun earlier in episode 14 is now closed with the post-Actium revival of Antony by Vorenus, the father and child reunions of both Vorenus with his children and Pullo with his son Caesarion/Aeneas and of course the union in death of Antony and Cleopatra, both perished and perched on their thrones and as effigies on Octavian's triumphal cart. Antony returns from the naval defeat at Actium (31 BCE) to a life of Alexandrian dissipation and an increasingly desperate and sober Cleopatra. The orgy scenes from the 'Inimitable Diers' phase (Plutarch, *Life of Antony* 71.4–5) are certainly busy, staffed with Italian porn actors and volunteers from the crew: 'whores, hermaphrodites, and lick spittle',[25] as Antony describes them while debating flight or suicide with Cleopatra.

Series creator Heller says on the DVD commentary to the final episode that he wanted to find a 'new way into something familiar', and he succeeds in doing so by injecting some neglected items from Plutarch and the filmic tradition, by omitting one of the most familiar of all Shakespearean scenes and by adding an episode from his own life. One of the neglected items from the tradition is Antony's challenge to single combat attested to in Plutarch (*Life of Antony* 75.1). While this appeared in the 1963 *Cleopatra*, here it is not invoked to redeem Antony's masculine bravery, but to show the depths of drunken effeminacy to which he has fallen and to demonstrate to Cleopatra the desperate situation she is in, motivating her decision to yield to the invitation from Octavian that has been slipped to Charmian. She sees this meeting with Octavian after the death of Antony as the only way to save herself, her children and her crown. The attempted seduction of Octavian was quite popular in later Western painting and sculpture, although it does not feature in Hollywood

The Twenty-first-Century 'Authentic' Cleopatras 151

Figure 8.2 Screen shot of Lindsey Marshal in HBO's *Rome*, episode 22 (Heller 2007).

films. In *Rome* it helps to close the ring begun in episode 14 when Cleopatra, using some of the same lines, attempted and failed to seduce Antony during their negotiations. To meet with Octavian, she again wears a diaphanous gown and oozes charm and promised cooperation. She fails to lure the soulless 'monster' but at least manages to conceal her panic and her immediate resolve to follow Antony in death.

The item from Heller's own life comes in Cleopatra's last words, when she rises up and hisses to Octavian with her last breath: 'You [...] have a rotten soul.' Heller relates that this random line was uttered to him one day in New York's Central Park by an elderly woman and here he redirects it toward Octavian.[26] In *Rome*, perhaps given the demands of the sudden shortening of the series, the story of Antony and Cleopatra is subordinate to the Augustan triumph and the death of the republic. Finally, the narrative omission involves the character of Charmion who has two big scenes in Shakespeare: the fortune-teller and her answer to the Roman's query: 'Was this well done of your lady?' Instead, her role has been totally transformed into an intermediary when she appears to a hung-over Antony with a bloodied dress and dagger. This in turn sets the scene for the rescue of Caesarion by Vorenus, after he has assisted Antony's final departure and has carefully outfitted his tattooed corpse as a real Roman.

The creators of *Rome* did find a new way into a familiar Shakespearean story, but they did it by re-reading and following Plutarch and emphasizing aspects of the existing reception that supported their themes. They did not shy away from invoking other films, especially those where Cleopatra was played by Claudette Colbert, Rhonda Fleming and Elizabeth Taylor. The very beginning and the very end of the love affair between Antony and Cleopatra witnessed the highest level of creative fabrication, but the core of their depiction of the relationship was firmly based in Plutarch. Since Plutarch himself was but an early phase of the reception of Cleopatra, his account cannot be called factual – indeed, facts are hard to come by in the life of the Queen – but it is at least not egregiously anachronistic. The care with which that relationship was allowed to play out before the audience is what makes this one of the most exceptional and satisfying contributions to the Cleopatra reception. The series tells the story of Antony and Cleopatra as a flawed couple, against the backdrop of a world changing in ways they cannot understand or control.

8.3 Historical novels

Almost half of the volumes in this section were published or written prior to the great recession of 2008, making it appear to be the heyday for this phase of the Cleopatra reception. They are also some of the most readable and creative selections. Essex (2001, 2002) would set the standard for some of the best of this period. She endeavoured to tell Cleopatra's whole story, but emphasized her early years where the lack of information but well-known outcomes serves the needs of a writer of historical fiction. Invented and enhanced characters provide insight to her *Kleopatra* in a third-person narrative. It is well researched and faithful to the sources, while at the same time inventive and engaging. The first volume focuses on the young Cleopatra and her conflicts with her dangerous family, dealing frankly with sex, love and violence. Since this period is the least well documented, Essex takes full advantage of the latitude provided. Cleopatra's liaison with Caesar is not consummated until the second novel which carries her story to her death. While this Cleopatra is intelligent and competent, we can see her darker side as well. She may be an exotic Queen, but the dangerous Oriental has been replaced by a formidable modern woman.

Saylor (2004) is part of a mystery series. The detective, Gordianus the Finder, goes to Alexandria with his Egyptian born freedwoman/wife so she can bathe in the Nile and finds himself in middle of the dynastic conflict. The focus is on Caesar and his relationship with Ptolemy, itself a stunningly clever addition to the tradition, so Cleopatra is once again a supporting character. Saylor notes, 'If she were to appear among the glitterati of today, I think we might conservatively classify her as mad, bad and dangerous to know.'[27] Roberts (2005) is also part of a mystery series (*SPQR*) set in 51 BCE on Cyprus just before the death of Ptolemy XII. His daughter Cleopatra is performing official duties there, when the Aedile/detective Decius arrives to deal with pirates and seeks the aid of the precocious princess.

Colleen McCullough (2002, 2007), on the other hand, used Cleopatra as a more central figure in the final two volumes of her *Masters of Rome* series, although Caesar, Antony, Octavian and the other alpha males get most of the attention. Her portrayal of Cleopatra is largely conventional: she is intelligent, has a lovely voice and took her royal role very seriously.[28] But she is also described as quite unattractive:

[N]o one would ever call Cleopatra beautiful by any standard. No breasts to speak of nor any hips; just straight up and down, arms attached to stark shoulders like sticks, a long and skinny neck and a head that reminded him [Caesar] of Cicero's – too big for its body. Her face was downright ugly, for it bore a nose so large and hooked that it riveted all attention upon it.[29]

The author drew her that way as well.[30] She is also portrayed as a sincere believer in her place as Pharaoh in the workings of the Egyptian cosmos as well as a competent player in Greco-Roman power games. Although no more authoritative than these other well-crafted receptions, McCullough's Cleopatra is plausible, well researched and tautly woven into her complex narrative. It certainly eclipses the romance trilogy by O'Banyon (2007–8), which keeps the Queen in the background.

The second decade of this century reflects the increased interest in the historical Cleopatra and several of those works, perhaps along with the popularity of HBO *Rome*, appear to have influenced these last five authors. Meyer (2011) joined the ever-growing offerings targeted at young adult readers. We will see more examples in the next section which treats novels about Cleopatra's children. *Cleopatra Confesses* is a first-person account of her entire life apparently dictated as the Queen awaits Octavian's will. The well-researched and age-appropriate narrative presents an intelligent, charming and ambitious Queen as a model (and cautionary tale) for young girls along the lines of Meyer's numerous other fictionalized biographies.

Three authors penned 'military page-turners' which feature the Queen as a supporting character. Told in the first person, three volumes are from the very prolific R. W. Peake (2012, 2013 and 2013a) in his self-published *Marching with Caesar* series.[31] Featuring the career of Centurion Titus Pullo (and later his protégé), Peake's works are well researched, tightly plotted and action-packed thrillers. In spite of the canons of this testosterone-laden genre, Peake treats Cleopatra rather sympathetically. Her introduction to Caesar bears the influence of Plutarch and HBO's *Rome* as Pullus initially finds her unattractive: 'A very tiny, very ugly woman, with a great big nose and hardly any chin at all.'[32] But then she speaks and he too is smitten. Later he credits her charm to her sparkling wit and bawdy jokes.[33] He also chronicles her steely determination and ruthlessness, especially toward her sister.[34] In the second volume the focus is on Antony. Peake uses the episode of her arrival in Tarsus and conquest of

Antony[35] to underscore her cunning intellect in a frank conversation with the Primus Pilus in which she also reveals her vulnerable side. In the third volume, the author has Pullus sum up his assessment of the Queen: 'Cleopatra is many things, but I don't believe she is evil.'[36] His is one of the more balanced accounts in fiction. On the other hand, Smith (2015) is a first-person narrative by an almost famous historical figure, Quintus Dellius, which thoroughly revises a reputation tainted as an opportunistic turncoat. Revisionism in fiction can be entertaining but it requires a better-known protagonist. The result here is too radical a whitewash, especially when paired with such an arbitrarily wicked Queen. The real Dellius, like the real Cleopatra, is much more interesting. Turney (2018, 2019) is also a highly productive self-published military writer who features Cleopatra in at least two volumes, with more to come.[37] Turney is a good storyteller, well versed in the Roman military in spite of the inferior maps. Cleopatra is introduced at the very end of volume 11 as she prepares to meet Caesar. Once she emerges from the grain sack and the war planning begins, there is chemistry with Caesar: 'She knew there were more handsome women in the Ptolemaic court than her, and yet she knew how to make herself desirable with barely a move.'[38] Turney's portrait of Cleopatra is, in his own estimation, 'less than flattering' and he seems to blame her for many of Caesar's problems both in Alexandria and back in Rome.[39] Her role may expand later, but here she has a less engaging supporting function.

Holleman (2015, 2017) is a refreshing and well written novel approach to the young Cleopatra. Both novels feature the youngest sibling, Arsinoë, but the second includes Ptolemy XIII as well concluding with his death during the Alexandrian war. Given the dearth of facts and details for this period, the author weaves a compelling portrait of a dysfunctional family within the constraints of the foreordained conclusion. Needless to say, Cleopatra's image while plausible is not unblemished. It is entertaining and I am eager to read how the author might handle the rest of Arsinoë's tragic life. Most recently, Rice and Tanzer (2019) explore a unique point of view by making Edmonia Lewis's statue of the dying Cleopatra one of the three speakers in a tale which attempts to weave together the stories of the artist, the Queen and the work of art. The result is more pedantic history than fiction and not as much fun as it could have been. Finally, Macleod (2020), while the story of a Vestal Virgin, features Cleopatra as a supporting character, historical anchor and counterpoint to the dutiful but conflicted priestess. Her Cleopatra is manipulative and murderous, but her actions are well explained and sympathetically portrayed. It is one of the more engaging, balanced and accurate fictional accounts I have read. Penner (2020, 2020a, 2021) is the most recent addition to the list.[40] It is a three-volume self-published contribution which draws heavily on Schiff (2010) as well as the ancient authors.[41] As with many of the other writers, he is most original and entertaining in the earlier periods, where he is free of the constraints of the Plutarchan narrative. His work, along with his fellow independent writers, has been made possible by the popularity of E-readers such as Kindle, which has clearly contributed to the sheer volume of Cleopatra fiction in recent years. Since this is a study of popular culture, it is clear that they cannot be arbitrarily excluded. Only a few have proven to be truly awful.

8.4 Historical novels about Cleopatra's children

A skeletal biography set against the rich and boisterous tapestry of the Roman revolution creates the ideal medium for the writer of historical and/or romantic fiction and this licence has been extended to fiction about her offspring. Cleopatra VII had four children. As the likely son of Julius Caesar, Caesarion (Ptolemy XV Philopator Philometor Caesar) would not survive Octavian's victory. He may have attempted to escape to the port of Berenice on the Red Sea in order to flee to India or was persuaded by his tutor Rhodon to return to Alexandria for a promised reconciliation, or even a combination of the two. Later there were pretenders who claimed to have survived, but the consensus is that he was executed in 30 BCE along with his half-brother Antonius Antyllus. After the twins, Alexander Helios and Cleopatra Selene, were born, all of the children eventually became the centre of Anthony's (and Cleopatra's) plans to organize the Eastern empire through client kingdoms, including the youngest Ptolemy Philadelphus. After the deaths of Antony and Cleopatra, the twins and their youngest brother were sent to Rome to march in Octavian's triumph in golden chains and to live with Octavia Minor, the sister of the princeps. There is no mention of Helios after Selene's marriage to Juba in *c.* 26 BCE. Even less is known about Ptolemy Philadelphus. He was seen as part of the dynastic plan, since at the 34 BCE Donations of Alexandria he had been awarded areas acquired by his namesake, the architect of the Ptolemaic empire. He may have marched in Octavian's triumph, but our main sources do not agree. He may have died of illness shortly after reaching malaria-ridden Rome.

Cleopatra Selene[42] not only survived defeat, orphanhood and humiliation, but also the gradual loss of her siblings. She would have spent most of her teenage years in the household of Octavia, technically her stepmother, along with Anthony's other children by several former wives along with the children of Marcellus and her hostess. Luckily for Cleopatra Selene, she was betrothed and married to Juba II of Numidia. Together they were enthroned as King and Queen of Mauretania, where they successfully ruled, prospered and moulded their new country and capital into a Hellenistic jewel. We have several portrait sculptures and coins reliably attributed as hers. They had heirs and an apparently harmonious union.

I am referring to the receptions of Cleopatra's offspring in several categories and across a much broader period than the rest of this chapter since they have emerged as a thematic cluster. They are all works of fiction with all of the rights and privileges appertaining thereto, but within my first category of historical fiction, I mean works which adhere more or less to actual events and people, respecting the right of the authors to reasonable fictional motivations, reasonable anachronisms and unattested outcomes within the realm of reasonable plausibility. My next type I will call young adult historical romance, where actual events and people are the backdrop for typical young-love plots. There are also a few examples of actual children's historical fiction. Next, I would include quasi-historical adult romances, better known as 'bodice-rippers', which are more character-driven plots. Further down my scale would be 'alternative history' or 'magical reality' novels which do not follow an actual historical narrative or, for that matter, the laws of physics.

While most of my examples make at least some mention of all of the children (unlike the films), only three devote equal attention to all of them. Desmond (1971) is early and rather pedestrian; Livingston (2015, 2016, 2017), while a lively read, veers off into fantasy; but Naomi Michison (1972) is actually literature and a delight to read. The story is told in converging threads in different time periods, demanding an engaged reader. She is as interested in the offspring of slaves and courtiers as in the royals and is quite explicit in her treatment of sexuality. Herself a free-love Fabian socialist, Michison applies a multicultural and feminist lens to these tumultuous times.[43]

Two of my best offerings deal with Caesarion. He is a significant character in McCullough (2007), the final instalment of her *First Man in Rome* series. She makes him a bit older and more mature than in actuality, but that serves to enhance his tragedy and his naiveté. Although interweaved with the stories of Antony, Cleopatra and Octavian, it is a very original tale of a bright kid who would have been a good king. He is, on the other hand, the sole focus of Bradshaw (2002), which has Caesarion survive execution to make a new life for himself. It is very well written, has a plausible plot, accurate Roman and Egyptian background and is a real page-turner. Unlike some 'What if?' plots, it does not posit an alternative course for subsequent imperial history.

Poor Ptolemy Philadelphus has never been granted his own novel or depiction. He remains a pitiful sidebar in the tales of other siblings. He or his brother Alexander Helios *may* have been renamed Lucius Antonius (the traditional second name for a male Antonius), and a clever novelist should be able to posit a role for him in the court of Augustus or the entourage of Tiberius.

It is not surprising that more novels feature Cleopatra Selene than the other siblings. Good receptions of ancient historical figures profit from a core of basic facts onto which the writers can embroider an original story or a least a twist. In the case of Selene, we know she was orphaned at ten, raised by Octavia, married to a client king and had at least one child who ruled Mauretania after his parents. She would have interacted with well-known figures such as Antony, Cleopatra, Octavian, Livia and the other wards and children of Octavia.

Moran (2009) features Juba as a social activist and a swashbuckling romantic hero. The resulting abolitionist subplot is quite anachronistic, but it reads well enough. Selene is an effective vehicle for the plot, while still sympathetic and consistent. Smith (2016) is more about Julia and Livia, who gets a rare positive portrayal. Alternating chapters from the POV of all three women add interest, but Selene does fade from view after her marriage, until she reappears for a surprising plot twist.

Schecter (2011) is age appropriate both for the young adult reader and for Cleopatra Selene. Since she had also written a children's book[44] about Cleopatra, the author is comfortable with the period and the locale. She also makes her Selene an intelligent and engaged young girl, a good match for the scholarly

Juba. *Cleopatra's Moon* is an excellent example of how realistic fiction is treating Cleopatra and her offspring.[45] It does take many liberties with the historical figures, especially Octavia, Livia and Juba, and treats the heroine as more Egyptian than Hellenistic Greek, but respects the general cultural background and the actual course of events. But it and most of its genre do treat Cleopatra and her daughter as modern females, which in the hands of a lesser storyteller might seem a glaring flaw. Schecter, along with Essex and Holleman, has set a high standard for fictionalizing Cleopatra and her daughter.

Receptions of anything from antiquity, whether it is literary, artistic or historical, represent a dialogue between the past and the present. Authors found the sad stories of these children compelling for very personal and for general cultural reasons. They chose to incorporate them into stories which they found relevant to their own times. Feminist values can transcend male power politics in Mitchison (1972); Bradshaw (2002) can show that the moral example of a kind peasant can be the salvation of a pampered and self-centred young man; and Shecter (2011) and Mitchison (1973) can show young girls their self-worth and inner strength.

9

The Twenty-first-Century Fantasy Cleopatras

Interest in the role of the classics in modern fantasy and science fiction has blossomed in recent years, largely due to the efforts of Brett Rogers and Benjamin Stevens and the many contributors to their collected volumes.[1] Numerous scholars have contributed insights into the influence of the classical world on a wide selection of works in an equally broad array of genres. More significantly, they have helped to focus the ongoing – and unresolved – debates on the still emerging theories of classical reception and how they apply to both high and popular culture. The short essay by Tony Keen is especially valuable.[2] As Keen also points out,[3] this debate has been coupled with differing definitions and categorizations of works of science fiction and fantasy. Since the Second World War, this study has already encountered works featuring a received Cleopatra which have been included under this rubric,[4] including comics, anime, alternative history, horror, time travel, magic, heroic fantasy and superheroes. The twenty-first century has already seen a substantial contribution to this diverse group. In deference to these disputes, I have included any work which was either labelled as one of the above or could be reasonably assumed to be 'unreal', but which clearly evoked the real Cleopatra. Individual works would of course warrant closer analysis as reception theory continues to mature, but for our purposes a broader approach seems reasonable. It is notable that the shift in Cleopatra's reception in the last twenty years is as radical as that of 100 years ago when the vamp faded from prominence. The result is the polar opposite of the 'realistic' or 'historical' Queen of the same period.

9.1 Horror and science fiction

As mentioned in the previous chapter, several of the novels featuring the children of Cleopatra also belong to these fantasy genres, whether pure science fiction, horror or magic. Davitt (2016) is an example of alternative history wherein Caesar survived and passed an empire to Caesarion. Davis (2015 and 2018) is also alternative history/fantasy romance in which Cleopatra and Antony win the Battle of Actium at the end of the first volume and rule the world until her death in 2 BCE, thanks to the protection of Isis. The Livingston trilogy (2015, 2016, 2017) is also in the magical-fantasy genre, but more restrained and much better written, evoking a *Game of Thrones*-style complexity. The covers evoke Vorenus, Juba and Cleopatra Selene, respectively. In this world, Juba is adopted by Caesar, Pullo and Vorenus have been co-opted from the *Bellum Gallicum* and the magical trident of Neptune and the Ark of the Covenant are featured. Great liberties are taken with historical events and the pop culture cross-references abound.[5]

Magic, fantasy and New Age Isis worship are staples of several trilogies focused on Cleopatra Selene. Desruisseaux (2012) is confusing, idiosyncratic and reads more like fan fiction. The trilogy by Dray (2011, 2011a, 2013) is in a similar vein, but is very well written, entertaining and internally consistent. The characters are relatable, as they, in Harry Potter fashion, have to learn about their powers and the forces behind them.

Scarborough (2002–4) is a more traditional science-fiction thriller. It is based on a realistic Cleopatra but with the twist that she had switched places with Charmion to prevent Octavian from burning her body and denying her an afterlife. Since she had arranged for her remains to rest in an unexpected location, the stage is set for a modern forensic archaeologist to find them along with her DNA which – as we are informed – can be blended with that of a living person – an Egyptian Egyptologist – in order to recover the memories and consciousness of the Queen. The story is clever and engaging enough to warrant a sequel, bolstered by careful research into Alexandrian archaeology, Cleopatra's character and genetics. The notion of Cleopatra loose in the modern world has always been fruitful, but the added dimension of a feminist filter makes these novels both entertaining and thoughtful. Also featuring an archaeological angle is *Cleopatra's Tomb* (2020),[6] a conventional grave robber mystery, rooted more in *Speed Racer* and *Scooby-Doo* than Plutarch.

Another contribution to this resurrection theme is *The Passion of Cleopatra* (2017), a collaboration between Anne Rice and her son Christopher. This sequel picks up the story of the *The Mummy* (1989) with a recovered Cleopatra seducing her doctor, but first co-author Christopher Rice has inserted a backstory for the elixir by introducing its inventor and her nemesis, who will drive this plot once everyone has reassembled in England for a nice country wedding, including an American novelist who, it turns out, has not only been channelling Cleopatra into all of her novels, but is actually siphoning off all her memories and emotions, prompting Cleopatra to find her way to the wedding on the eve of the First World War. It is in fact her 'passion' story, her suffering and mental disorientation brought on by her resurrection and sudden immortality. In the Rices' universe, corpses can be reanimated by the elixir, but they become 'Nochtin' and lose their memories to whomever their soul has transmigrated. As a result, Cleopatra takes on a much larger role here, but the featured players are Christopher's new characters: Sybil the writer and Bektaten the original immortal, who seems to owe a lot to H. Rider Haggard's *She* (1887). Ramses, Julie, Alex and Elliot (who is secretly gay) remain consistent with the first tale but are reduced to supporting actors in a rather thin plot which many online reviewers found disappointing, although they do get the bulk of the sex scenes. What interests me about both contributions is what they add to the rich tapestry of the Cleopatra reception.

Like Anne, Christopher Rice makes Cleopatra beautiful, sexual and a dabbler in poisons, but in flashbacks to before her reanimation, the details of her life are quite historical. She is shown as having been concerned with finances and competent in their management (28–9); her memories of Alexandria (48–57) reveal a wide reading and an appreciation of the nature of Ptolemaic culture; Rice has her read and critique modern (1914) accounts of Augustan propaganda (52); she displays her extensive education and reading (53); and it is her vanishing memory which deceives the villain (Saqnos) into doubting her real identity when she does not remember she had fought her brother. Sybil Parker not only retains the soul of Cleopatra and shares her memories, but has also read 'too much Plutarch', as her mother chided. She had immersed herself in the Queen and Alexandria although as a concession to her idiot editors she had consciously conflated Pharaonic and Ptolemaic Egypt. She is aware of the real Cleopatra and admires her enough to risk all in her aid and salvation. In the end it is a complete set of Sybil's novels which help to restore Cleopatra's reality. Christopher has continued both Anne's novel and that tradition by bringing Cleopatra even further into the horror fantasy genre.

Nevertheless, this portrayal of Cleopatra reflects thoughtful research and a great familiarity with both the historical and pop-cultural traditions.

The third volume was published early in 2022 after Anne's death at the end of the previous year. Since the focus is on Ramses and a growing troop of immortals battling a family of deranged Russian monarchists in the early days of the First World War, Cleopatra's role is reduced and marginalized along with her psychic connection to her past, the hack novelist Sybil. It continues in the vein of supernatural thrillers, requiring more than the usual willing suspension of disbelief. The abstinence of the immortals from intervention in the Great War seemed to me derivative of similar apologies made for Superman during the Second World War, but the lively action and pointed dialogue keeps the reader engaged and titillated. The revisionist mythologizing become tedious at times, but on the whole the Rices are excellent storytellers.

Although her appearances are rare and early, the portrayal of Cleopatra is consistent with the rest of the series as she continues to heal and to accept her identity, which is in doubt: 'the question of whether or not she was truly Egypt's last queen reborn, or a fragmented clone residing within her resurrected skin and bones'.[7] The Rices do explore her character and relationship with Sibyl and Alex in the third chapter, and while it is largely backstory, it does underscore Cleopatra's self-doubts and the mellowing effects of her entwinement with her mortal saviour. Bektaten confirms her identity in chapter 10 and her 'passion' is complete. Her only plot-related appearance is in chapter 12, when the calm and reflective Cleopatra can help the others to understand the perilous resurrection of a recently deceased character in order to recover essential intelligence about the dangers ahead. She does not appear again until chapter 27, where she in effect endorses Julie's relationship with Ramses. Her transformation is now complete:

> Something quieted within the former queen. Some persistent, gnawing hostility vanished from her, and after a long moment, she settled farther back into her chair and gestured with one hand to the empty chair across from her. A small invitation that was also momentous. Julie accepted.[8]

Cleopatra's story arc in these three novels reflects the trends in her reception over the last thirty years, moving from monster mummy to suffering revenant to restored and gracious Queen. It remains to be seen if the dark and dangerous

Cleopatra is to return to her symbolic repose in the Cairo Museum or enrich the lives of her mortal lovers and mediums.

In addition to the following comics, there have also been several other novels focusing on magic, Isis worship and the supernatural featuring either Cleopatra or her daughter Selene. Magic, demons and lots of teenage sex are featured in Windham (2006), which is centred on Auletes' absence in Rome and Berenike's usurpation. Graham (2009) also mixes actual events with religious mysticism but tells the story from the first-person point of view of Charmian, here an Egyptian. The engaging story features frequent interactions with the gods which qualifies it for inclusion in this section. In terms of readability, it ranks with Rice and Dray. Another example is, Headley (2011), who has made Cleopatra the very first vampire in an entertaining romp which starts historically and realistically and then careens wildly from Egypt, the underworld and onto Rome itself, where she finally bites into the elderly neck of Augustus before walking off toward a sequel. Langlais (2014) is a graphically sexual 'bodice ripper' featuring a Cleopatra just released from hell and hiding from Antony with a powerful vampire. While the occasional references to her actual life are reasonably realistic, the post-mortem stories are pure fiction, thinly trowelled between the lurid sex. Finally, Roberts (2020) posits an ancient arms race which fails to change the outcome of Actium.

9.2 Comics and graphic novels

As we have noted above, in the twentieth century Cleopatra appeared in over forty comic books and graphic novels, most of them reflecting the 1963 film starring Elizabeth Taylor in the title role.[9] Toward the end of the century, a much darker version of the Egyptian Queen began to emerge, perhaps influenced by Anne Rice's novel *The Mummy* and the subsequent graphic version.[10] This trend has continued into the twenty-first century with five new graphic novels on the Queen appearing: Kurt Busiek's *Astro City* (WildStorm, 1995–2019); Fiona Kay Avery's *Cursed* 1–4 (Top Cow, 2003–4); Kenton Daniel's *Tony and Cleo* 1–4 (Bluewater, 2010–13); Anthony Del Col's *Assassin's Creed Origins* 1–4 (Titan Comics, 2018); and Mike Maihack's *Cleopatra in Space* 1–6 (Scholastic, 2014– 20).

Kurt Busiek's *Astro City* (1995–2019) is abundantly endowed with costumed superheroes, social and economic liabilities and super villains to exploit them. It is quite well written and well drawn, although a few storylines are more like sermons than science fiction. Cleopatra appears in sixteen of the seventeen collected volumes, but not in all of the individual issues.[11] Usually each issue is a self-contained story, but some of the story arcs take up multiple fascicles. Individual superheroes and their backstories will reappear in various story arcs. Cleopatra is a costumed, but never masked, superheroine who can fly, survive in space and fight evil with super strength and a cobra headed 'Sun Staff of RA', which she refers to as magic.[12] No connection has been made to the historical Cleopatra, but her vulture headdress is standard to the iconography. She is a member of the Honor Guard and regularly appears in their group shots and group fights but is little more than an extra in most of her appearances until Volumes 9 and 13, where she is elevated to a supporting actress role.[13] But *Astro City* has seen two Cleopatras.

The first Cleopatra was white, more simply attired, who appears in 1958,[14] but only in stories set in the late 1950s and 1960s which appear in seven different volumes.[15] *Astro City* covers several generations of heroic and real time, so this is not unique to her character. She is described in Volume 7, page 18 thus: 'The old one –– she'd been white, blonde, like 5'4" – always perky, reassuring, like she'd save the day and then hand out Rice Krispy squares.'[16] She lacked the super strength of her successor.[17] Being white was possibly intended to reflect the prevailing reception of Cleopatra in this period, although that is never specifically addressed. She very much recalls the white Cleopatras of films from the peplum era of the early 1950s through to the 1963 Lizpatra. Her disappearance from non-pornographic film until 1999 is perhaps alluded to in the dramatic origin story of the second, and Black, Cleopatra.

The Black Cleopatra has a fairly elaborate backstory, but never gets a story or arc of her own. But then only three of the Honor Guard members have been so featured, perhaps because Winged Victory is another empowered feminist icon (modelled on Athena Nike) from an ancient context and many Black and urban issues were cleverly and extensively explored in 'The Dark Age: Brothers in Arms'.[18] In fact, her origin story is embedded in this Black narrative, narrated by the brothers. She was Sarah Brandeis, apparently a colleague or assistant of the archaeologist Dr McGillicuddy. Since she later has to get to a lecture, she appears to have continued in his footsteps.[19] Before Hellsignor can take possession of the Gem of Thebis, hero Pointman of the Omega Rangers flings it around her neck, saying, 'Sorry ... you seem like an OK chick.'[20] She is transformed into Cleopatra, costume, staff and all: 'She's a fine figure of a woman, strong and solid ... but no marshmallow treats for her, you know what I mean?'[21] The event is historicized by a precise date – 3 May 1982.

Busiek has coyly left open any connections to the historical or legendary Cleopatra, but the *Astro City* Cleo is as fierce and courageous a warrior as was her namesake. They were both vulnerable and experienced injury and defeat.[22] While she often mentors women,[23] the *Astro City* Cleo also routinely assists males. She frequently speaks in the third person, as did the real Cleo's first Roman, Julius Caesar. Like her Shakespearian version, the *Astro City* Cleo sometimes speaks in a pompous and stilted tone. She is very attractive, with a more sexualized costume than her white predecessor. We see in a locker-room vignette in Volume 8 that she keeps her hair fashionably short and her figure trim.[24]

This Cleo's most prominent roles all come in three unconnected stories in Volume 9, where she mentors female characters and dispenses kindly wisdom in between fierce battles. This reflects recent trends in her reception in an Afrocentric context: Cleopatra was a caring and effective monarch and a responsible steward of her land and people. While few scholars would identify her as Black, she was definitely an African Queen who fell victim to European males. It is not surprising that she would become a sign for African Americans, beginning in the nineteenth century.[25] Busiek seems to be quite aware of these trends and has cleverly referenced this social change and perhaps also the shift in the focus of Cleo's reception by keeping the two Cleopatras in our focus. She really deserved her own story, but alas, *Astro City* seems now to be defunct.

The four remaining exempla of graphic novels have some connection to the historical Cleopatra, however tenuous that might be. In the *Cursed* storyline,[26] Cleopatra never actually died, but has existed under numerous aliases, currently Klara Peterson. She is white, beautiful and has to shed her skin periodically with the assistance of a willing human sacrifice. Reality is swept aside and she is treated as a product of Pharaonic Egypt, ignoring her Macedonian context. The story arc is about Shan Beaumont who has inherited a piece of the Osiris Amulet craved by evil German archaeologist Victor Hahn.

Shan has been chosen to assist Osiris, a job Victor has sought. Klara keeps her alive. In the third issue, Klara recounts the death and rebirth of Cleopatra and makes mention of Octavian, but she quickly reverts to a rather muddled version of the Isis-Osiris myth. In the final instalment, Shan's photographer turns into Thoth and explains why Shan has been chosen. After defeating Victor, Klara instructs Shan to find the other twelve pieces of the amulet in order to restore the reign of Osiris. Shan has had twelve years to work on this, but so far, no sequel. The art is mediocre and the writing confusing. While contributing nothing new, the *Cursed* series does exploit several recent themes from the reception: focus on Isis worship, use of magic and the presence of zombies/mummies.

Tony and Cleo,[27] on the other hand, is conscious of both the historical and received Cleopatra. Daniels rather cleverly combines Rice's dangerous resurrection plot with elements of time travel common in earlier comics. While the artwork is not appealing to me, it at least does not distract from the story. Tony is a Black bodyguard of dubious moral character (he is a Cubs fan) who had assisted in Cleopatra's resurrection in 2003. She is depicted as a diva, white and highly sexualized. Octavian is aware of her resurrection and is arranging a surrogate assassination from the past through terrible magic. In a flashback to the death of Antony, she is dressed in the usual Cleopatra attire, while her modern clothes are barely there. Most significantly, although she attempts to mould her circumstances around her every whim, in fact every aspect of her life to this point is dependent on males: Antony and Octavian in her own time, the Scottish archaeologist and Tony now and a lunatic assassin transcending both periods. She even distances herself from her adoring female assistant and cat-suited bodyguard 'Tilda'.

In the second issue we learn more about the 'Ides of March' time-bending plot. Cleopatra dreams of fighting her assassin who not only defeats her but is unmasked as Tony. She loses faith in her protector, unjustifiably. In the dream, she wears a cat suit similar to Tilda's, with a 'fascinator' version of a vulture headdress. She determines to return to Egypt and retrieve her magic 'crooks'.

Next, we learn the details of the plot to kill Cleopatra and how a mother in Alabama has been training her son to do the deed. In his search for Cleo, the killer finds and kills the Scottish archaeologist who discovered and revived her. Just as with Caesar and Antony, Cleo is once again losing the males whom she has relied on to protect her. As she moves toward empowerment, she adopts a cat suit similar to Tilda's and is now armed with the magic crooks she had in her tomb.

The final episode begins with a flashback to 2003 when the Prof and Tony found and revived Cleopatra, dressed in conventional pseudo-Egyptian attire. That was five years earlier, when she was not ready to fend for herself. But now, dressed as a dominatrix with enormous breasts and pulsating crooks, she does solo battle with her assassin and prevails on her own. Thus, she avenges Antony and thwarts Octavian. When she encounters Tony, she accepts that he is an ally, accepts that he is her equal and agrees that the two of them should start again at the 'beginning'. She becomes more self-reliant than she had ever been before Actium.

Finally, there is *Cleopatra in Space*,[28] a six-part children's graphic novel that begins with the more or less historical Cleopatra at age fifteen. Since we know little about her before 51 BCE, this is fairly safe. However, she and her environment are depicted as purely Egyptian, but later references call her father Auletes, Greek for flute player, her sidekick is named Antony and her nemesis is Octavian. Maihack clearly tries to weave elements of Cleopatra's real story into his fiction, rather skilfully. In his version, Cleopatra has been zapped to a future and distant galaxy, for which she has been prophesied as a saviour against Xaius Octavian and his troops, the Xerx. His power and his longevity are due to his possession of the magical Sword of Kebechet. He turns out to share part of Cleopatra's world. She hated school in Egypt and is appalled that she has been transported to a space academy. The only classes she likes are combat – at which she excels because she too is a Warrior Princess. There are lessons embedded here about the value of friendship and respect for learning (as one ten-year-old consultant remarks, 'She should have gone to those classes! They taught stuff she needed to know!').

The second volume is a more straightforward adventure, but we meet her Antony and by actually showing up at her birthday party, she begins to form her team of rivals. She even finds crucial clues in the books in the Library of Alexandria. The third volume draws many threads together, culminating in a battle royal and a harsh education for Cleopatra. Maihack even has her sneak into Hykosis City in a carpet. In Book Four, she foils Octavian's attempt to gain control of an energy source called the Golden Lion, gaining the trust of her cat mentor Kenshu. In the process, she reunites with the roguish Antony (who is dark-skinned), dons a very sexy two-piece outfit and they kiss. Book Five begins and ends with flashbacks to Octavian's origins in Egypt as Gozi and his early friendship with Cleopatra. Two years after Cleopatra was transported to the future, Egypt was destroyed and plundered by wandering space pirates who also took Gozi. Cleo continues to learn what it means to be responsible for the well-being of others. The final volume brings the story full circle back to Egypt, where Cleo returns to the past (with Antony) to defeat both the space aliens and the Romans and establish a new world order. In the process, Cleopatra defeats Octavian with his own sword, saves the Pharoah, restores the academy and liberates the Nile Galaxy, fulfilling the prophecy repeated throughout the story.

This is intended for children, but it goes beyond comic escapism and afterschool specials. The art is gorgeous, the situations are relatable and the ugliness of life is not glossed over (kids and cats die). It has been heartily endorsed by several precocious children of my colleagues. They like a girl who kicks butt, but they want her to stay in school, trust her friends and listen to the cats. While this Cleopatra is depicted as white, Egyptian and not Macedonian, she is not completely disconnected from the context of the actual princess.

9.3 Video games

Assassins Creed Origins is a graphic novelization of an electronic game of the same name, the tenth instalment in the *Creed* franchise published by Ubisoft in 2017.[29] The background history and the architecture are surprisingly realistic for the genre, which is all about the fighting between the Brotherhood of Assassins (who are allied with Cleopatra) and the Order of the Ancients.[30] The portrayal of Cleopatra on the other hand is more in line with other recent receptions than with the historical queen. Campbell notes, in an online review for Polygon.com, that in this game Cleopatra is 'tough, smart and ruthless. But she is often clothed in slinky, revealing outfits. She is a femme fatale: exotic, sensual, flirtatious and beautiful.'[31] It even includes the charge from Aurelius Victor that she traded a lover's death for one night of sex with her. This scene occurs at a party early in the game, cementing the characterization. Rose

Milnes has explored this portrayal in a 2020 Classical Association of the Middle West and South paper which I have not seen.[32]

The game focuses on the 'test and quest' adventures of the Assassins Bayet and his wife Aya (later Amunet). Since it is set in Ptolemaic Egypt, their adventures intersect with historical figures and events, including Cleopatra, especially during her association with Julius Caesar. The writers are quite willing to subordinate facts to their own alternate reality of violent covert struggles between shadowy forces. History does manage to follow its true course in the end, but the underlying conspiracies seem to be behind it all. As a true twenty-first-century tale, the lines between good and evil are blurry to say the least. Being in essence a supporting actor, Cleopatra does not come across as either the hero or villain of the piece. She serves more to add sex, glamour and tragedy to this dystopian past.

The graphic novel version begins with an introduction titled 'Loading Memory ...', which places this excerpt in the context of the video game story arc. Aya has set out for Rome to establish a branch of the 'Hidden ones' in order 'to assassinate those who would seek to control the free will of the people'.[33] By switching back and forth between Alexandria in 30 BCE and Rome in 44 BCE the writers are able to connect the two narratives, although Aya drives the plot. Since the Cleopatra narrative is limited to the days around Octavian's capture of Alexandria, she is limited to one rather scanty outfit. Mark Antony and his children are absent, although he appears in the Ides of March narrative. Iras and Charmion have been replaced by a single attendant named Akira. Cleopatra is depicted as dark-skinned but only has distinctly Black features on Cover 4A drawn by a different artist. Cover 4B also has a number of anomalies including a snake despite its banishment from this narrative, but this kind of cover art autonomy and variety is common in contemporary graphic novels.

Chapter/Issue 1 begins in Alexandria in 30 BCE as Octavian is closing in on the city in the wake of the defeat at Actium the year before. Cleopatra oversees the execution of a captured female warrior in Roman armour who reminds her of Aya. We flash back to Rome in 44 BCE where Aya has pursued her mission to oppose tyranny. She is assisting Brutus in his plot to kill Caesar and she strikes the first blow. Throughout, the writers demonstrate their erudition with famous phrases, in this instance, 'You too my child?'

Chapter/Issue 2 returns to Alexandria where Caesarion is losing a training duel to a masked soldier. As they conclude their bout, they see a fire set by the Romans in the distance and make an unsubtle allusion to the discord after Caesar's death. Mark Antony incites the crowd and Aya must fight them at every turn, largely in homage to the main attraction of the video game but interspersed with sophomoric musings about violence and justice.

In Chapter/Issue 3, Cleopatra and Caesarion are attacked by an assassin, but Caesarion manages to bludgeon him to death with a torch. Cleopatra then orders him to stab the masked soldier who had left them alone. Meanwhile back in Rome in 44 BCE, Aya is thrown to angry hippos which she fights until rescued by Brutus and Cassius only to be blocked by Antony and his mob. This makes *Origins* one of the rare works sympathetic to Brutus and the tyrannicides.

Chapter/Issue 4 begins with Octavian's troops storming Alexandria (which did not happen) and includes Cleopatra's famous quote from Livy: 'I will not be triumphed over.' Cleopatra vows to fight on when the doors to her throne room are smashed open. The scene then shifts back to Rome for yet another battle royal until Aya convinces Brutus to leave Rome to Antony. After a one-page summary of the next fourteen years (omitting the entire Antony–Cleopatra narrative), we return to the crashing doors to find, not Octavian and his soldiers, but Aya, with a new outfit and name – Amunet. After only five panels of shouting, Cleopatra agrees to stop the fighting if Aya will take Caesarion with her. Aya gives her a vial of poison and leaves with her son. They are last seen sailing past the Pharos off to rid the world of more tyrants.

9.4 Animation

Clone High (2002–3),[34] a Canadian effort (although it is placed in Minnesota and aired primarily on MTV), only lasted for one season and thirteen episodes. It failed to catch on but has since developed a minor cult following. The premise is that a secret military project, overseen by the Board of Shadowy Figures who only appear in the shadows, cloned historic figures for their own undefined aim. The clones are now all in high school at a secure undisclosed location near Saint Paul, having been raised by alarmingly inappropriate foster parents. The dastardly principal has his own evil schemes to exploit them in an amusement park named Cloney Island. The clones are all victims of their DNA, but as teenagers they also strive to rebel. Joan of Arc becomes an angst-ridden Goth girl, who panics when she hears the voice of God, but it is only an AM Gospel station she picks up on her retainer. *Clone High* is structured as a parody of issue-themed high school dramas. For example, Gandhi, who strives to be a party animal, is ostracized because he has ADHD and therefore must be contagious as is the case in all diseases known primarily by their initials. The clones are obsessed with sex, alcohol and social position, and the situations and the humour are frequently scatological or downright obscene. It is fast paced, has original music and has an anime style of animation known as pose-to-pose. As a certified arrested adolescent, I find it hilarious.

One of the principal characters is the clone of Cleopatra. Except for a very brief excerpt from her self-serving film class project, little is used from her backstory. Every male lusts for her, but especially Abe and JFK. Cleo is the archetypal TV mean girl. She is a cheerleader, class president since freshman year and abundantly endowed. She is also vain, nasty and completely self-absorbed. Cleopatra has attached herself to JFK, but taunts Abe relentlessly to the point that he cannot see that Joan of Arc is in love with him. Her connection to the real Cleopatra VII is superficial and is limited to occasional artefacts and jewellery. Her characterization is still drawn from her image as a man-eating, power-hungry bombshell familiar from most of American popular culture. If she only had a snake bra, she could be the Theda Bara of the twenty-first century. This Cleopatra is not dependent on her men nor a victim of their successes and failures, but clearly the mistress of her domain – even if it is a dysfunctional high school.

Scooby-Doo: Where's My Mummy? (Hanna-Barbera, 2005)[35] with its slick Warner Brothers animation is the only animated feature-length film for this period, yet it still bears some traces of Lizpatra influence. The plot is mostly copied from the *Speed Racer* story,[36] where once again an archaeologist succumbs to treasure lust and attempts to abscond with the loot by posing as the reincarnation of the mummy of Cleopatra. It is mostly a vehicle for Scooby Doo and his buddies to do their shtick. One saving grace is that Virginia Madsen does the voice of Cleopatra.

10

Her Infinite Variety

10.1 Trends 1889–2022

Throughout the period of this study there have always been an infinite variety of Cleopatra images existing simultaneously, especially in the last three decades. As Lucy Hughes-Hallett (1990) has shown, this had always been the case throughout Western culture, but to her canonical eight categories we should now also add the fantasy/magical Cleopatra.[1] In fact, we can see most of these types at the end of the nineteenth century in England and France (e.g., Haggard 1889), where we began our survey, before the next phase of her reception broke into American culture through the infant film industry (e.g., Gaskill 1912). As the 'New Woman' and the vamp grew out of fashion, so too the silent film Cleopatra as *femme fatale*.

How that image came to be replaced by a softer and gentler Queen of the 1920s and 1930s is harder to explain in strictly social historical terms, but the shocks of the First World War, the influenza epidemic and the constitutional victory of 1920[2] seem to have made some forms of hedonism acceptable in the 1920s. We cannot entirely rule out the possibility that the light-hearted beauty campaigns for Palmolive Soap were as much a cause as an effect in relation to the specific image of Cleopatra. While in fiction we continued to see the *femme fatale*, Barrington (1929) first showed us a laughing Queen who would become quite common in the interwar receptions, notably in DeMille (1934). Although some of the finest examples of this trend were British and outside the scope of this study, Butts (1935), Lindsay (1935) and Berners (1941) are well worth reading.

The immediate postwar contributions, especially Pascal (1945) and Wilder (1948), continued along these lines, but the numerous examples from the pepla, pulp fiction and comics frequently reverted to a curious potpourri of

Figure 10.1 Fanny Davenport as a stage Cleopatra (1894). From the author's collection.

killers, lovers and maidens in distress. Those from the early 1960s generally reflected the hype around the coming Lizpatra (Mankiewicz 1963) or were attempts to cash in on the interest being generated. Although Castle (1953) starring Rhonda Fleming cleverly drew from older traditions, most examples from this period emphasized Cleopatra's beauty, sexuality and dangerous allure. Complicating this portrayal was the postwar tendency for films to depict Romans as Paleo-Nazis.[3]

Major films had twice marked watersheds in the development of the Cleopatra reception, but in the case of the 1963 Lizpatra, the aftermath was not as positive. For reasons much discussed by others, it was a box-office disaster, although it did have some redeeming features. None of those, however, could overcome the bad acting, worse editing and public hostility to the stars. Although it attempted to draw on some of the more interesting developments in her reception since Theda Bara, Lizpatra made the real Cleopatra (and all ancient epic films) into box-office poison for the next forty years. Pornography was the principal exception.

While the next several decades were not without some interesting and high-quality anomalies, such as Drake (1968), Tezuka (1970), Aaron (1985) and Chase-Riboud (1987), no reception could be said to have become part of American popular culture in the wider sense until Anne Rice published *The Mummy* in 1989. Because of her high profile as a fantasy/horror novelist and the serialization of the story as a graphic novel, interest in Cleopatra surged in the 1990s. Even the more historical Queen profited with a novel – George (1997) and its TV adaptation Roddam (1999) – but more notable were the appearances in science fiction/fantasy novels, comics and TV shows as diverse as *Xena* (Campbell 1997) and *Bettie Page* (Silke 1999–2000).

This has remained the pattern for the first two decades of the new millennium. Interest in the historical Cleopatra has remained quite high, with numerous excellent biographies and studies having appeared throughout the world. Some of these no doubt inspired the works of historical fiction which proliferated as well. While these can be very inventive, especially when dealing with Cleopatra's less well documented early years and the fates of her children and known associates, they still strive for a degree of verisimilitude and historical realism. At the other end of the spectrum is the fantasy Cleopatra whose story has been appropriated and adapted into the popular genres of science fiction, fantasy and horror and displayed in not only fiction, but also graphic novels, animation and electronic games. More remarkably, Cleopatra often escapes the late twentieth-century tropes of the updated *femme fatale* and becomes a teenage role model, sympathetic mummy or multifaceted model of a modern woman. She can still be as scary as Theda Bara, but the strength and resiliency of Helen Gardner shines through with frequent glimpses of a laughing Claudette Colbert. Custom indeed cannot stale her infinite variety.

10.2 Primacy of Plutarch and Shakespeare

Perhaps the most striking observation to emerge from this study is the enduring power and incredible influence of Shakespeare's *Antony and Cleopatra* and *his* primary source, Plutarch's *Life of Antony*, in spite of the continued outpouring of both scholarly research and well documented non-fiction. Often the influence is clearly second- or third-hand, but the trail is generally easy to follow. This was especially evident in the British made HBO *Rome* series, where it was evident that the writers – and some of the actors – had actually read Plutarch and were intimately familiar with the text and nuance of Shakespeare. Both authors have frequently been treated as if they were the primary sources for her life instead of the receptions that they were and still are. This study has focused primarily

Figure 10.2 Screen shot of Beyoncé as Cleopatra in *Dreamgirls* (2006).

on the English language receptions popular in the USA, but the impact is seen everywhere, especially in Europe and Japan.

10.3 Endurance of Orientalism

Starting in the 1990s we have also seen a return to the darker side of Cleopatra's reception in a revival of Orientalism (which has never completely disappeared) and the 'Killer Kleopatra' of Haggard and Theda Bara. Her image had been softened and modernized by the 'New Woman' trends of the interwar period, but that was derailed for a while by the negative reaction to Lizpatra. This reborn Orientalism has become especially prevalent in graphic novels and horror fiction and will doubtless endure.[4] A truly ground-breaking film could shatter the stranglehold of Shakespeare and Orientalism, but only time and Gal Gadot can tell.

10.4 Changing role of film in influencing other reception genres

For most of the period covered by this study, which begins at the very start of the age of film, there has been a direct and two-way relationship between major films and other receptions of Cleopatra. The Bara film grew from Victorian Orientalism – and Haggard in particular – and spawned the vamp and then Palmolive's reimaging of Cleopatra as a more approachable flapper. That campaign and the 'New Woman' movement in general softened her image, as seen, for example, in the Barrington novel and the Colbert film. Lizpatra grew from the pepla and novels of the postwar era and inspired numerous imitations and spoofs but muddled the contemporary reflections by mindlessly pilfering the incompatible images from both Shaw and Shakespeare. This pattern seems to have changed and there has not been a successful theatrical release of a major film about Cleopatra in over half a century. It is therefore remarkable that major developments in her reception did occur in this period without a Hollywood blockbuster to spark the popular imagination. Instead, shifts in her image seemed to have been initiated by other genres such as horror novels, comics, video games and even art exhibits. The pattern could revert to 'normal' if any of the proposed films ever emerge from development hell.

10.5 As a reflection of changing gender roles

Gender roles have changed dramatically over our time period, perhaps more rapidly and profoundly than in any other. It is as if for every shift in the contemporary attitudes towards women, Cleopatra has been invoked to either attack the changes or to celebrate them. As a woman of power entangled romantically with powerful men, she was a ready-made sign. She readily fit into multiple polarities: male–female, East–West, Greek–Roman, European–African and so on.

10.6 As a reflection of changing racial perceptions

Cleopatra's race has been an issue since her own lifetime, but debate intensified in the nineteenth century due to a number of factors including colonialism, Orientalism and American slavery. If treated as an 'other' in any of these scenarios, she tended to be assigned to most if not all of the polarities being imposed upon her story. In reaction to this, many African Americans embraced her as a Black African Queen. Since she was born in Alexandria, she was African – as much as the South African-born Charlize Theron. The lack of clear evidence as to her skin colour and parentage has not deterred either side on this question. Since she was probably at least one-quarter Macedonian and one-half Egyptian, the question should be moot, but alas it rages on, as we saw in the media frenzy when Angelina Jolie was rumoured to be in line for the role in the Scott Rudin production.

10.7 Gal Gadot in a snake bra?

These issues resurfaced recently with the announcement that Gal Gadot would produce and star in a feature-length film on the Queen, to be written by Laeta

Kalogridis (writer of Oliver Stone's *Alexander*) and directed by Patty Jenkins, who directed *Wonder Woman*. I welcome the news since it would involve a talented Mediterranean actress with box-office appeal, a writer familiar with the period and a proven female director. The press reports offered few clues to the content or time frame of the film, but the *Wonder Woman* franchise did use a young actress to portray her as a youth and one might expect to see the same here. I sincerely hope we are spared another thirty-something trying to play a teenager. I would expect Shakespeare and Plutarch to be quite visible in the narrative, but one can hope to see the influence of some of the other receptions discussed in this volume, such as Mary Butts, Barbara Chase-Riboud or Karen Essex.

I am prepared to be disappointed, as I have been with the several proposed films which have failed to materialize in recent years, but I was dismayed by the intensity of the ideological and racist reactions from across the political and social spectrum. One can see a representative and thoughtful discussion which appeared on the website of the Society for Classical Studies,[5] although I find their positions rather extreme and unfair since no one has actually seen the script, much less the final film. We will have to wait and see.

10.8 Video games and graphic novels

Based on the proliferation of electronic games and comics over the last two decades, I would not be surprised if we see them dominate the Cleopatra receptions of the twenty-first century. New novels keep appearing, although too many of them are salacious, poorly edited and sub-literary. While sex, vampires and sex with vampires does sell, the audience seems too small to be considered broadly popular. The cleverest of the historical novels I have read lately tend to focus on the marginal characters of Cleopatra's reception: her children, siblings and servants. Computer games seem to reach more people, especially those like *Assassin's Creed: Origins* which tie into a run of graphic novels. There are several new games based on ancient myths and history, so Cleopatra could be next. Stand-alone graphic series do well, especially if aimed at a younger audience such as *Cleopatra in Space*. We should expect steady production in these areas, but I doubt we will see many major feature-length theatrical films any time soon.

10.9 A modest pitch for a TV series

With the explosion of streaming services and the tragic demise of movie theatres, I would suspect that television would offer the best platform for Cleopatra to return as a major presence in the popular imagination. The previous pages are testimony to what can be achieved outside of the broadcast network establishment, whether as one-off movies or as miniseries. As an example, I would indulge your patience with a modest pitch of my own if only to illustrate what could be done.

I would like to propose a nine-episode miniseries focusing on the main turning points in Cleopatra's history: her perilous youth in conflict with her siblings; her struggle to succeed her father on the throne; her affair with Julius Caesar; her lone rule, culminating with the meeting with Antony at Tarsus; her entanglement with Antony; the adventures of the inimitable livers; the war with Octavian and his propaganda; the plot of Jack Lindsay's 1935 novel; the end game and her children.

The sequence is traditional, but I would want to film all of them on the same sets as Alexandria and Rome, with the secondary characters played by the same actors as far as possible, but with Cleopatra played by a different age-appropriate actress and with nine different directors (including as many women of colour in both roles as possible). I have my favourites in mind for both roles, but I would like to see as much racial, skin tone and body diversity as possible. I would also call on a number of the writers from this volume, both living and dead. They could provide the material to represent every type of Cleopatra including the killer, the vamp, the clever Cleo, the sex kitten, the Hellenistic ruler, the deadly monster and the manifestation of destiny. As a promo, I would show each actress and a few living former Queens in a Spartacus-like scene where a belligerent Roman centurion barges into the throne room set and demands that the Queen identify herself. Each in turn would rise and declare to the camera 'No, I am Cleopatra', after Sophia Loren has had a turn. It would send a clear if jarring message about the infinite variety of Cleopatra's reception, because truly she was a lass unparalleled.

Notes

1 'A Lass Unparalleled'

1 Hughes-Hallett 1990. Ellis 1947 is an earlier study of elite receptions up to Shaw. See also Marquart 2016.
2 Hamer 1993, 2nd edn, 2008.
3 For example, Walker and Higgs 2001, Walker 2004, Walker and Ashton 2006 and Ashton 2008.
4 Wenzel 2005.
5 Wyke 1997, 2002 and 2011.
6 Shakespeare, *Antony and Cleopatra*, 2.2.236.
7 Ashton 2008: xi.
8 Macurdy 1932.
9 Roller 2010. Shorter treatments such as Jones 2006a and Walker and Ashton 2006 are also reliable.
10 Other well done recent comprehensive biographies include Grant 1972, Ashton 2003, Burstein 2004, Kleiner 2005, Jones 2006b, Fletcher 2008, Tyldesely 2008, Preston 2009, Schiff 2010 and Goldsworthy 2010.
11 See Appendix A which is based on Roller 2010: App. I 159–61.
12 Huss 1990 and Roller 2010: 167–8.
13 Livia Capponi said in a recent online Q&A that she will soon publish an argument for the later date.
14 Roller 2003 and 2018.
15 Beneker 2014: 508.
16 Roller 2010: 61 and 107.
17 Walker and Higgs 2001.
18 Representative examples of these coins may be found in Walker and Higgs 2001.
19 Higgs 2001: 209.
20 Walker 2004: esp. 47–64.
21 Walker 2004: reference is to illustration 19, pp. 42–3.
22 Jones 2006a: 78–88.
23 Benario 1970.
24 Hughes-Hallett 1990: 64.
25 Jones 2006a: 209.

26 Tatum 2008: 115.
27 Jones 2006b: 18–19.
28 Useful discussions may be found in MacDonald 2002, Royster 2003 and Trafton 2004.
29 Jenkins in development.
30 Huss 1990: 191–204.
31 Haley 1993: 23–43.
32 On Plutarch's biographical agenda, see Geiger 2014: 292–303.
33 For surveys of the early receptions see Ellis 1947, Hughes-Hallett 1990, Royster 2003, Jones 2006a, Hamer 2008 and Marquart 2016.

2 The *Femme Fatale*

1 In my opinion, Shaw only qualifies as popular culture when the film version appeared and it will be discussed in that context.
2 Haggard 1967.
3 Ellis 1978: 1–42 is the source for most of the biographical information.
4 Katz 1987: 24.
5 Hilton 2011: 107–28.
6 Ellis 1978: 278.
7 Reeve 2018: 6.
8 Eugene Delacroix. 'Cleopatra and the Peasant' 1838.
9 Lawrence Alma-Tadema, 'Antony and Cleopatra' Opus CCXLVI 1883, in Ash 1990: plate 13; Smith 2011: 159–64.
10 Algernon Swinburne, 'Cleopatra' 1866, in Jones 2006a: 263–9.
11 Arthur O'Shaughnessy, *An Epic of Women*: Cleopatra I 1870, in Jones 2006a: 256–9.
12 Alexander Pushkin, *Egyptian Nights*: 'Cleopatra and her lovers' 1825, in Jones 2006a: 260–3.
13 Gauthier 1838.
14 Sextus Aurelius Victor, *De Viris Illustribus Urbis Romae* 86.2.
15 Charlotte Bronte, *Villette* 1853, excerpt of Chapter 19, in Jones 2006a: 250–4.
16 Image in Trafton 2004: 182.
17 Nathaniel Hawthorne, *The Marble Faun* 1860: Chapter 14.
18 Trafton 2004: 181.
19 Abbott 1879.
20 Hilton 2011.
21 Hilton 2011: 110–11.

22 Haggard 1926: 215–16.
23 Haggard 1889: 45.
24 Haggard 1889: 90: 'Her breast was bare, but under it was a garment which glistened like the scaly covering of a snake, everywhere sewn with gems.' On the snake bra, see Daugherty 2013a: 183–94.
25 Haggard 1889: 91.
26 Shaw 1895: 725–7.
27 Dubar 1994: 239–40.
28 Ducrey 2017: 298, n. 1.
29 Dubar 1994: 245; Ducrey 2017: 278.
30 Ducrey 2017: 266–8.
31 Ducrey 2017: 261–466. An English translation is available: Morlock 2010.
32 Ducrey 2017: 270. Cf. Dubar 1994: 241.
33 Humbert 2016: 26, citing Dewachter 2004.
34 For example, Humbert 2016: figures 7 and 8.
35 Ducrey 2017: 295, n. 1.
36 Act 1, Scene 5. Ducrey 2017: 314.
37 Haggard's book had been out for a year and Sardou was proficient in English as well as Latin and Greek.
38 Pliny, *Natural History* 9.119–21; see Jones 2006a: 106–8.
39 Ducrey 2017: 353, n. 1 and 273–5; Humbert 2016: figure 7.
40 There were apparently some substantial alterations to this scene in later texts. Ducley 2017: 432, n. 1.
41 For example, Hughes-Hallett 1990: plate 10.
42 Ducley 2017: 278.
43 Dubar 1994: 246.
44 Hall 1891. The photographic illustrations appear to be from a later film.
45 Ducley 2017: 278.
46 Hughes-Hallett 1990; Hamer 2008; Wyke 2011: 173–7.
47 Trafton 2004: 165–221.
48 Hughes-Hallett 1990: 252.
49 See Richardson and Willis 2001 for context and examples.
50 Matthews 2003: 13.
51 See Wenzel 2005: 195–8 for a discussion of this lost film. Surviving stills plates 40–4.
52 Wentzel 2005: 296–368. Some of the entries may not be unique films as she duly notes.
53 Hughes-Hallett 1990; Hamer 1997 and 2008; Wyke 1997, 2002, 2011 and 2017.
54 For a discussion of the 1910 French version, see Wenzel 2005: 140–9.

55 McCaffrey 1999: 81.
56 Wenzel 2005: 245, n. 56.
57 Wenzel 2005: 150–62 is the most complete and best documented discussion. It was also featured in a well-informed but more popular style online review: Kramer 2017.
58 Wenzel 2005: 245, n. 55.
59 Wenzel 2005: 151–6.
60 Sextus Aurelius Victor, *De Viris Illustribus Urbis Romae* 86.2; Gauthier 1838.
61 Alma-Tadema, 'Antony and Cleopatra' Opus CCXLVI 1883; example in Ash 1990: plate 13. See also Smith 2011.
62 Wenzel 2005: 161–2. Some of her posed stills do appear to show Theda Bara in dance mode.
63 Wenzel 2005: 309–10, 163–75.
64 Ball 1968: 168.
65 Wenzel 2005: 170–1.
66 Hughes-Hallett 1990: 225–51; Wenzel 2005: 171–5; Pucci 2011: 195–207.
67 Wyke 2002: 251 = Wyke 1997: 78.
68 Wenzel 2005: 175.
69 Said 1985 is essential.
70 Wyke 2002: 256 = Wyke 1997: 79–80.
71 Wyke 2002: 258–64.
72 Zemon-Davis 2000: 141, n. 5. calls Wyke's approach 'an example of film criticism subordinating any aesthetic or historical components in films to present-day purposes and messages'.
73 Doering 2008: 158–60.
74 Doering 2008 and 2018.
75 Wenzel 2005: data 312–13 and discussion 177–95. See also Wyke 2017: 66–71 for an overview. Most recently, see the extensive treatment by Dye 2020.
76 Golden 1996 is a comprehensive biography.
77 Both reproduced in Golden 1996: xii–xiii.
78 Wyke 2011: 178. See also Golden 1996: 129–34.
79 Zierold 1973: 37. Contains many amusing anecdotes from her PR campaigns. Dye 2020 relates even more.
80 Marquis 1927: 17. Entitled 'ii mehitable was once cleopatra'. This occurred in the second instalment of the 'archie and mehitable' series which had started running in New York newspapers in 1916.
81 As Wenzel 2005: 193–5. See also Bronfen 2013: 145–6.
82 F. Scott Fitzgerald, *The Beautiful and Damned*, New York: Scribner's, 1922: 95.
83 Wyke 2002: 171. See also Lant 2013: 54.

84 Wenzel 2005: 181–2. She follows Thompson 1996: 68–70, as shall I. Film historian Dye 2020 makes greater use of the early scenario by Adrian Johnson. His reconstruction is quite plausible, but frequently based on conjecture and publicity stills. He is working on a video reconstruction based on them. For an excerpt, see http://www.lostcleopatra.com/.
85 Wenzel 2005: 267–8, 306–7.
86 Dye 2020: 109–10 accepts Haggard as the original inspiration but acknowledges other influences in the same chapter.
87 On this costume in general, see Wenzel 2005: 184–5. This is part of a larger discussion of all of the costumes.
88 Haggard 1889: 90.
89 Compare the engraving '"I've won," She Cried' facing Haggard 1889: 152 by M. Greiffenhafgen.
90 Dye 2020: 164–89.
91 Thompson 1996: 78.
92 Thompson 1996: 75.
93 Dye 2020: 270–83 quotes many of the contemporary reviews at length.
94 Hubbard 1910: 67–77.
95 Wyke 2002: 277.
96 Zierold 1973: 57.
97 Golden 1996: 237.
98 Since her poem was published in Birmingham, she might be English.
99 Hughes-Hallett 1990: 226.
100 Ironmonger 1924: 38.
101 Ironmonger 1924: 9.
102 Ellis 1984 and Taves 2006.
103 Taves 2006: 21.
104 Ellis 1984: 89–91.
105 Taves 2006: 256–7.
106 Taves 2006: 38–9.
107 Taves 2006: 254.
108 Ellis 1984: 149.
109 Taves 2006: 148–9, 240–59. See also Taves 1985.
110 Ellis 1984: 185–6.
111 Taves 2006: 148.
112 Taves 2006: 209–10.
113 Ellis 1984: 161.
114 Ellis 1984: 149.
115 Mundy 1929: 180.

116 Mundy 1929: 189.
117 Mundy 1929: 285.
118 Mundy 1929: 335.
119 Well documented in works such as Bram Dijkstra 1986, *Idols of Perversity: Fantasies of Feminine Evil in Fin-De-Siecle Culture*, and Bram Dijkstra 1996, *Evil Sisters: The Threat of Female Sexuality in Twentieth-Century Culture*.

3 A Kinder, Gentler Cleopatra

1 Matthews 2003: 107.
2 Although outside the scope of this study, similar receptions can be found in the British poetry of Ironmonger 1924 and the novels of Lindsay 1935, Butts 1935 and Berners 1941. On Butts, see especially Blondell 1998.
3 Robinson 1954: 21–5.
4 Sivulka 1998: 107ff.
5 Daugherty 2015: 188–9.
6 https//www.youtube.com/watch?v=FP1SJ_sLHyE.
7 Taylor Swift, 'Blank Space' on *1989*, Big Machine Records, 2014.
8 https//www.youtube.com/watch?v=61-ptVgYfNk.
9 Rowland 2011: 141–2.
10 Wyke 2011: 186–7.
11 Sivulka 2001: 143–8. See Wieber 2020 for these and similar ads featuring Zenobia and Dido.
12 Foster 1975: 10–16.
13 Hopkins 1998: 134–45.
14 Wenzel 2005: 301–13.
15 Gaskill 1912, Guazzoni 1913 and Edwards 1917
16 Rowland 2011: 141–2.
17 Cruikshank 2010: 241.
18 https//adage.com/article/adage-encyclopedia/resor-helen-lansdowne-1886-1964/98850.
19 Sivulka: 1998 110.
20 Sivulka 1998: 112.
21 Cruikshank 2010: 104–7.
22 Hopkins 1998: 135–6.
23 Sivulka 2001: 145.
24 Hopkins 1998: 140.
25 An eBay search for 'Palmolive soap ads' will turn up a representative sample.

26 Foster 1975: 9.
27 Foster 1975: 16–17.
28 Most of these are not accessible for free, but for this and a 1960s effort, see a useful summary at https//cleopatrasboudoir.blogspot.com/2013/11/cleopatra-soap.html.
29 See page 24. Haggard 1889.
30 Aubert 2008: 196, fig. 202.
31 Wenzel 2005: 102–3, 313–19.
32 Wenzel 2005: 195–8, plates 40–4.
33 Wenzel 2005a: 124–5.
34 For an overview, see Bruce F. Campbell, *Ancient Wisdom Revived: A History of the Theosophical Movement* (Berkeley: University of California Press, 1980).
35 A popularizing work is aimed at a general reader, avoids untranslated Latin and Greek and either limits or eliminates footnotes or references.
36 http//www.gatewaytotheclassics.com/browse/authors_browse_one.php?author=abbott.
37 For a list of titles, see https//en.wikipedia.org/wiki/Philip_Walsingham_Sergeant.
38 Sergeant 1909: 338. Weigall even mentions him as an authority in the same sentence with Ferrero and Mommsen.
39 https//seriesofseries.owu.edu/hutchinsons-library-of-standard-lives/.
40 See the biography by his granddaughter, Hankey 2001.
41 Hoberman 1997: 138.
42 Weigall 1924: v.
43 Weigall 1924: 425–6.
44 Hankey 2001: 197–200.
45 Quoted by Hankey 2001: 198.
46 Weigall 1924: 123–6.
47 Hughes-Hallett 1990: 252–7; cf. Hankey 2001: 199.
48 Hoberman 1997: 148, n. 2.
49 Delayen 1934: xi–xii.
50 See Hankey 2001: 199–200 for a sample of reviews.
51 Wertheimer 1931: 322.
52 Tyldesley 2008: 1, 217.
53 Barrington 1929: preface.
54 For a biography and criticism, see Blondel 1998: especially 380–8.
55 Butts 1994: 280. This repaginated reprint is more generally available than the 1935 edition.
56 Butts 1994: 345.

57 I am passing over the conventional novels of Claude Ferval (1927) and Emil Ludwig (1937) because they had minimal impact on American popular culture and were not originally written in English, although they both circulated in the USA in translation.
58 Marquis 1927: 17–18.
59 Gross 1928: 67–75.
60 Thomas 1942: 3–15.
61 Sigler 1997: 361.
62 Barnard 1950.
63 My source for this paragraph comes from https//abcbookworld.com/writer/beck-lily-adams/.
64 Barrington 1929: 5.
65 Barrington 1929: 174.
66 Barrington 1929: 264–70.
67 Plot summary at https//www.goodreads.com/book/show/26865986-the-laughing-queen.
68 Wenzel 2005: 319–20. It is no. 29 in her catalogue.
69 Hamer 2008: 104–34; Hughes-Hallett 1990: 269–71 and passim; Wenzel 2005: 198–217 and passim; Winkler 2009: 264–72; Wyke 2002: 281–302.
70 Birchard 2004: 275.
71 Birchard 2004: 276.
72 Birchard 2004: 276.
73 Birchard 2004: 276–7.
74 Dick 2008: 77–99.
75 For example, Hughes-Hallett 1990: 269 and Schiff 2010: 340, n. 261, who cites Lovic 2001: 83.
76 Birchard 2004: 254; Dick 2008: 66.
77 DeMille 1959: 322.
78 For a more detailed plot summary and commentary, see Wenzel 2005: 200–12.
79 https//www.phrases.org.uk/meanings/close-your-eyes-and-think-of-england.html.
80 Wenzel 2005: 202 is her first reference to Wertheimer 1950.
81 Winkler 2009: 269.
82 Wenzel 2005: 216–17.
83 Wenzel 2005: 199.
84 Wenzel 2005: 199.
85 https//www.imdb.com/title/tt0020578/?ref_=nm_flmg_wr_27.
86 https//www.imdb.com/title/tt0024991/fullcredits?ref_=tt_ov_wr#writers/.

87 Wertheimer 1931: 231–2.
88 Birchard 2004: 277.
89 Noted along with other tie-ins by Hamer 2008: 148, n. 19.
90 For documentation and discussion of this effort, see Wyke 2002: 293–302.
91 Wenzel 2005: 215.
92 Hamer 2008: 120–1.
93 Hamer 2008: 121–4; Wyke 2002: 293–302.
94 https//en.wikipedia.org/wiki/Claudette_Colbert. Citing Sol Chaneles, *The Movie Makers* (London: Octopus Books, 1974), 97.
95 Hughes-Hallett 1990: 225–51.
96 Pelling 1988: 187–8; Hillard 2002: 551–3; Peek 2011: 606, n. 63.
97 Britchard 2004: 279.
98 Hughes-Hallett 1990: 292–4; Hamer 2008: 128–30; Wyke 2002: 291; Winkler 2009: 264–72.
99 Hughes-Hallett 1990: 294.

4 Thoroughly Modern Cleopatra

1 Lindsay 1935.
2 Butts 1935.
3 Berners 1941.
4 See Blondel 1998.
5 For more information, see https://jacklindsayproject.com/.
6 Amory 1998 is an authoritative biography.
7 See section 3.1.
8 On its reception of Cleopatra, see Hughes-Hallett 1990: 252–4. For an insightful discussion, see Couchman 1973: 43–50.
9 Deans 1947. Contrast Wenzel 2005: 105–6.
10 Bean 2013: 92.
11 As cited in https://en.wikipedia.org/wiki/Caesar_and_Cleopatra_film:. See also Bean 2013: 94.
12 Bean 2013: 115.
13 Cited by Wenzel 2005: 105.
14 Bean 2013: 93.
15 Deans 1947: 65.
16 Hughes-Hallett 1990: 254.
17 Balderson 1948: 188–97.
18 Tarn 1934: 35–42, 66–83.

19 *Cleopatra and Caesar; a play, adapted from A goddess to a god*, by John L. Balderston and Sybil Bolitho. Hollywood, California, Studio Script Service, c. 1950. New York Public Library nos 19501 and 19491.
20 Hughes-Hallett 1990: 298.
21 For overview, see http://www.twildersociety.org/works/the-ides-of-march/.
22 According to my professor Lloyd Stow, who knew and admired Wilder during his tenure at the University of Chicago, from 1930 to 1936.
23 For overview, see http://www.twildersociety.org/works/the-woman-of-andros/.
24 MacKendrick 1948: 65–7.
25 Hughes-Hallett 1990: 272–3.
26 Wilder 1948: 51. The Roman numerals in this section refer to Wilder's divisions.
27 Wilder 1948: 93.
28 MacKendrick 1948: 65.
29 Wilder 1948: 113.
30 Wilder 1948: 121.
31 Wilder 1948: 122.
32 Wilder 1948: 169.
33 Wilder 1948: 243–4.
34 Solomon 2001: 12–13.
35 Castle 1953; Wenzel 2005: 108–9, 323–4.
36 Solomon 2001: 67 calls it 'cheap and disappointing'. Summary and analysis in Hatchuel 2011: 170–2.
37 Wenzel 2005: 108.
38 Hughes-Hallett 1990: 286.
39 In many ways the film foreshadows themes that will appear in *Spartacus* (1960).
40 Hughes-Hallett 1990: 269.
41 Wenzel 2005: 108–10, 324–5.
42 Summary and analysis in Hatchuel 2011: 177–9.
43 Hatchuel 2011: 179.
44 Sextus Aurelius Victor, *De Viris Illustribus Urbis Romae* 86.2.
45 On this motif in film, see Winkler 2009a.
46 Wenzel 2005: 110–11, 328.
47 https://www.imdb.com/list/ls072907762/.
48 Wenzel 2005: 329–30.
49 Solomon 2001: 67.
50 Hatchuel 2011: 173.
51 Correctly omitted by Wenzel.
52 Hatchuel 2011: 174–6.

53 Wenzel 2005: 112, 274–5, 331–2.
54 Hatchuel 2011: 173–4.
55 Wenzel 2005: 113, 334.
56 Warner 1960: 282.
57 Gardner 1962: 59–60.
58 Gardner 1962: 86–8.
59 A version of this section appeared previously in Daugherty 2009. Where the writer is not listed, I have given as full reference as possible.
60 Emile Gauvreau, 'Caesar and Cleopatra by George Bernard Shaw', *Picture News in Color and Action* 1, no. 4 (Bridgeport, CT: 299 Lafayette Street, April 1946): 25–7. Another three-page version of the love story with another ravishingly beautiful but cruel and manipulative Cleopatra appears in 'Famous Love Affairs: Antony and Cleopatra', *Lovelorn: Stirring Stories of Real Romance* 3 (New York: Best Syndicated Features, 1949).
61 'Antony and Cleopatra: All for the Love of a Woman!' *Ideal: A Classical Comic* 1, no. 1 (New York: Timely Comics, July 1948): 1–38.
62 During the 1950s, *HA HA Comics*, ran a recurring feature on a Dog/Cat odd couple named Antony and Cleopatra. Antony is dumb, inarticulate and completely at the mercy of Cleopatra the cat. That the names alone provide the framework for the repeated joke shows public familiarity with her and general acceptance of a devious and manipulative Cleopatra. Cf. 'Antony and Cleopatra', *HA HA Comics* 83 (St. Louis: Creston, May 1952): 1–7.
63 Finger 1951: 1–12.
64 Page 9, fifth panel.
65 Metal and/or snake bras appear as early as 1917 in the Theda Bara film and in Palmolive ads from 1917 to 1923.
66 'Across the Ages', *Strange Adventures* 60 (Sparta, IL: National Comics, September 1955): 1–6.
67 'The Three Prophecies', *House of Secrets* 3 (Sparta, IL: National Comics, March–April 1957): 17–22.
68 Rich 1962.
69 Baldwin 1963.
70 https://en.wikipedia.org/wiki/Wilson,_Keppel_and_Betty.

5 Lizpatra and Its Aftermath

1 The term Lizpatra was coined by critic Dwight Macdonald in *Esquire* in 1965 according to Wyke 2002: 310.

2 Mankiewicz 1963.
3 Cyrino 2005: 121–58.
4 Zacky 2001. Included on the Twentieth Century Fox 5 Star Collection DVD (2001).
5 Solomon 2001: 75. See also Wenzel 2005: 217–20.
6 See, for example, Wenzel 2005: 220–39 for a detailed discussion of the deleted scenes.
7 Solomon 2001: 67.
8 Franzero 1957.
9 Wyke 2002: 303–6.
10 Wenzel 2005: 242; 'intelligenter und gebildeter'
11 Royster 2003: 93–118.
12 Royster 2003: 97.
13 Hatchuel 2011.
14 Hatchuel 2011: xiii.
15 Hatchuel 2011: 135.
16 Hatchuel 2011: 145.
17 Winkler 2009: 264–81.
18 Hughes-Hallett 1990: 278.
19 Royster 2003: 51–4.
20 Wenzel 2005: 215.
21 Mitchison 1973.
22 Anderson 1977: 12.
23 Anderson 1977: 29.
24 Anderson 1977: 33.
25 Dana 1963.
26 Griffith 1964.
27 Reiner 1973.
28 In general, see Hughes-Hallet 1990: 263–5 and Wenzel 2005: 279–80.
29 Cull 2001.
30 Cull 2001: 162.
31 Hatchuel 2011:181–9.
32 Zacky 2001.
33 An earlier version of this section appeared in Daugherty 2009.
34 Kogen 1964: 4–5.
35 *Laugh* 148 (St Louis: Close Up, July 1963): cover; *Archie's Girls, Betty and Veronica* 88 (St Louis: Close Up, April 1963): cover.
36 O'Shea 1963: 1–13.

37 O'Shea 1966, http://perlypalms.com/herbie/herbie.htm#1966-08.
38 His talking dog, Harvard-Harvard, summarizes her characterization: 'Watch out, Mahstah! This is the DEADLY Cleopatra.' 'A Comedy of Eras', *The Adventures of Bob Hope* 89 (National Periodical Publications, DC Comics, October–November 1964): 17.
39 She is merely fodder for two jokes, including her phone number scratched in a mummy crypt. Drake 1966: cover and 8.
40 Goscinny 1965 and 1970. Page references are to the English version.
41 'Cleopatra's nose, had it been shorter, the whole face of the world would have been changed.' Blaise Pascal, *Pensées*, 1670: No. 32.
42 This issue has been turned into a cartoon and a live action movie starring Monica Bellucci. Goscinny 1968 and Chabat 2002.
43 'Superboy's Romance with Cleopatra', *Adventure Comics* 291 (Sparta, IL: National Comics, December 1961).
44 'The Cleopatra of the Future', *Adventures of the Fly* 22 (Sparta, IL: Radio Comics, December 1962): 1–9.
45 Lee 1963: 1–13.
46 Lee 1964.
47 'Jimmy Olson meets Cleopatra!', *Superman's Pal, Jimmy Olson* 71 (Sparta, IL: National Periodical, September 1963): 11–20.
48 'The Day when Superman Proposed', *80 Page Giant Magazine: Lois Lane* 14 (Sparta, IL: National Periodical Publications, DC Comics, September 1965): 35.
49 Moulton 1966.
50 'The Web and the Flame', *The Amazing Spiderman* 4 (New York: Non-Pareil Publishing Marvel Comics Group, November 1967): 10.
51 Robbins 1969.
52 Miller 1964.
53 Miller 1964a.
54 Diggs 1977, https://en.wikipedia.org/wiki/Harry_Driggs.
55 Donahue 1991, http://www.thelooniverse.com/strips/cleopatra/cleopatra.html.
56 http://www.animenewsnetwork.com/encyclopedia/anime.php?id=3253&page=22.
57 Haggard 1967. See Chapter 2 for a discussion of the novel.
58 Maggin 1975: 3–31.
59 Cf. Carolly Erickson, *Lilibet: An Intimate Portrait of Elizabeth II* (New York: Macmillan, 2004).
60 Loew 1974: 7–18. Cleopatra is also in *Vampirella* 38.
61 In general, see McCarthy 2009: 121–43.
62 Tezuka 1963.

63 Tezuka 1969.
64 Tezuka 1969: 104.
65 Tezuka 1969: 21.
66 Tezuka 1969: 67.
67 Tezuka 1970, http://www.imdb.com/title/tt0065588/?ref_=nm_flmg_wr_72.
68 Power 2009: 137.
69 In addition to Power 2009, I have benefitted from Ban 2016 and McCarthy 2009.
70 See the short features collected in Tezuka 2009.
71 A twelve-volume unfinished series. For an overview, see https://en.wikipedia.org/wiki/Phoenix_manga.
72 Tezuka 1970a.
73 Wieber 2017 has an excellent summary and analysis.
74 Power 2009: 137.
75 Tezuka 2009.
76 For example, Kelly 2014.
77 Wenzel 2005: 280–2 is a thoughtful discussion of the *regina meretrix*.
78 Perry 1970.
79 Hatchuel 2011: 181.
80 Brown 1982. See also Wenzel 2005: 281.
81 Todd 1983.
82 Willis 1969: 24–5.
83 Drake 1993.
84 http://www.leslieuggams.com/about_leslie.php.
85 Johansen 2020. She has treated Cleopatra in numerous other musical renditions. See the handout at https://camws.org/filebrowser/download/1551.
86 Buckley 1996: 26–8.
87 *New York Times*, 21 October and 3 November 1968, respectively.
88 Mandelbaum 1991: 209–11.
89 d'Usseau 1977.
90 http://www.steveallen.com/television_pioneer/meeting_of_minds.htm.
91 Allen 1978: 17–22, 47–9.

6 Eighties' Ladies

1 An earlier version of this section appeared as Daugherty 2013a.
2 Aaron 1985.
3 Actually, a clip of Carol Lombard from *The Campus Vamp* (1928).
4 Finney 1973.

5 Jack Finney, *The Bodysnatchers* (1955), *Time and Again* (1970) and *From Time to Time* (1995). Films: *Invasion of the Body Snatchers* (1956); *Invasion of the Body Snatchers* (1978), *Body Snatchers* (1993) and *The Invasion* (2007).
6 Royster 2003: 145–69.
7 Todd 1983.
8 http://www.judytenuta.com/video.php?video=pepper.
9 An earlier version of this chapter appeared as Daugherty 2013b.
10 http://www.africanburialground.gov/ABG_Artwork.htm.
11 Selz 1999: 128–32.
12 Chase-Riboud 2022. See Spencer 2009c: 746.
13 Quoted in Barbara Chase-Riboud, 1939–, 'Pasadena College Artist in Residence, 1990', http://www.paccd.cc.ca.us/library/artists/barbara_chase.htm. For a similar quote, see Anderson 2000: 111.
14 Selz 1999: 8–10, 60.
15 Selz 1999: 33, 42, 48.
16 Basualdo 2014.
17 Chase-Riboud 1974: 3–5.
18 Selz 1999: 63.
19 Selz 1999: 65–8.
20 As in *Anna* 13: 'Any history will do / for those who have none.' Chase-Riboud 1974: 45.
21 As in *Anna* 3: 'Did she remember / the Nile?' Chase-Riboud 1974: 35.
22 On this aspect of her poetry, see Armand 2009: 981–98.
23 For example, Wells 2005: 64.
24 Chase-Riboud 2014.
25 Chase-Riboud 1989.
26 Wells 2005: 65.
27 Barbara Chase-Riboud, *Sally Hemmings* (New York: Morrow, 1979).
28 Chase-Riboud 1986.
29 Chase-Riboud 1994.
30 Chase-Riboud 2003.
31 Spencer 2009d.
32 Chase-Riboud 2022. Sample chapter in Chase-Riboud 2009: 999–1013.
33 Spencer 2009c: 746.
34 Chase-Riboud 2022: 397.
35 Chase-Riboud 2022: 15.
36 Chase-Riboud 2022: 41, 44, 57, 76, 90–1, 97, 108, 158 and 161 are examples of her infatuation.

37 Chase-Riboud 2022: 315.
38 Chase-Riboud 2022: 375.
39 Daugherty 2013b.
40 An example is in Selz 1999: 76.
41 Spencer 2009c: 752.
42 Selz 1999: 49.
43 This work is currently located in the lobby of Cramton Auditorium of Howard University in Washington, DC.
44 Currently in a private collection in New York City.
45 Robinson 1996: 24; Janson 1997: 16; Selz 1999: 120. Lewis was celebrated in 2022 with a commemorative stamp issued by the US Post Office.
46 Selz 1999: 49.
47 Trafton 2004: 213.
48 Selz 1999: 51.
49 Armand 2009: 995-6. She also sees the connection with the poem.
50 Spencer 2009c: 756-7.
51 Chase-Riboud has not clarified which drawing triggered the response she details in the Introduction.
52 Chase-Riboud 1987: 16.
53 Armand 2009: 995-7 explores her use of the oxymoron in this poem.
54 For more information and the complete score, see his website at http://www.andyvores.com/WORKS/WORKS%20PAGES/Voice/Voice/VoiceFrameset.htm and Vores 2009: 898-909.
55 Daugherty 2013b.
56 http://chaseriboud.free.fr/Poet2004.htm.
57 Shwartz 1987.
58 Shwartz 1987: 29.
59 McEveety 1982.
60 Rice 1989 and Rice 1990-2.
61 Roberts 1994: 93.
62 Roberts 1994: 94.
63 For fuller summaries, see Roberts 1994: 94-7 or Smith 1996: 115-22.
64 http://annerice.com/Bookshelf-Mummy.html 4/4/2017.
65 Hoppenstand 1996a.
66 Rice 1989: 252.
67 Hoppenstand 1997: 290.
68 Smith 1996: 118.
69 Rice 2017.

7 The Fantasy Queen of the Nineties

1. For example, Thomas 1927, Mundy 1929, Barrington 1929, Butts 1935, Lindsay 1935, Gerson 1956 and Mitchison 1972.
2. Massie 1986.
3. Massie 1997.
4. Massie 1986: 145–50, 196–200.
5. Massie 1986: 149.
6. Massie 1997: 74–7.
7. Massie 1997: 75.
8. For a list, see https://margaretgeorge.com/.
9. George 1997: 958–64.
10. Roddam 1999.
11. See also Wenzel 2005: 120, 280; Winkler 2009: 280–1; Hatchuel 2011: 153–5; and Magerstädt 2019: 112.
12. Bradshaw 2000.
13. Private email from the actress.
14. Gregory 1999.
15. Gregory 1999: 9.
16. Wenzel 2005: 119.
17. According to the director's DVD commentary, this was suggested by Ben Stiller.
18. Marshall 1993.
19. Campbell 1997.
20. https://www.youtube.com/watch?v=LeiFF0gvqcc.
21. For example, DeMille 1934, Drake 1968, Perry 1970, Busiek 1995–2017, Hurst 1997, Bradshaw 2000.
22. Hurst 20000.
23. https://en.wikipedia.org/wiki/Penelope_Lively.
24. Bulis 1994.
25. For details, see https://tardis.fandom.com/wiki/State_of_Change_novel:.
26. Bulis 1994: 172 establishes Caesarion's affection for his mother as Peri recounts her reception.
27. Tarr 1994.
28. Hughes-Hallett 1990: 17.
29. Tarr 1994: 401.
30. McCullough 2002: 47.
31. Tierres 1990: 9–10.
32. Crane 2000.
33. Parent 1997.

34 Silke 1999–2000.
35 Lopresti 1998.
36 Wagner 2000.
37 Wagner 2000: 8.

8 The Twenty-first-Century 'Authentic' Cleopatras

1. Wenzel 2005: 124–5 noted that Rice 1989 and Essex 2001 were then in development. Schiff 2010 also appears stuck in 'development hell' according to numerous entertainment press reports. Gal Gadot is the latest to join the fray (Jenkins forthcoming) with a script from *Alexander* writer Laeta Kalogridis.
2. For catalogue, see Walker 2001. It concluded at the Field Museum in Chicago in 2002.
3. Rice 1989 and the subsequent serialization as a graphic novel in Rice 1990–2.
4. Scott 2000.
5. For example, Ashton 2008, Burstein 2004, Capponi 2021, Fletcher 2008, Goldsworthy 2010, Jones 2006b, Kleiner 2005, Preston 2009, Roller 2010, Schiff 2010 and Walker 2006.
6. Winkler 2009b is an excellent resource for this film.
7. In general, see Cyrino 2005: 207–56 and Winkler 2004.
8. Chabat 2002.
9. Lefebvre 2015.
10. Ouali 2009.
11. Edel 2002.
12. Young 2003.
13. For background on the series, see Cyrino 2015: 1–5 and Cyrino 2017: 293–9.
14. Burstein 2004: 93–154 and Jones 2006a: 31–204.
15. Jones 2006a: 78–87.
16. Plutarch, *Life of Caesar* 49.
17. Play: Shaw 1901. Film: Pascal 1945.
18. Heller 2007.
19. Quoted in the DVD commentary to episode 22, 'De Patre Vostro' (About Your Father).
20. Daugherty 2013: 183–94.
21. For a reasonable account and bibliography, see Roller 2010: 71–5.
22. Toscano 2013: 125.
23. See Lucan, *Pharsalia* 10.141; on Coan 'silk', see Pliny, *Natural History* 6.20.
24. On this aspect of the reception of Antony, see Kelly 2014.

25 The line may be an allusion to Antony's famously coarse wit, what Plutarch calls *bomolochia* at *Life of Antony* 29.4.
26 The New York story is noted in the episode 22 synopsis in the trivia section on the HBO Rome *Wikia.com* site.
27 Saylor 2004: 288.
28 McCullough 2007: 44.
29 McCullough 2002: 47.
30 Younger version, McCullough 2002: 4; older Cleopatra, McCullough 2007: 266.
31 For an overview, see http://marchingwithcaesarbookseries.com/.
32 Peake 2012: 194.
33 Peake 2012: 296.
34 Peake 2012: 442.
35 Peake 2013: 180–94.
36 Peake 2013a: 35, 40–2.
37 For lists and summaries, see https://simonturney.com/series/marius-mules/.
38 Turney 2018: 401.
39 Turney 2019: 405–6. For an example, see 49–54.
40 See https://www.jaypenner.com/#the-last-pharaoh for background.
41 Penner 2021: 240.
42 Roller 2004 and 2018.
43 While English, Mitchison appears to have been widely read in the USA.
44 Schecter 2013; Vicky Alvear. *Cleopatra Rules: The Amazing Life of the Original Teen Queen* (Honesdale, PA: Boyd's Mill, reprint, 2013).
45 Also remarkably well done is Mitchison 1973 a children's book which portrays Selene's thirst for knowledge and adventure on an equal footing with her twin brother. Ashton 1979 and Chandler 2016 have little redeeming value while Breem 1974 only features Selene in a cameo role in a gone girl mystery.

9 The Twenty-first-Century Fantasy Cleopatras

1 Rogers 2015, 2017 and 2019.
2 Keen 2019: 9–17.
3 Keen 2019: 14–15.
4 See sections 4.5, 5.2, 5.4, 6.3, 7.3 and 7.4.
5 Weiringa 2011 owes only its title to Cleopatra's son, being the story of a Dutchman born in Alexandria to a missing father and a doomed mother. It bears only thematic relationship to Cleopatra but is quite good as an evocation of another tragic childhood.

6 Steele 2020.
7 Rice 2022: 10.
8 Rice 2022: 331.
9 Daugherty 2009.
10 Rice 1989 and 1990–2 (twelve volumes).
11 See Yau 2018 for a detailed if confusing chronology of events and characters from medieval to future times.
12 Busiek 1995: Vol. 1, 22.
13 Busiek 2015: Vol. 9, 50, 81–4; Vol 13, 60–84.
14 First appearance with Honor Guard Busiek 1995: Vol. 1, 51.
15 Vol. 1, 51; 5, 50; Vol. 6, 12; Vol. 7, 18; Vol. 8, 69; Vol. 10, 95; Vol. 13, 19, 60, 69, 147.
16 Busiek 2011: Vol. 7, 18.
17 Busiek 2015: 78.
18 Busiek 2011: Vols 6–7.
19 Busiek 2014: Vol. 8, 58.
20 Busiek 2011: Vol. 7, 14–19.
21 Busiek 2011: Vol. 7, 18.
22 The first Cleopatra lies insentient or dead at the feet of Living Nightmare in a backstory flashback about his 'defeat' (Vol. 13, 147). In this story the monster is tamed by a later Honor Guard including the second Cleopatra.
23 Busiek 2015: Vol. 9, 50, 81–4; Vol. 13, 60–84.
24 Busiek 2014: Vol. 8, 58.
25 See Haley 1993, Royster 2003 and Trafton 2004.
26 Avery 2003–4.
27 Daniels 2010–13.
28 Maihack 2014–20.
29 Guesdon 2017. Although this game is not discussed, Rollinger 2020 is an excellent introduction to this genre.
30 https://en.wikipedia.org/wiki/Assassin%27s_Creed_Origins.
31 Campbell 2017: https://www.polygon.com/features/2017/11/2/16593124/assassins-creed-origins-cleopatra.
32 https://camws.org/sites/default/files/meeting2020/abstracts/2276AncientCharacterinModernMedia.pdf.
33 Del Col 2018: not paginated.
34 Lawrence 2002–3.
35 Sichta 2005.
36 Kuri 1967.

10 Her Infinite Variety

1 Hughes-Hallett 1990: 11–307.
2 See Matthews 2003: 158–83.
3 See Winkler 2009a.
4 See now Carlà-Uhink and Wieber 2020 for an excellent set of essays.
5 https://classicalstudies.org/scs-blog/three-ancient-historians/blog-part-i-casting-cleopatra-it%E2%80%99s-all-about-politics; https://classicalstudies.org/scs-blog/three-ancient-historians/blog-part-ii-casting-cleopatra-it%E2%80%99s-all-about-politics.

Appendices

Appendix A: Brief chronology of Cleopatra VII Philopator (adapted from Roller 2010: 159–62)

All dates are BCE.

69	Born in Alexandria; mother unknown.
58	Ptolemy XII flees to Rome; Eldest daughter Berenike IV seizes power.
55	Ptolemy XII restored by Gabinius; Berenike IV executed.
52	Ptolemy XII names Cleopatra and brother Ptolemy XIII as joint heirs.
51	Joint rule until *c.* August; Buchis Bull ceremony, March. Bibulus' sons murdered.
50	Ptolemy XIII gains control by October.
49	Joint rulers send aid to Pompey. Cleopatra flees to Thebes.
48	Cleopatra to Syria. Pompey murdered after Pharsalus. Caesar and the Alexandrian war.
47	Ptolemy XIII dies. Ptolemy XIV and Cleopatra joint rulers. Caesarion born?
46	Caesar's triumph. Arsinoe pardoned. Cleopatra in Rome. Home by August.
45	Cleopatra in Egypt.
44	Cleopatra back in Rome. Caesarion born? Caesar killed, March. Ptolemy XIV dies.
43	Second Triumvirate. Cleopatra attempts to send aid before Philippi (42).
41	Meets Antony at Tarsus. He kills Arsinoe and goes to Alexandria.
40	Antony to Syria and Rome. Fulvia dies. Marries Octavia. Twins born.
37	Antony, Cleopatra and twins to Antioch for Parthian war preparations.
36	Ptolemy Philadelphus born. Parthian disaster. Antony to Alexandria.
35–34	Parthian campaign renewed. Triumph and Donations of Alexandria.

33   Intense propaganda campaigns on both sides. Cleopatra main target of Octavian.
32   Antony's will read in Rome. War declared on Cleopatra.
31   Battle of Actium. Cleopatra to Egypt. Negotiations fail.
30   Octavian invades Egypt. Suicides by August. Caesarion killed. Egypt a province of the Roman Empire.

Appendix B: Bibliography of secondary works cited in the text

Abbott, Jacob (1879), *History of Cleopatra, Queen of Egypt*, New York: Harper.
Amory, Mark (1998), *Lord Berners: The Last Eccentric*, London: Chatto and Windus.
Anderson, Wayne (2000), 'Looking at Sculpture Darkly: The Sculpture of Barbara Chase-Riboud', *Art Journal* 59 (3): 110–12.
Angela, Alberto (2018), *Cleopatra: The Queen Who Challenged Rome and Conquered Eternity*, Milan: HarperVia.
Armand, Claudine, Andre Kaenel and Claire Omhovere (2006), *Ancrages/Passages*, Nancy: Presses Universitaires de Nancy.
Armand, Claudine (2006a), 'Interview with Barbara Chase-Riboud', in Armand 2006: 15–37.
Armand, Claudine (2008), 'Entre poésie et sculptures: la voix de Barbara Chase-Riboud', in Rédouane 2008: 185–207.
Armand, Claudine (2009). 'In the Interstices of Sculpture and Poetry: Sewing and Basting', *Callaloo* 32 (3): 981–98.
Ash, Russell (1990), *Sir Lawrence Alma-Tadema*, New York: Abrams.
Ashton, Sally-Ann (2003), *The Last Queens of Egypt*, Edinburgh: Pearson.
Ashton, Sally-Ann (2008), *Cleopatra and Egypt*, Oxford: Blackwell.
Aubert, Natacha (2008), 'Roger Moore en Romulus. Tite-Live lu par Cinecitta (*L'Enlevement de Sabines*), Richard Pottier, 1961', in Lochman 2008: 194–201.
Ball, Robert H. (1968), *Shakespeare on Silent Film: A Strange Eventful History*, London: Allen and Unwin.
Ban, Toshio and Tezuka Productions (2016), *The Osamu Tezuka Story: A Life in Manga and Anime*, trans. Frederik L. Schodt, Berkeley, CA: Stone Bridge.
Basualdo, Carlos (2014), *Barbara Chase-Riboud: The Malcolm X Steles*, Philadelphia: Philadelphia Museum of Art.
Bean, Kendra (2013), *Vivien Leigh: An Intimate Portrait*, Philadelphia: Running Press.
Beck, Mark, ed. (2014), *A Companion to Plutarch*, Oxford: Wiley Blackwell.

Benario, Janice M. (1970), 'Dido and Cleopatra', *Vergilius* 16: 2–6.
Beneker, Jeffrey (2014), 'Sex, Eroticism and Politics', in Beck 2014: 503–15.
Birchard, Robert S. (2004), *Cecil B. DeMille's Hollywood*, Lexington: University of Kentucky Press.
Blondell, Nathalie (1998), *Mary Butts: Scenes from the Life*, Kingston, NY: McPherson.
Bloom, Harold, ed. (1990), *Cleopatra*, New York: Chelsea House.
Bronfen, Elizabeth (2013), 'Cleopatra's Venus', in Renger and Solomon 2013: 137–50.
Buckley, Michael (1996), 'Leslie Uggams: Madam's Adams', *Theater Week* 9 (35 Issue 451, 1 April): 24–30.
Burstein, Stanley M. (2004), *The Reign of Cleopatra*, Westport, CT: Greenwood.
Campbell, Colin (2017), https://www.polygon.com/features/2017/11/2/16593124/assassins-creed-origins-cleopatra.
Capponi, Livia (2021), *Cleopatra*, Rome: Laterza.
Carlà-Uhink, Filipo and Anja Wieber (2020), *Orientalism and the Reception of Powerful Women from the Ancient World*, London: Bloomsbury Academic.
Couchman, Gordon W. (1973), *This Our Caesar: A Study of Bernard Shaw's Caesar and Cleopatra*, The Hague: Mouton, 43–50. Reprinted in Bloom 1990: 118–25.
Cruikshank, Jeffrey L. and Arthur W. Schultz (2010), *The Man Who Sold America: The Amazing (But True!) Story of Albert D. Lasker and the Creation of the Advertising Century*, Boston: Harvard Business Review Press.
Cull, Nicholas J. (2001), '"Infamy! Infamy! They've All Got It in for Me!" *Carry On Cleo* and the British Camp Comedies of Ancient Rome', in Joshel 2001: 162–90.
Cyrino, Monica S. (2005), *Big Screen Rome*, Oxford: Blackwell.
Cyrino, Monica S. (2017), 'Premium Cable Television', in Pomeroy 2017: 293–305.
Cyrino, Monica S., ed. (2008), *Rome, Season One: History Makes Television*, Oxford: Blackwell.
Cyrino, Monica S., ed. (2013), *Screening Love and Sex in the Ancient World*, New York: Palgrave Macmillan.
Cyrino, Monica S., ed. (2015), *Rome, Season Two: Trial and Triumph*, Edinburgh: Edinburgh University Press.
Daugherty, Gregory (2008), 'Her First Roman: A Cleopatra for Rome', in Cyrino 2008: 141–52.
Daugherty, Gregory (2009), 'The Greatest Story Ever Drawn: Cleopatra in American Comics', *International Journal of Comic Art* 11 (2): 208–30.
Daugherty, Gregory (2013a), 'Glenn Close in *Maxie* (1985): A Chapter in the Social History of the Snake Bra', in Cyrino 2013: 183–94.
Daugherty, Gregory (2013b), 'Barbara Chase-Riboud's Multimedia Receptions of Cleopatra', *New Voices in Classical Reception Studies* 8, http://www2.open.ac.uk/ClassicalStudies/GreekPlays/newvoices/Issue8/issue8index.htm.

Daugherty, Gregory (2015), 'Rome, Shakespeare, and the Dynamics of the Cleopatra Reception', in Cyrino 2015: 182–92.

Deans, Marjorie (1947), *Meeting at the Sphinx: Gabriel Pascal's Production of Bernard Shaw's Caesar and Cleopatra*, London: Macdonald.

Delayen, Gaston (1934), *Cleopatra*, trans. Farrell Symons, New York: Dutton. French version 1932.

DeMille, Cecil B. (1959), *The Autobiography of Cecil B. DeMille*, ed. Donald Hayne, Englewood Cliffs, NJ: Prentice Hall.

Dick, Bernard F. (2008), *Claudette Colbert: She Walked in Beauty*, Jackson: University of Mississippi Press.

Doering, James M. (2008), 'In Search of Quality: George Colburn, George Kleine, and the Film Score for "Antony and Cleopatra" (1914)', *Musical Quarterly* 91 (3/4): 158–99.

Doering, James M. (2018), 'Grand Ideas and Second Thoughts: Lessons from George Colburn's Personal Score to *Antony and Cleopatra* (Cines-Kleine, 1914), *American Music (Silent Film Music)* 36 (1): 46–69.

Dubar, Monique (1994), 'Cleopatra or Hamlet? Sarah between Sardou and Shakespeare', in Holger Klein and Jean-Marie Maguin (eds), 233–61, *Shakespeare Yearbook 5: Shakespeare and France*, New York: Mellen.

Ducrey, Guy and Sylvie Humbert-Mougin (2017), *Drames et pieces historique de Victorien Sardou V: Theodora, Cleopatre, Gismonda*, Paris: Classiques Garnier, 261–466.

Dye, Phillip (2020), *Lost Cleopatra: A Tale of Ancient Hollywood*, Orlando, FL: BearManor Media.

Ellis, Oliver (1947), *Cleopatra in the Tide of Time*, London: Williams and Norgate Ltd.

Ellis, Peter Beresford (1978), *H. Rider Haggard: A Voice from the Infinite*, London: Routledge.

Ellis, Peter Beresford (1984), *The Last Adventurer: The Life of Talbot Mundy 1879–1940*, West Kingston, Jamaica: Grant.

Faxon, Alicia Craig (1999), 'Review of Jontyle Theresa Robinson (1996), *Bearing Witness: Contemporary Works by African American Women Artists*, New York: Rizzoli', *Woman's Art Journal* 19 (2): 55–6.

Fitzgerald, F. Scott (1922), *The Beautiful and Damned*, New York: Scribner's.

Fletcher, Joann (2008), *Cleopatra the Great: The Woman behind the Legend*, London: Hodder & Stoughton.

Foster, David R. (1975), *The Story of Colgate-Palmolive: One Hundred and Sixty-Nine Years of Progress*, New York: Newcomen Society.

Foy, Roslyn Reso (2000), *Ritual, Myth and Mysticism in the Works of Mary Butts: Between Feminism and Modernism*, Fayetteville: University of Arkansas Press.

Franzero, Carlo Maria (1957), *The Life and Times of Cleopatra,* London: Redman.

Geiger, Joseph (2014), 'The Project of the Parallel Lives: Plutarch's Conception of Biography', in Beck 2014: 292–303.

Golden, Eve (1996), *Vamp: The Rise and Fall of Theda Bara*, Vestal, NY: Emprise.

Goldsworthy, Adrian (2010), *Antony and Cleopatra*, New Haven, CT: Yale University Press.

Grant, Michael (1972), *Cleopatra: A Biography*, New York: Dorset.

Gruen, Erich S. (2001), 'Cleopatra in Rome: Facts and Fantasies', in Miles 2011: 37–53.

Haggard, H. Rider (1926), *The Days of my Life: An Autobiography in Two Volumes*, London: Longman's.

Haley, Shelley P. (1993), 'Black Feminist Thought and Classics: Re-membering, Re-claiming, Re-empowering', in Rabinowitz 1993: 23–43. Excerpted in Jones 2006: 282–6.

Hamer, Mary (2008), *Signs of Cleopatra: Reading an Icon Historically*, 2nd edn, Exeter: Exeter University Press.

Hankey, Julie (2001), *A Passion for Egypt: Arthur Weigall, Tutankhamun and the 'Curse of the Pharoahs'*, London: Tauris.

Hatchuel, Sarah (2011), *Shakespeare and the Cleopatra/Caesar Intertext: Sequel, Conflation, Remake*, Madison, NJ: Fairleigh Dickinson University Press.

Higgs, Peter (2001), 'Searching for Cleopatra's Image: Classical Portraits in Stone', in Walker and Higgs 2001: 200–9.

Hillard, T. W. (2002), 'The Nile Cruise of Cleopatra and Caesar', *Classical Quarterly* 52 (2): 549–54.

Hilton, J. L. (2011), 'Andrew Lang, Comparative Anthropology and the Classics in the African Romances of Rider Haggard', *Akroterion* 56: 107–28.

Hoberman, Ruth (1997), *Gendering Classicism: The Ancient World in Twentieth-Century Women's Historical Fiction*, Albany, NY: SUNY Press.

Hopkins, Claude C. (1998 reprint), *My Life in Advertising* [1923] *& Scientific Advertising* [1923], Chicago: NTC Business Books.

Hoppenstand, Gary (1997), 'Anne Rice's Pastiche of the British "Thriller": Comparing *The Mummy* to Arthur Conan Doyle's "Lot No. 249"', in Ramsland 1997: 286–304.

Hoppenstand, Gary and Ray B. Brown (1996), *The Gothic World of Anne Rice*, Bowling Green, OH: Bowling Green University Popular Press.

Hoppenstand, Gary and Ray B. Brown (1996a), 'Introduction: Vampires, Witches, Mummies, and Other Charismatic Personalities: Exploring the Anne Rice Phenomenon', in Hoppenstand 1996: 1–12.

Hughes-Hallett, Lucy (1990), *Cleopatra: Histories, Dreams and Distortions*, New York: Harper & Row.

Humbert, Jean-Marcel (2016), 'Ancient Egypt on Stage from Bonaparte's Military Campaign up to the Present Time', *Journal of Ancient Egyptian Interconnections* 8: 26–48.

Huss, Werner (1990), 'Die Herkunft der Kleopatra Philopator', *Aegyptus* 70 (1–2): 191–203.

Janson, Anthony F. (1997), *Barbara Chase-Riboud, The Monument Drawings*, Wilmington, NC: St. Johns Museum of Art.

Johansen, Jordan (2020), 'Let's Call her Cleopatra, Cleopatra', presentation at CAMWS, 2020, https://camws.org/sites/default/files/meeting2020/abstracts/2344LetCallHer Cleopatra.pdf; handout: https://camws.org/filebrowser/download/1551.

Jones, Prudence (2006a), *Cleopatra: A Sourcebook*, Norman: Oklahoma University Press.

Jones, Prudence (2006b), *Cleopatra: The Last Pharoah*, London: Haus.

Joshel, Sandra R., Magaret Malamud and Donald T, McGuire, Jr, eds (2001), *Imperial Projections: Ancient Rome in Modern Popular Culture*, Baltimore, MD: Johns Hopkins University Press.

Katz, Wendy R. (1987), *Rider Haggard and the Fiction of Empire*, Cambridge: Cambridge University Press.

Keen, Tony (2019), 'More "T" Vicar? Revisiting Models and Methodologies for Classical Reception in Science Fiction', in Rogers 2019: 9–17.

Kelly, Rachel (2014), *Mark Antony and Popular Culture: Masculinity and the Construction of an Icon*, New York: Tauris.

Kleiner, Diana E. E. (2005), *Cleopatra and Rome*, Cambridge, MA: Harvard University Press.

Kramer, Fritzi (2017), '*Cleopatra* (1912) A Silent Film Review', in *Movies Silently: Celebrate Silent Film*, 15 October 2017, http://moviessilently.com/2017/10/15/cleopatra-1912-a-silent-film-review/.

Lant, Antonia (2013), 'Cinema in the Time of the Pharaohs', in Michelakis and Wyke 2013: 53–73.

Lindner, Martin, ed. (2005), *Drehbuch Geschichte: Die Antike Welt im Film*, Muenster: Lit.

Lochman, Tomas, Thomas Spaeth and Adrian Staehli, eds (2008), *Antike im Kino: Auf dem Weg sur eine Kulturgeschichte des Antikenfilms*, Basel: Skulpturhalle.

Lovic, Michelle (2001), *Cleopatra's Face: Fatal Beauty*, London: British Museum.

MacDonald, Joyce Green (2002), *Women and Race in Early Modern Texts*, Cambridge: Cambridge University Press.

MacKendrick, Paul (1948), 'The Ides of March', *Classical Journal* 44 (1): 65–7.

Macurdy, Grace Harriet (1932), *Hellenistic Queens: A Study of Woman-Power in Macedonia, Seleucid Syria, and Ptolemaic Egypt*, Baltimore, MD: Johns Hopkins University Press.

Magerstädt, Sylvie (2019), *TV Antiquity: Swords, Sandals, Blood and Sand*, Manchester: Manchester University Press.

Maier, Angelica J. (2021) '"Is Cleopatra Black": Examining Whiteness and the American New Woman', *Humanities* 10 (68), https://doi.org/103390/h10020068.

Mandelbaum, Ken (1991), *Not Since Carrie: Forty Years of Broadway Musical Flops*, New York: St. Martins.

Marquart, Joerg (2016), *Cleopatra*, in Moellendorff 2016: 133–44.

Matthews, Jean V. (2003), *The Rise of the New Woman: The Women's Movement in America, 1875–1930*, Chicago: Dee.

McCaffrey, Donald W. and Christopher P. Jacobs (1999), *Guide to the Silent Years of American Cinema*, Westport, CT: Greenwood.

McCarthy, Helen (2009), *The Art of Osamu Tezuka, God of Manga*, New York: Abrams.

Michelakis, Pantelis and Maria Wyke, eds (2013), *The Ancient World in Silent Cinema*, Cambridge: Cambridge University Press.

Miles, Margaret ed. (2011), *Cleopatra: A Sphinx Revisited.* Berkeley: California University Press.

Moellendorf, Joerg, Annette Simonis and Linda Simonis (2016), *Brill's New Paully Supplements 7: Figures of Antiquity and their Reception in Art, Literature and Music*, Leiden: Brill.

O'Bell, Leslie (1984), *Pushkin's Egyptian Nights: The Biography of a Work*, Ann Arbor, MI: Ardis.

Peek, Cecilia M. (2011), 'The Queen Surveys her Realm: The Nile Cruise of Cleopatra VII', *Classical Quarterly* 61 (2): 595–607.

Pelling, C. B. R. (1988), *Plutarch: Life of Antony*, Cambridge: Cambridge University Press.

Pomeroy, Arthur (2017), *A Companion to Ancient Greece and Rome on Screen*, London: Wiley Blackwell.

Power, Natsu Onoda (2009), *God of Comics: Osamu Tezuka and the Creation of Post-World War II Manga*, Jackson: University of Mississippi Press.

Preston, Diana (2009), *Cleopatra and Antony: Power, Love and Politics in the Ancient World*, New York: Walker.

Pucci, Giuseppe (2011), 'Every Man's Cleopatra', in Miles 2011: 195–207.

Rabinowitz, Nancy Sorkin and Amy Richlin, eds (1993), *Feminist Theory and the Classics*, London: Routledge.

Ramsland, Katherine (1997), *The Anne Rice Reader*, New York: Ballantine.

Rédouane, Abouddahab (2008), *Textes d'Amériques: Ecrivains et artistes américains, entre américanéité et originalité*, Lyon: Presses Universitaires de Lyon.

Reeve, Richard (2018), *The Sexual Imperative in the Novels of Sir Henry Rider Haggard*, London: Anthem.

Renger, Almut-Barbara and Jon Solomon (2013), *Ancient Worlds in Film and Television: Gender and Politics*, Leiden: Brill.

Richardson, Angelique and Chris Willis (2001), *The New Woman in Fiction and Fact: Fin-de-Siecle Feminisms*, London: Palgrave Macmillan.

Roberts, Bette B. (1994), *Anne Rice*, New York: Twayne.

Robinson, Jontyle Theresa (1996), *Bearing Witness: Contemporary Works by African American Women Artists*, New York: Rizzoli.

Robinson, Murray (1954), 'Everybody's Making Like Cleopatra', *Colliers*, 26 November 1954, 21–5.

Rogers, Brett and Benjamin Stevens, eds (2015), *Classical Traditions in Science Fiction*, Oxford: Oxford University Press.

Rogers, Brett and Benjamin Stevens, eds (2017), *Classical Traditions in Modern Fantasy*, Oxford: Oxford University Press.

Rogers, Brett and Benjamin Stevens, eds (2019), *Once and Future Antiquities in Science Fiction and Fantasy*, London: Bloomsbury.

Roller, Duane W. (2003), *The World of Juba II and Kleopatra Selene: Royal Scholarship on Rome's African Frontier*, London: Routledge.

Roller, Duane W. (2010), *Cleopatra: A Biography*, Oxford: Oxford University Press.

Roller, Duane W. (2018), *Cleopatra's Daughter and Other Royal Women of the Augustan Era*, Oxford: Oxford University Press.

Rollinger, Christian (2020), *Classical Antiquity in Video Games: Playing with the Ancient World*, London: Bloomsbury.

Rowland, Ingrid (2011), 'The Amazing Afterlife of Cleopatra's Love Potions', in Miles 2001: 132–49.

Royster, Francesca T. (2003), *Becoming Cleopatra: The Shifting Image of an Icon*, New York: Palgrave Macmillan.

Said, E. W. (1985), *Orientalism*, London: Peregrine.

Schiff, Stacy (2010), *Cleopatra: A Life*, New York: Little, Brown.

Selz, Peter and Anthony F. Janson (1999), *Barbara Chase-Riboud: Sculptor*, New York: Abrams.

Sergeant, Philip W. (1909), *Cleopatra of Egypt: Antiquity's Queen of Romance*, London: Hutchison.

Shaw, George Bernard (1895), 'Sardoodledom', *Saturday Review*, 1 June 1895, 725–7.

Sigler, Carolyn (1997), *Alternative Alices: Visions and Revisions of Lewis Carroll's Alice Books: An Anthology*, Lexington: Kentucky University Press.

Sivulka, Juliann (1998), *Soap, Sex and Cigarettes: A Cultural History of American Advertising*, Belmont, CA: Wadsworth.

Sivulka, Juliann (2001), *Stronger Than Dirt: A Cultural History of Advertising Personal Hygiene in America, 1875 to 1940*, New York: Humanity.

Smith, Jennifer (1996), *Anne Rice: A Critical Companion*, Westport, CT: Greenwood.
Smith, Margaret Mary Demaria (2011), 'HRH Cleopatra: The Last of the Ptolemies and the Egyptian Paintings of Sir Lawrence Alma-Tadema', in Miles 2011: 150–71.
Solomon, Jon (2001), *The Ancient World in Cinema*, New Haven, CT: Yale University Press.
Spencer, Suzette A. (2009c) 'On Her Own Terms: An Interview with Barbara Chase-Riboud', *Callaloo* 32 (3): 736–57.
Spencer, Suzette A. and Carlos A. Miranda (2009b), 'Abrading Boundaries: Reconsidering Barbara Chase-Riboud's Sculpture, Fiction and Poetry', *Callaloo* 32 (3): 711–15.
Spencer, Suzette A. and Carlos A. Miranda (2009d), 'Omnipresent Negation: *Hottentot Venus* and *Africa Rising*', *Callaloo* 32 (3): 910–33.
Spencer, Suzette A. and Carlos A. Miranda, eds (2009a), *Barbara Chase-Riboud: A Special Issue. Callaloo: A Journal of African Diaspora Arts and Letters* 32 (3), Baltimore, MD: Johns Hopkins University Press.
Tarn, W. W. (1934), 'Cleopatra', in *Cambridge Ancient History X: The Augustan Age*, 35–42, 66–71 and passim, Cambridge: Cambridge University Press.
Tatum, W. Jeffrey (2008), *Always I am Caesar*, Oxford: Blackwell.
Taves, Brian (1985), 'Philosophy Into Popular Fiction: Talbot Mundy and The Theosophical Society', *Southern California Quarterly* 67 (2): 153–86.
Taves, Brian (2006), *Talbot Mundy, Philosopher of Adventure: A Critical Biography*, Jefferson, NC: McFarlane.
Thomas, Henry and Dana Lee Thomas (1942), *Living Biographies of Famous Women*, Boston: Stratford.
Thompson, Frank (1996), *Lost Films: Important Movies That Disappeared*, New York: Citadel.
Toscano, M. M. (2013), 'The Womanizing of Mark Antony: Virile Ruthlessness and Redemptive Cross-Dressing in Rome Season Two', in Renger 2013: 123–35.
Trafton, Scott (2004), *Egypt Land: Race and Nineteenth Century American Egyptomania*, Durham, NC: Duke University Press.
Tydesley, Joyce (2008), *Cleopatra: Last Queen of Egypt*, New York: Basic Books.
Vores, Andy (2009), 'Forward', *Callaloo* 32 (3): 897–905.
Walker, Susan (2004), *The Portland Vase*, London: British Museum Press.
Walker, Susan and Sally-Ann Ashton (2006), *Cleopatra*, London: Bristol Classical Press.
Walker, Susan and Peter Higgs (2001), *Cleopatra of Egypt: From History to Myth*, Princeton, NJ: Princeton University Press.
Weigall, Arthur (1924), *The Life and Times of Cleopatra, Queen of Egypt*, New York: Garden City. First Edition 1914.

Wells, Monique Y. (2005), 'Barbara Chase-Riboud, visionary woman: in words and art the renowned author and sculptor breathes life into the history of the forgotten female', *Black Issues Book Review* 7 (2): 64–5.
Wenzel, Diana (2005), *Kleopatra im Film: Eine Koenigin Aegyptens als Sinnbild fuer orientalische Kultur*, Remscheid: Gardez! Verlag. Her married name is Fragata.
Wenzel, Diana (2005a), 'Von kindlichen und komischen Kleopatras', in Lindner 2005: 124–36.
Wenzel, Diana (2008), '"Her infinite variety": 1001 Kleopatra Konstruktion', in Lochman, Spaeth and Staehli 2008: 158–69.
Wertheimer, Oskar von (1931), *Cleopatra: A Royal Voluptuary*, London: Lippincott.
Wertheimer, Oskar von (1950), *Kleopatra: Die genialste Frau des Altertums*, Berlin: Reese.
Wieber, Anja (2017), 'Non-Western Approaches to the Ancient World', in Pomeroy 2017: 336–40.
Wieber, Anja (2020), 'Die palmyrenische Koenigin Zenobia als Werbeikone fuer Seife', *Thersites* 11: 277–323, https://thersites-journal.de/index.php/thr/article/view/169.
Willis, John (1969), *Theatre World: 1968–1969 Season*, Vol. 25, New York: Crown.
Winkler, Martin M. (2009), *Cinema and Classical Texts: Apollo's New Light*, Cambridge: Cambridge University Press.
Winkler, Martin M. (2009a), *The Roman Salute: Cinema, History, Ideology*, Columbus: Ohio State University Press.
Winkler, Martin M., ed. (2004), *Gladiator: Film and History*, Oxford: Blackwell.
Winkler, Martin M., ed (2009b), *The Fall of the Roman Empire: Film and History*, Oxford: Wiley-Blackwell.
Worteck, Susan Willand (1982), '"Forever Free": Art by African American Women, 1862–1980, an Exhibition', *Feminist Studies* 8 (1): 97–108.
Wyke, Maria (1997), *Projecting the Past: Ancient Rome, Cinema and History*, New York: Routledge.
Wyke, Maria (2002), *The Roman Mistress: Ancient and Modern Representations*, Oxford: Oxford University Press.
Wyke, Maria (2017), 'From 1916 to the Arrival of Sound', in Pomeroy 2017: 66–71.
Wyke, Maria and Dominic Montserrat (2011), 'Glamour Girls: Cleomania in Mass Culture', in Miles 2011: 172–94.
Yau, Danny (2018), *The Astro City Chronology*, self-published.
Zacky, Brent and Kevin Burns (2001), *Cleopatra: The Film That Changed Hollywood*, AMC documentary, Prometheus Entertainment, https://www.imdb.com/title/tt0282417/.
Zemon-Davis, Natalie (2000), *Slaves on Screen: Film and Historical Vision*, Cambridge, MA: Harvard University Press.
Zierold, Norman (1973), *Sex Goddesses of the Silent Screen*, Chicago: Regnery.

Appendix C: Bibliography of Cleopatra in prose fiction

Allen, Steve (1978), *Meeting of the Minds: First Series*, Buffalo: Prometheus.
Anderson, Poul (1977), *A World Named Cleopatra*, New York: Pyramid.
Ashton, Andrea (1979), *Cleopatra's Daughter*, New York: Bantam Books.
Balderston, John L. and Sybil Bolitho (1948), *A Goddess to a God*, New York: Macmillan.
Barnard, Allan, ed. (1950), *Cleopatra's Nights: The Life and Loves of the Queen of Egypt*, New York: Dell.
Barrington, E. [Lily Adams Beck] (1929), *The Laughing Queen*, New York: Grosset & Dunlap. Reprinted as *Cleopatra, The Laughing Queen* (c. 1934) with endplates and jacket images from the DeMille film.
Berners, Lord (Baron) [Gerald Hugh Tyrwhitt-Wilson] (1941), *The Romance of a Nose*, London: Constable. Perhaps not released until 1942.
Berners, Lord (Baron) [Gerald Hugh Tyrwhitt-Wilson] (1999), *Collected Tales and Fantasies*, New York: Turtle Point.
Bostock, William (1977), *I, Cleopatra*, New York: Warner.
Bradshaw, Gillian (2002), *Cleopatra's Heir*, New York: Forge Books.
Breem, Wallace (1974), *The Legate's Daughter: A Novel of Intrigue in Ancient Rome*, London: Gollancz.
Bulis, Christopher (1994), *State of Change* (*Dr. Who, The Missing Adventures* #5), London: Virgin Books.
Butts, Mary (1935), *Scenes from the Life of Cleopatra*, London: Heinemann. Reprinted in Butts, Mary (1994), *The Classical Novels*, New York: McPherson, 121–345.
Chandler, Sanchia F. (2016), *Cleopatra Selene: We The Great Are Misthought*, Cambridge: Vanguard.
Chase-Riboud, Barbara (1979), *Sally Hemmings*, New York: Morrow.
Chase-Riboud, Barbara (1986), *Valide: A Novel of the Harem*, New York: Morrow.
Chase-Riboud, Barbara (1989), *Echo of Lions*, New York: Morrow.
Chase-Riboud, Barbara (1994), *The President's Daughter*, New York: Crown.
Chase-Riboud, Barbara (1994a), *Roman Egyptien*, trans. D. Armand-Canal, Paris: Felin.
Chase-Riboud, Barbara (2003), *Hottentot Venus*, New York: Crown.
Chase-Riboud, Barbara (2009), Excerpt of *Central Park*, *Callaloo* 32 (3): 999–1013.
Chase-Riboud, Barbara (2022), *The Great Mrs. Elias: A Novel*, New York: Amistad.
Cowlin, Dorothy (1970), *Cleopatra, Queen of Egypt: A Biographical Novel*, London: Wayland.
Davis, Helen R. (2015), *Cleopatra Unconquered*, Honolulu: Savant.
Davis, Helen R. (2019), *Cleopatra Victorious: Book Two in the Cleopatra Reimagined Series*, Honolulu: Savant.

Davitt, Deborah L. (2016), *Ave, Caesarion (The Rise of Caesarion's Rome*, Volume 1), self-published.

Desmond, Alice Curtis (1971), *Cleopatra's Children*, New York: Dodd, Mead & Co.

Desruisseaux, Sharon (2012), *'Legacy of the Moon' (Book One)*, CreateSpace Independent Publishing Platform.

Dray, Stephanie (2011), *Lily of the Nile: A Novel of Cleopatra's Daughter*, New York: Berkley.

Dray, Stephanie (2011a), *Song of the Nile: A Novel of Cleopatra's Daughter*, New York: Berkley.

Dray, Stephanie (2013), *Daughters of the Nile: A Novel of Cleopatra's Daughter*, New York: Berkley.

Essex, Karen (2001), *Kleopatra*, New York: Warner Books.

Essex, Karen (2002), *Pharoah: Volume II of Kleopatra*, New York: Warner Books.

Falconer, Colin (2000), *When We Were Gods: A Novel of Cleopatra*, New York: Crown. Reissued in multiple formats as *Cleopatra: Daughter of the Nile*.

Ferval, Claude [Marguerite Thomas-Galline Aimery de Pierrebourg] (1927), *The Life and Death of Cleopatra*, New York: Garden City. Translation of *La Vie et la mort de Cléopâtre*, Paris: A. Fayard (1922).

Finney, Jack (1973), *Marion's Wall*, New York: Simon and Schuster.

Gardner, Jeffrey [Gardner F. Fox] (1962), *Cleopatra*, New York: Pyramid.

Gauthier, Theophile (1882), *One of Cleopatra's Nights and Other Fantastic Romances*, New York: Worthington. Translation of *Une Nuit de Cleopatre*, Paris: Ferroud (1838).

George, Margaret (1997), *The Memoirs of Cleopatra: A Novel*, New York: St. Martins.

Gerson, Noel B. (1956), *That Egyptian Woman*, New York: Dell.

Graham, Jo (2009), *Hand of Isis*, New York: Orbit.

Gregory, Kristiana (1999), *Cleopatra VII: Daughter of the Nile*, New York: Scholastic.

Gross, Milt (1928), *'Clipettra' Famous Fimmales Witt Odder Ewents From Heestory*, Garden City, NY: Doubleday, 67–75.

Haggard, H. Rider (1889), *Cleopatra: Being an Account of the Fall and Vengeance of Harmachis, The Royal Egyptian, as Set Forth by his Own Hand*, London: Longman's.

Hall, A. D., trans. (1891), *Sardou's Cleopatra: A Novelization of the Celebrated Play*, New York: Street and Smith.

Hawthorne, Nathaniel (2002), *The Marble Faun*, Oxford: Oxford University Press, Chapter 14, 96–101. Originally published 1860.

Headley, Maria Dahvana (2012), *Queen of Kings: A Novel of Cleopatra, the Vampire*, New York: New American Library.

Holleman, Emily (2015), *Cleopatra's Shadows*, New York: Little, Brown.

Holleman, Emily (2017), *The Drowning King*, New York: Little, Brown.
Hornblow, Leonora (1961), *Cleopatra of Egypt*, New York: Landmark Random House.
Hubbard, Elbert (1910), *The Mintage: Being Ten Stories and One More*, East Aurora, NY: Roycrofters.
Langlais, Eve (2014), *Cleopatra's Return*, 2nd edn, self-published.
Leighton, Margaret (1969), *Cleopatra. Sister of the Moon*, New York: Farrar, Straus.
Lindsay, Jack (1935), *Last Days with Cleopatra*, London: Ivor Nicholson and Watson.
Lively, Penelope (1993), *Cleopatra's Sister*, New York: HarperCollins.
Livingston, Michael (2015), *The Shards of Heaven*, New York: Tor.
Livingston, Michael (2016), *The Gates of Hell*, New York: Tor.
Livingston, Michael (2017), *The Realms of God*, New York: Tor.
Ludwig, Emil (1937), *Cleopatra: The Story of a Queen*, New York: Viking.
Macleod, Debra May (2020), *Brides of Rome*, Ashland, OR: Blackstone.
Marquis, Don (1927), *archie and mehitabel*, New York: Doubleday.
Massie, Allan (1986), *Augustus*, London: Hodder and Stoughton.
Massie, Allan (1997), *Antony*, London: Hodder and Stoughton.
Matthews, Kevin (1958), *Woman of Egypt*, New York: Popular Library.
McCullough, Colleen (2002), *The October Horse: A Novel of Caesar and Cleopatra*, New York: Simon & Schuster.
McCullough, Colleen (2007), *Anthony and Cleopatra*, New York: Simon & Schuster.
Meyer, Carolyn (2011), *Cleopatra Confesses*, New York: Simon & Schuster.
Mitchison, Naomi (1972), *Cleopatra's People*, Glasgow: Kennedy & Boyd.
Mitchison, Naomi (1973), *Sun and Moon*, New York: Nelson. First published 1970.
Moran, Michelle (2009), *Cleopatra's Daughter: A Novel*, New York: Crown.
Mundy, Talbot [William Lancaster Gribbon] (1929), *Queen Cleopatra*, Indianapolis: Bobbs Merrill.
Mundy, Talbot [William Lancaster Gribbon] (1935), *Purple Pirate*, New York: Appleton.
O'Banyon, Constance [Evelyn Gee] (2007), *Sword of Rome*, New York: Dorchester.
O'Banyon, Constance [Evelyn Gee] (2007a), *Lord of the Nile*, New York: Dorchester.
O'Banyon, Constance [Evelyn Gee] (2008), *Daughter of Egypt*, New York: Dorchester.
Peake, R. W. (2012), *Marching with Caesar Volume Three – Civil War*, self-published.
Peake, R. W. (2013), *Marching with Caesar Volume Four – Antony and Cleopatra Part I – Antony*, self-published.
Peake, R. W. (2013a), *Marching with Caesar Volume Five – Antony and Cleopatra Part II – Cleopatra*, self-published.
Penner, Jay (2020), *The Last Pharoah – Book I: Regent*, self-published.

Penner, Jay (2020a), *The Last Pharoah – Book II: Queen*, self-published.

Penner, Jay (2021), *The Last Pharoah – Book III: Empress*, self-published.

Pushkin, Alexander (1916), *Egyptian Nights*, in *The Prose Tales of Alexander Poushkin* by Alexander Pushkin, trans. T. Keane. Kindle version. Originally published 1835.

Rice, Anne (1989), *The Mummy or Ramses the Damned*, New York: Random House.

Rice, Anne and Christopher Rice (2017), *Ramses the Damned: The Passion of Cleopatra*, New York: Anchor Books.

Rice, Anne and Christopher Rice (2022), *Ramses the Damned: The Reign of Osiris*, New York: Anchor Books.

Rice, John and Gail Tanzer (2019), *The Ghost of Cleopatra: Edmonia Lewis and her Lost Masterpiece*, self-published.

Roberts, John Maddox (2005), *SPQR IX: The Princess and the Pirates*, New York: St. Martin's.

Roberts, Tom (2020), *Lost Scrolls of Archimedes*, Pensacola, FL: Raven Cliffs.

Rofheart, Martha (1976), *The Alexandrian*, New York: Crowell.

Saylor, Steven (2004), *The Judgement of Caesar*, New York: St. Martin's.

Scarborough, Elizabeth Ann (2002), *Channeling Cleopatra*, New York: Ace.

Scarborough, Elizabeth Ann (2004), *Cleopatra 7.2*, New York: Ace.

Schecter, Vicky Alvear (2011), *Cleopatra's Moon*, New York: Levine.

Shwartz, Susan (1987), *Byzantium's Crown*, New York: Popular Library.

Smith, Craig (2015), *The Horse Changer*, Newcastle upon Tyne: Myrmidon.

Smith, Phyllis T. (2016), *The Daughters of Palatine Hill*, Seattle: Lake Union.

Steele, Nellie H. (2020), *Cleopatra's Tomb: A Maggie Edwards Adventure*, self-published.

Tarr, Judith (1994), *Throne of Isis: A Novel of Cleopatra*, New York: Tor. Ebook issued as *Throne of Isis: A Thrilling Tale of Cleopatra in Ancient Egypt* (*The Three Queens Book 1*), Canelo Adventure (22 July 2019).

Thomas, Henry [H. T. Schnittkind] (1927), *Cleopatra's Private Diary*, Boston: Stratford.

Turney, S. J. A. (2018), *Marius' Mules XI: Tides of War*, self-published.

Turney, S. J. A. (2019), *Marius' Mules XII: Sands of Egypt*, self-published.

Vickery, Walt (1962), *Cleopatra's Blonde Sex Rival*, Hollywood, CA: France Book.

Warner, Rex (1960), *Imperial Caesar*, Boston: Little Brown.

Wieringa, Tommy (2011), *Caesarion*, London: Portobello.

Wilder, Thornton (1948), *The Ides of March*, New York: Harper.

Windham, Dharma (2006), *Reluctant Goddess: Kleopatra and the Stolen Throne*, West Conshohocken, PA: Infinity.

Appendix D: Bibliography of Cleopatra in films and TV shows

(Due to similar titles, these are listed chronologically by name of director with the name of the actress playing Cleopatra followed by Wenzel 2000: 300–68 references or IMDB links.)

Melies, Georges Dir. (1899), *Le vol de la tombe de Cleopatre* (*Robbing Cleopatra's Tomb*), France: Star Film, possibly with Je(h)anne d'Alcy = Wenzel #1.

Gaskill, Charles L. Dir. (1912), *Cleopatra*, USA: Vitagraph and Helen Gardner Picture Players, starring Helen Gardner = Wenzel #11.

Guazzoni, Enrico Dir. (1913), *Marcantonio e Cleopatra*, Italy: Cines, starring Gianna Terribili Gonzales = Wenzel #12.

Edwards, J. Gordon Dir. (1917), *Cleopatra*, USA: Fox, starring Theda Bara = Wenzel #16.

Neill, Roy William Dir. (1928), *Cleopatra*, USA: Metro-Goldwyn Mayer, star unknown = Wenzel #25.

DeMille, Cecil B. Dir. (1934), *Cleopatra*, USA: Paramount, starring Claudette Colbert = Wenzel #29.

Pascal, Gabriel Dir. (1945), *Caesar and Cleopatra*, UK: Gabriel Pascal Productions, starring Vivien Leigh = Wenzel #31.

Castle, William Dir. (1953), *Serpent of the Nile: The Loves of Cleopatra*, USA: Columbia, starring Rhonda Fleming = Wenzel #34.

Mattoli, Mario Dir. (1953), *Two Nights with Cleopatra*, Italy: Excelsa-Rosa Film, starring Sophia Loren = Wenzel #35.

Allen, Irwin Dir. (1957), *The Story of Mankind*, USA: Warner Brothers, starring Virginia Mayo = Wenzel #40.

Cottafavi, Vittorio Dir. (1959), *The Legions of Cleopatra*, France and Italy: Alexandra-Film, starring Linda Crystal = Wenzel #42.

Cerchio, Fernando Dir. (1960), *Cleopatra's Daughter*, Italy: Explorer Film '58, https://www.imdb.com/title/tt0054289/

Rich, John Dir. (1962), 'Somebody has to Play Cleopatra', *Dick Van Dyke Show* Season 2, Episode 14, USA: Calvada, with Mary Tyler Moore. [TV] https://www.imdb.com/title/tt0559804/?ref_=ttep_ep14

Pierotti, Piero Dir. (1962), *A Queen for Caesar*, France: Les Films S.R., starring Pascal Petit = Wenzel #45.

Mankiewicz, Joseph L. Dir. (1963), *Cleopatra*, USA: 20th Century Fox, starring Elizabeth Taylor = Wenzel #49.

Cerchio, Fernando Dir. (1963), *Toto and Cleopatra*, Italy: Liber Film, starring Magali Noël = Wenzel #48.

Thomas, Gerald Dir. (1964), *Carry On, Cleo*, UK: Adder Productions, starring Amanda Barrie = Wenzel #52. [TV]

Baldi, Ferdinando Dir. (1964), *The Son of Cleopatra*, Italy: Seven Film, https://www.imdb.com/title/tt0056510/.

Perry, Peter Dir. (1970), *The Notorious Cleopatra*, USA: Global Pictures, starring Sonora = Wenzel #60.

d'Usseau, Loring Dir. (1977), *Meeting of the Minds*, Shows 1 and 2, USA: PBS. With Jayne Meadows =Wenzel #67. [TV]

Brown, Edwin Dir. (1982), *Irresistible*, USA: Essex Distributing, with Starr Wood, https://www.imdb.com/title/tt0086313/

McEveety, Bernard Dir. (1982), 'Cleo and the Babe', in *Voyagers!* Season 1, Episode 8, USA: James D. Parriott Productions, Airdate November 14,1982, with Andrea Marcovicci. [TV] https://www.imdb.com/title/tt0083500/

Todd, Cesar Dir. (1983), *The Erotic Dreams of Cleopatra*, France and Italy: Film Sr 1-Naja, starring Marcella Petri = Wenzel #71.

Aaron, Paul Dir. (1985), *Maxie*, USA: Aurora with Elsboy Entertainment, starring Glenn Close, https://www.imdb.com/title/tt0089569/

de Jong, Ate Dir. (1991), *Highway to Hell*, USA: Goodman, with Amy Stiller = Wenzel #79.

Campbell, Bruce Dir. (1997), 'The King of Assassins', *Xena, Warrior Princess*. Season 3, Episode 8, USA: Renaissance Pictures (Air date 17 November 1997), with Gina Torres = Wenzel #83. [TV]

Roddam, Franc Dir. (1999), *Cleopatra*, USA: Hallmark Entertainment, starring Leonor Varela = Wenzel #84. [TV miniseries]

Hurst, Michael Dir. (2000), 'Antony and Cleopatra', *Xena, Warrior Princess*. Season 5, Episode 18, USA: Renaissance Pictures, with Josephine Davison and Lucy Lawless = Wenzel #85 [TV]

Bradshaw, Randy Dir. (2000), *The Royal Diaries: Cleopatra – Daughter of the Nile*. USA: Scholastic Entertainment, starring Elisa Moolecherry =Wenzel #86. [TV]

Scott, Ridley Dir. (2000), *Gladiator* USA: Dreamworks.

Chabat, Alain Dir. (2002), *Asterix et Obelix: Mission Cleopatre*, France: Katharina, starring Monica Bellucci = Wenzel #87.

Edel, Uli Dir. (2002), *Julius Caesar: His Time Has Come*, USA: Five Mile River Films, with Samuela Sardo = Wenzel #89. [TV mini-series]

Young, Peter Dir. (2003), *Imperium: Augustus*, Germany and Italy: Lux Vide/RAI Fiction, with Anna Vale = Wenzel #92.

Heller, Bruno Dir. (2005), *Rome: Season One,* UK: BBC/HBO, with Lindsey Marshal, https://www.imdb.com/title/tt0384766/. Episode 8. [TV]

Heller, Bruno Dir. (2007), *Rome: Season Two,* UK: BBC/HBO, with Lindsey Marshal, https://www.imdb.com/title/tt0384766/. Episodes 14, 20, 21, and 22. [TV]

Ouali, Kemal Dir. (2009), *Cleopatre: La Derniere Reine d'Egypte,* France: CLN Spectacles, starring Sofia Essaidi. [Taped Musical in Palais des sports de Paris] https://fr.wikipedia.org/wiki/Cl%C3%A9op%C3%A2tre_(com%C3%A9die_musicale)

Lefebvre, Philippe Dir. (2015), 'Cleopatre IX', *Peplum* Saison 1, Episode 1, France: KaBo, with Nadia Roz. [TV] https://www.imdb.com/title/tt4119154/?ref_=nv_sr_srsg_0

Villeneuve, Denis Dir. (in development), *Unnamed Cleopatra Film,* USA: Rudin Films, based on Schiff (2010).

Jenkins, Patty Dir. (in development), *Unnamed Cleopatra Film,* USA: Paramount, starring Gal Gadot. https://deadline.com/2020/10/cleopatra-gal-gadot-patty-jenkins-movie-deal-paramount-pictures-wonder-woman-reteam-laeta-kalogridis-writing-1234595246/. https://www.imdb.com/title/tt13258918/?ref_=nm_flmg_act_2

Appendix E: Bibliography of Cleopatra in comics and graphic novels

(Listed by writer where identified, otherwise by date of publication.)

'Caesar and Cleopatra by George Bernard Shaw', ed. Emile Gauvreau, *Picture News in Color and Action* 1 (4), Bridgeport, CT: 299 Lafayette Street Corp, April 1946: 25–7.

'Antony and Cleopatra: All for the Love of a Woman!', *Ideal: A Classical Comic* 1 (1), New York: Timely Comics, July 1948: 1–38.

'Famous Love Affairs: Antony and Cleopatra', *Lovelorn: Stirring Stories of Real Romance* 3, New York: Best Syndicated Features, 1949.

'Antony and Cleopatra', *HA HA Comics* 83, St. Louis: Creston, May 1952: 1–7.

'Across the Ages', *Strange Adventures* 60, Sparta, IL: National Comics, September 1955: 1–6.

'The Three Prophecies', *House of Secrets* 3, Sparta, IL: National Comics, March–April 1957: 17–22.

'Superboy's Romance with Cleopatra', *Adventure Comics* 291, Sparta, IL: National Comics, December 1961.

'The Cleopatra of the Future', *Adventures of the Fly* 22, Sparta, IL: Radio Comics, December 1962: 1–9.

'Jimmy Olson meets Cleopatra!', *Superman's Pal, Jimmy Olson* 71, Sparta, IL: National Periodical, September 1963: 11–20.

Archie's Girls, Betty and Veronica 88, St. Louis: Close Up, April 1963: cover.

Laugh 148, St. Louis: Close Up, July 1963: cover.

'A Comedy of Eras', *The Adventures of Bob Hope* 89, Sparta, IL: National Periodical Publications (DC Comics), October–November 1964: 17.

'The Day when Superman Proposed', *80 Page Giant Magazine: Lois Lane* 14, Sparta, IL: National Periodical Publications (DC Comics), September 1965: 35.

'The Web and the Flame', *The Amazing Spiderman* 4, New York: Non-Pareil Publishing (Marvel Comics Group), November 1967: 10.

Avery, Fiona Kay (2003–4), *Cursed* 1–4, Los Angeles: Top Cow.

Busiek, Kurt (1995–2019), *AstroCity* 1–17, Burbank, CA: DC Comics (as Wildstorm and Vertigo). Also published as individual issues. Original numbers are on masthead page.

Busiek, Kurt (2015), *Astro City: A Visitor's Guide (2004–) #1,* Kindle Edition (VTG/DC Comics). Included in Vol. 10 of Busiek (1995–2019).

Crane, Walter S. IV (2000), *Sheba. Volume One: The Sands of Seth*, Cambridge MA: Sick Mind Press.

Daniels, Kenton (2010–13), *Tony and Cleo* 1–4, Portland, OR: Bluewater.

Del Col, Anthony (2018), *Assassin's Creed Origins*, London: Titan Comics. Based on video game *Guesdon* (2017). Contains all four individual issues published separately.

Diggs, R. (1977), *The Life and Loves of Cleopatra*, 3rd edn, San Francisco: self-published.

Drake, S. (1966), 'A Boy's Best Friend is his Mummy', *Jerry Lewis* 94, Sparta, IL: National Periodical Publications (DC Comics): cover and 8.

Finger, Bill (1951), 'Bodyguards to Cleopatra', *Detective Comics* 167, New York: National Comics: 1–12.

Goscinny, Rene and Albert Uderzo (1965), *Asterix et Cleopatre*, Paris: Dargaud Editeur.

Goscinny, Rene and Albert Uderzo (1970), *Asterix and Cleopatra*, New York: William Morrow.

Haggard, H. Rider (1967), 'Cleopatra', *Classics Illustrated* 161, New York: Gilberton.

Kogen, Arnie (1964), 'Movie Ads with Behind the Scenes Gossip', *Mad* 1 (88), New York: E.C. Publications: 4–5.

Lee, Stan (1964), 'The Lady from Nowhere', *Strange Tales* 124, New York: Vista Publications (Marvel Comics), September 1964: 9 pages.

Lee, Stan (plot) and R. Berns (script) (1963), 'The Mad Pharoah', *Tales of Suspense* 44, New York: Vista (Marvel Comics), August 1963: 1–13.

Loew, Flaxman (1974), 'The Vampire of the Nile', *Vampirella* 36, New York: Warren Publishing: 7–18.

Lopresti, Aaron (1998), 'Bloodlines', *Xena: Warrior Princess* 1 (1–2), New York: Topps Comics.

Maggin, Elliot S. (1975), 'Cleopatra, Queen of America', *The Superman Family* 22 (171), New York: National Periodical Publications (DC Comics): 3–31.

Maihack, Mike (2014–20), *Cleopatra in Space* 1–6, New York: Graphix (Scholastic).

Miller, Jack E. (1964), 'Cleopatra's Deadly Trap', *Rip Hunter . . . Time Master* 19, Sparta, IL: National Periodical Publications (DC Comics): 25 pages.

Miller, Jack E. (1964a), 'The Beauty Contest of the Ages', *Rip Hunter . . . Time Master* 21, Sparta, IL: National Periodical Publications (DC Comics): 25 pages.

Moulton, Charles (1966), 'The Curse of Cleopatra', *Wonder Woman* 161, Sparta, IL: National Periodical Publications (DC Comics).

O'Shea, Shane (1963), 'Herbie goes to the Devil', *Forbidden Worlds* 116, Sparta, IL: Best Syndicated Features (American Comics Group): 1–13.

O'Shea, Shane (1966), 'Egyptian Conniption', *Herbie* 19, Sparta, IL: Best Syndicated Features, http://perlypalms.com/herbie/herbie.htm#1966-08.

Parent, Dan and Bill Golliher (1997), 'The Cleopatra Chronicles I–III', *Sabrina, The Teenage Witch* 1–3, New York: Archie Comic Publications.

Rice, Anne (1990–2), *The Mummy or Ramses the Damned*, adapted Faye Perozich, Tampa: Millennium: 12 issues.

Robbins, Frank (1969), 'I Chose Eternal Exile', *Superboy* 160, New York: National Periodical Publications (DC Comics).

Silke, Jim (1999–2000), *Bettie Page: Queen of the Nile*, 'Episode 1: Buried Alive', 'Episode 2: Mad Love', 'Episode 3: She Devil', Milwaukee: Dark Horse Comics.

Tezuka, Osamu (1969), 'The Secret of the Egyptian Conspirators', *Astro Boy* 9, Milwaukee: Dark Horse (2002): 7–110. Originally serialized in *Shonen* magazine in 1969.

Tezuka, Osamu (1970a), *Apollo's Song*, New York: Vertical. Original Japanese serial *Aporo No Uta* in *Shukan Shonen Kingu* in 1970.

Tierres, Michael (1990), 'Cleopatra's Asp', *The Phantom* 964, Sydney: Frew (King Features): 9–10.

Wagner, John (2000), 'The Slave Trail', *Xena: Warrior Princess* 5, Milwaukie, OR: Dark Horse Comics.

Wagner, John (2000a), 'Sacrifice', *Xena: Warrior Princess* 6, Milwaukie, OR: Dark Horse Comics.

Appendix F: Bibliography of Cleopatra in animation

Baldwin, Gerald (1963), 'Cleopatra' episode of 'Peabody's Improbable History' of *The Rocky and Bullwinkle Show*, USA: Jay Ward Productions, 1963, https://www.imdb.com/title/tt4397876/

Goscinny, Rene, Albert Uderzo and Georges Dargaud (1968), *Asterix & Cleopatra*, Paris: Dargaud Films = Wenzel #56.

Kuri, Ippei (1967), 'Race Against Time Parts 1 and 2', *Speed Racer* Season 1 (28-9), Japan: Tatsunoko Production, https://www.imdb.com/title/tt0061300/

Lawrence, Bill, Phil Lord and Christopher Miller (2002-3), *Clone High*, USA: MTV Network, https://www.imdb.com/title/tt0305011/?ref_=nv_sr_srsg_0.

Marshall, Dave (1993), 'Disasterpiece Theatre/Hercule Yakko/Home on De-Nile/A Midsummer Night's Dream', *Amimaniacs* Season 1, Episode 25, USA: Amblin Entertainment, https://www.imdb.com/title/tt0856334/?ref_=ttep_ep25.

Sichta, Joe (2005), *Scooby-Doo: Where's My Mummy?*, USA: Hanna-Barbera, https://www.imdb.com/title/tt0480461/

Tezuka, Osamu (1963), *Astro Boy*, Episodes #44 'Cleopatra's Heart' and #45 'The Return of Cleopatra' (US air dates 1963-5), https://tezukaosamu.net/en/anime/30.html.

Tezuka, Osamu (1970), *Kureopatora*, Japan: Mushi =Wenzel #61.

Tezuka, Osamu (2009), *The Astonishing World of Osamu Tezuka*, New York: Kimstim.

Appendix G: Bibliography of Cleopatra in electronic games

Gagnon, Lisa (writer) (2000), *Pharoah – Cleopatra Queen of the Nile*, USA: Sierra Entertainment.

Guesdon, Jean (2017), *Assassin's Creed Origins*, Canada: Ubisoft.

Appendix H: Bibliography of Cleopatra on the stage

Balderston, John L. and Sybil Bolitho (1950), *Cleopatra and Caesar; a play, adapted from A goddess to a god*, Hollywood, CA: Studio Script Service.

Cossa, Pietro (1879), *Cleopatra: poema drammatico in sei atti*, Turin: Bona.

Drake, Ervin (1968), *Her First Roman*, premier 20 October 1968, starring Leslie Uggams.

Ducrey, Guy and Sylvie Humbert-Mougin (2017), *Drames et pieces historique de Victorien Sardou V: Theodora, Cleopatre, Gismonda*, Paris: Classiques Garnier.

Morlock, Frank J. (trans.) (2010), *Victorien Sardou, Cleopatra: A Play in Five Acts*, Rockville, MD: Borgo Press.

Sardou, Victorien (1890), *Cleopatre. Drame en cinq actes et six tableaux. Represente pur la premiere fois au Theatre de la Porte-Saint-Martin le 24 octobre 1890*, in Ducrey 2017: 261–466.

Shakespeare, William (1607), *Antony and Cleopatra*, New York: Pelican, 1960.

Shaw, George Bernard (1901), *Caesar and Cleopatra: A History*, New York: Penguin 1979.

Appendix I: Bibliography of Cleopatra in poetry, recordings and music

Chase-Riboud, Barbara (1974), *From Memphis & Peking*, New York: Random House.

Chase-Riboud, Barbara (1987), *Portrait of a Nude Woman as Cleopatra*, New York: Morrow.

Chase-Riboud, Barbara (2014), *Everytime a Knot is Undone, A God is Released: Collected and New Poems 1974–2011*, New York: Seven Stories.

Coogan, Jack (1917), *Cleopatra Had a Jazz Band*. No further information.

Dana, Bill (1963), 'Jose and Cleopatra', Track A4 in *Jose Jimenez in Jollywood*, Kapp Records – KS-3332.

Drake, Ervin (1993), *Her First Roman. 25th Anniversary Cast Recording*, Lockett-Palmer.

Endor, Chick (1925), *Who Takes Care of The Caretaker's Daughter (While The Caretaker's Busy Taking Care)*. No further information

Griffith, Andy (1964), 'Andy and Cleopatra', on *The Wit and Wisdom of Andy Griffith*, EMI Capitol.

Ironmonger, C. Edith (1924), *Cleopatra, A Narrative Poem*, Birmingham: Cornish Brothers.

Reiner, Carl and Mel Brooks (1973), 'Anthony and Cleopatra', on *Excerpts from the Complete 2000 Year Old Man*, Hollywood, CA: Rhino Records.

Index

Page numbers in **bold** refer to figures.

A Queen for Caesar (film, 1962), 80–1, 82
Aaron, Paul, 177
Abbott, Jacob, 16, 53–4
advertising, 41, 42–3
    atmospheric, 48
    Dr Pepper, 111
    Orientalism, 50
    Palmolive, 43–8, **45**, **49**, 50, **51**, 52–3, 63, **63**, 64, 69–70, 107, 175
    Second World War, 69–70
Afrocentrists, 10
air travel, 42
Alexander Helios, 3, 156–7, 158
Allen, Steve, 106–7
Alma-Tadema, Sir Lawrence, 16, 28, 44
Amyot, 11
Anderson, Poul, 94
Animaniacs, 132–3
animation, 132–3, 172–3
anti-Semitism, 20
Antony, Marc, 1, 3–4, 5, 9, 19, 22, 23–4, 28–9, 34–5, 61, 72, 75, 77–8, 79, 79–80, 81, 92, 103, 104, 105, 112, 113, 120–2, 130, 146–9, 152
Apollodorus, 6
approachability, 66–7
Archie, 95, 136
Art Deco, 48
Ashton, Sally-Ann, 2
Asinius Pollio, 4
Assassins Creed Origins (Del Col), 170–2
Asterix et Obelix: Mission Cleopatre (film), 141
Asterix series, 96
Astro Boy, 99–101, **100**, 101
Astro City (Busiek), 136, 165, 166–7
atmospheric advertising, 48
audiences, female, 35
Avery, Fiona Kay, 165, 167–8

Balderston, John L., 71–2
Ball, Lucille, 36
Bara, Theda, 19, 26, 32–6, **34**, 38, 39, 52, 63, 67, 75, 78, 90, 107, 109, 111, 112, 124, 146, 177, 179
Barnard, Allan, 83
Barnes, Clive, 106
Barrie, Amanda, 113
Barrington, E., 38, 56, 57–8, 60, 63–4, **63**, 83, 113, 175, 179
Batman and Robin, 85, **86**, 87
Bean, Kendra, 71
Bellucci, Monica, 141
Benario, Janice, 8
Berners, Lord, 69, 175
Bernhardt, Sarah, 20–4, 27, 36
Beyoncé, **178**
biographers and biographies, 53–6
BJ Johnson Soap Co, 43–4, 44, 47
Bocaccio, 9
Bolitho, Sybil, 71–2
Bona Dea scandal, 74
Bradshaw, Gillian, 159
British Museum/Chicago exhibition, 7, 139–40
Bronte, Charlotte, 16
Brooks, Mel, 94
Burr, Raymond, 77
Burrs, Leslie, 119
Burton, Richard, 89, 91
Busiek, Kurt, 136, 165, 166–7
Butts, Mary, 56, 67, 69, 72, 175

Caesar, C. Julius, 3, 5, 6, 8, 33, 58, 60–1, 65, 71, 72, 72–5, 83–4, 90–1, 103, 103–4, 130, 142–4, 147
Caesar and Cleopatra (film, 1945), 25–6, 70–1, 144
Caesarion, 73, 82, 92, 103, 142–3, 152, 156, 158, 162, 171–2

Campbell, Colin, 170
camp-Cleopatras, 92
Canada, 52
Carry On Cleo (film, 1964), 94–5, 113
Cartier, 42
cartoons, 88
Castle, William, 176
censorship, 59
Chase-Riboud, Barbara, 114–16, 118–22, 177
   Cleopatra's Bed, 118
   Cleopatra's Chair, 118
   Cleopatra's Door, **117**, 118
   Portrait of a Nude Woman as Cleopatra, 115, 118–22
Cicero, 8
Classics Illustrated, 15, 98–9
Cleomania, 35
Cleopatra (film, 1912), 26, 27–30, **39**, 44
Cleopatra (film, 1917), 26, 32–6, **34**, 63, 109, 111, 112, 146
Cleopatra (film, 1928), 53
Cleopatra (film, 1934), 58, 59–67, 87, 90, 91, 111, 112–13, 144, 146
   anachronisms, 60
   arming scene, 61
   barge scene, 61, 65–6
   Barrington influence, 63–4
   battles, 62
   casting, 59
   costumes, 63, 64
   focus on India, 64, 65
   guiding narrative, 62
   omissions, 64
   plot, 59–62
   political thesis, 62–3
   script, 62
Cleopatra (film, 1963), 88, 89–92, **90**, 111, 113, 144–5, 146, 148, 179
   aftermath, 93–107, 177
   backlash, 135
Cleopatra (Haggard), 15, 16–20, 124
Cleopatra (TV miniseries), 128, **129**, 130
Cleopatra, A Narrative Poem (Ironmonger), 36–7
Cleopatra in Space (Maihack), 169–70
Cleopatra Jones–Wong–Schwartz trend, 111
Cleopatra legend, 36

Cleopatra: Queen of Sex, see *Kureopatora* (film, 1970)
Cleopatra Selene, 3, 156–7, 158–9, 162
Cleopatra VII Philopator
   ancient sources, 4–5
   beauty and appearance, 6–10, 43, 44, 90, 135, 176
   biography, 2–6
   brother/husband, 3
   children, 3, 4, 92, 156–9, 161–2, 177
   chronology, 205–6
   early receptions, 10–13, **12**
   family background, 3
   image, 2
   impact on men, 9
   and Marc Antony, 3–4, 5, 9, 19, 23–4
   nose, 81–2, 96
   pharaonic divinity, 5
   race, 6, 10, 16, 133, 180
   raced, 10
   reception during antiquity, 7–9
   religious role, 7
   reputation, 1
   Roman propaganda, 4, 9, 10–11
   sexualized, 5
   suicide, 4, 20, 22, 29, 35
   supporting characters, 5–6
   visit to Rome, 8
Cleopatra's Bed (Chase-Riboud), 118
Cleopatra's Chair (Chase-Riboud), 118
Cleopatra's Daughter (film, 1960), 80
Cleopatra's Door (Chase-Riboud), **117**, 118
Cleopatra's needle, 43
Cleopatra's Private Diary (Thomas), 57
Cleopatra's Sister (Lively), 134
Cleopatre (Sardou), 20–5
Clone High (TV series), 173–4
Close, Glenn, 109–14, **110**
Coca, Imogene, 42
coins, 7
Colbert, Claudette, 32, 43, 52–3, 59–67, 75, 78, 87, 90, 107, 111, 112–13, 144, 146, 152, 178, 179
Colburn, George, 31–2
Coleman, Ronald, 79
Colgate, 52
Colliers, 42
colonialism, 37

comics, 85, **86**, 87, 95–9, 125, 165, 177, *see also* graphic novels
Cormack, Bartlett, 62
Cossa, Pietro, 30
costumes, 17, 21, 28, 34, **34**, 48, 52, 59, 63, 64, 77, 79, 91, 109, 111–13
Cottafavi, Vittorio, 79–80
Cowlin, Dorothy, 93
Crystal, Linda, 80
Cull, Nicholas, 94
Cursed (Avery), 167–8
Cyrino, Monica S., 89

d'Alcy, Jeanne, 26
Dalton, Timothy, 130
Daniel, Kenton, 165, 168–9
Dante, 11
Davenport, Fanny, 24–5, 36, **176**
Davis, Helen R., 162
Davitt, Deborah L., 162
Dawson, Josephine, 133–4
Deans, Marjorie, 70–1
Del Col, Anthony, 165
Delayen, Gaston, 55–6
Dellius, Quintus, 4, 8, 9, 19
DeMille, Cecil B., 43, 52–3, 58, 76, 90, 91
Designated Sympathetic Roman, the, 6
Desruisseaux, Sharon, 162
Detective Comics, 85, **86**, 87
Dick Van Dyke Show (TV programme), 88
Dido, 8
Dio Cassius, 7, 9
Doering, James, 31
Dr Pepper, 111
Dr. Strange, 97
Dr Who: The Missing Adventures, 134–5
Drake, Ervin, 106, 177
Dray, Stephanie, 162
Dreamgirls (film), **178**
Dryden, John, 11, 85
Dubar, Monique, 21, 24
Ducrey, Guy, 21
Dye, Phillip, 33, 34

early receptions, 10–13, **12**
Edwards, J. Gordon, 26, 32–6
Edwards-Burrs, Lisa, 119
Egyptian religion, 5
Egyptomania, 21, 25, 42

Eliot, Gertrude, **12**
Ellis, Peter Beresford, 16
Erotic Dreams of Cleopatra, The (film, 1983), 106, 111
Essex, Karen, 153, 159
eugenics, 33

Falconer, Colin, 128
fashion, 42–3
female audiences, 35
feminine mystique, 88
feminist values, 159
femme fatale, 20, 27, 30, 30–1, 32, 33, 38–9, 52, 107, 137, 175, 177
Ferval, Claude, 83
fiction, 57–8
  about Cleopatra's children, 156–9, 161–2
  Anne Rice, 123–6, 140
  Butts, Mary, 69
  children and young adults, 93
  historical, 93, 127–8, 153–9
  postwar, 71–5
  pulp, 36, 36–8, 39, 82–5
  science fiction/fantasy, 85, **86**, 87, 93–4, 123, 134–5, 161–5
film, changing role of, 179–80
film noir, 39
Film that Changed Hollywood, The (documentary), 89
Finney, Jack, 110–11
Fitzgerald, F. Scott, 33
flapper, the, 39, 63, 66–7, 114, 179
Fleming, Rhonda, **76**, 77–8, 90, 107, 144, 152, 176
Foster, David R., 50
Fragata, Diana Wenzel, 2

Gadot, Gal, 10, 179, 180–1
Gahagan, Helen, 16
Gardner, Helen, 26, 27–30, 36, **39**, 44, 84, 124, 177–8
Gaskill, Charles L., 26, 27–30, **39**
Gaslight (film, 1944), 72
Gauthier, Theophile, 16, 83, 104, 122, 144
gender, 43
gender roles, 87, 180
George, Margaret, 128
George Kleine Attractions, 31, 32

Gerson, Noel B., 83
Gladiator (film), 140
Goldberg, Whoopie, 43
Gonzales, Gianna Terribili, 26, 30–2, 44
Graham, Jo, 165
graphic novels, 136–7, 165–70, 170–2, 181, *see also* comics
Griffith, Andy, 94
Gross, Milt, 56
Guazzoni, Enrico, 26, 30–2

Haggard, H. Rider, **18**, 22–3, 25–6, 27, 28, 30, 34, 36, 37, 44, 52, 67, 75, 98–9, 107, 135, 175, 179
  Cleopatra, 15, 16–20, 124
  She, 16, 17, 124
  She and Allan, 16
hair style, 7
Haley, Shelley, 10
Hamer, Mary, 1–2, 64
Hatchuel, Sarah, 78, 80, 90–1, 94–5, 105
Hawthorne, Nathaniel, 16, 25
Headley, Maria Dahvana, 165
Heller, Bruno, 145, 150, 152
Her First Roman, 106
Herbie, 95–6
Higgs, Peter, 7
Highway to Hell (film), 132
Hilton, J. L., 17
Hind, Ciaran, 145
historical fiction, 93, 127–8, 153–9
Hoberman, Ruth, 55
Holleman, Emily, 155, 159
Hope, Bob, 96
Hopkins, Claude, 44, 47
Horace, 8, 10, 36
Hornblow, Leonora, 84
Hubbard, Elbert, 35
Hughes-Hallett, Lucy, 1, 8–9, 26, 36, 36–7, 55, 65, 66, 71, 72, 77, 91–2, 135, 175
Humbert, Jean-Marcel, 21
humorous approaches, 56, 78–9, 81–2, 94–5, 95–6, 107, 141
Hunter, Rip, 97–8
Huss, Werner, 10
Hutchinson's Library of Standard Lives, 54

Ideal: A Classical Comic, 85
Ides of March, The (Wilder), 72–5

imperialism, 16–17, 31
India, 58, 64, 65
infantilized Queen-to-be, 70–1
influenza pandemic, 41
interwar period, 41, 58
invisible women of color, 115–16
Iron Man, 96–7
Ironmonger, C. Edith, 36–7, 41
Irresistible (film, 1982), 106
Isaic mysticism, 91
Isis identification, 92
Italy, 76–7, 78–9, 79–82

Jackson, Michael, 133
Jenkins, Patty, 180–1
jewellery, 42
Jimenez, Jose, 94
Johnson, Adrian, 32, 33
Jolie, Angelina, 180
Jones, Prudence, 9–10
Jones, Spike, 36

Kalogridis, Laeta, 180–1
Keen, Tony, 161
Kerr, Walter, 106
Killer-Kleopatra, 31, 32, 65, 179
Kipling, Rudyard, 16, 37
Kureopatora (film, 1970), 98, 101–5

Landau, Martin, 91
Lang, Andrew, 16, 17
Langlais, Eve, 165
Langtry, Lily, 36
Lasker, Albert D., 44, 46, 46–8, 52
Laughing Queen, The (Barrington), 57–8, 63–4, **63**
Le vol de la tombe de Cleopatre (Robbing Cleopatra's Tomb) (film, 1899), 26, 26–7
Lee, Stan, 96–7
Legions of Cleopatra, The (film), 79–80
Leigh, Vivien, 25, 71, 75, 107
Leighton, Margaret, 93
Lewis, Edmonia, 25
Lewis, Jerry, 96
Lifebuoy, 44
Lindsay, Jack, 67, 69, 72, 175
Lively, Penelope, 134
Livingston, Michael, 157, 162

Livy, 9
Lizpatra, see *Cleopatra* (film, 1963); Taylor, Elizabeth
Loren, Sophia, 78–9, 104, 144
Love Boat, The (TV programme), 111
Lucan, 9
Ludwig, Emil, 83
Lundigan, William, 77

McCullough, Colleen, 135, 153–4, 158
MacKendrick, Paul, 72
Macleod, Debra May, 155–6
Macurdy, Grace Harriet, 2
Mad Magazine, 95
Madsen, Virginia, 174
magic, 91, 92, 135, 137, 162, 165
Maihack, Mike, 165, 169–70
manga and anime, 98, 99–105, **100**
Mankiewicz, Joseph, 90, 135
Marcantonio e Cleopatra (film, 1913), 26, 30–2, 44, 87
March, Fredric, 59
Marion's Wall (Finney), 110–11
Marquis, Dan, 32, 56
Marshal, Lindsey, 42, 141–2, **141**, 143–4, 145, 149, **151**
MASH (TV programme), 111
Massie, Allan, 127–8
Matthews, Jean V., 25, 41, 83
Maxie (film, 1985), 109–14, **110**
Mayo, Virginia, 79
Meadows. Jayne, 106–7
Meeting of the Minds (talk show), 106–7
Melies, Georges, 26, 26–7
Meyer, Carolyn, 154
Middle Ages, 9, 11
Milnes, Rose, 171
miscegenation, dangers of, 33
Mitchison, Naomi, 93, 107, 157–8, 159
Mithridates of Pontus, 5
Monroe, Marilyn, 36
Moolecherry, Elisa, 130, **131**
Moore, Mary Tyler, 88
Moran, Michelle, 158
Moreau, Émile, 44
mummies, 97, 136–7
Mummy, The (Rice), 123–6, 140, 177
Mundy, Talbot, 37–8, 41, 67, 83
musical theatre, 106

Nation, The, 55
New Woman, the, 15, 25–6, 33, 41, 95, 175, 179
Newmar, Julie, 77
nineteenth century, 11–13, **12**, 15, 15–26
Noel, Magalí, 82
Northwest Orient Airlines, 42
Notorious Cleopatra (film, 1970), 98, 105

O'Banyon, Constance, 154
Octavian, 1, 4, 8, 8–9, 24, 61–2, 104, 105, 147
Olson, Jimmy, 97
Orientalism, 16–17, 28–9, 30, 31, 32, 50, 53, 77, 95, 179

Paget, Debra, 80
Palmolive, 43–8, **45**, **49**, 50, **51**, 52–3, 63, **63**, 64, 69–70, 107, 175
Pascal, Gabriel, 70–1, 96, 175
Passion of Cleopatra, The (Rice and Rice), 162–5
Patty Duke Show, The (TV programme), 111
Peake, R. W., 154–5
pearl in vinegar story, 42
Penner, Jay, 156
peplum genre, 75–82, **76**, 107
perfume, 43
Petit, Pascale, 80–1
Petrarch, 11
pharaonic divinity, 5
Pliny the Elder, 23, 42
Plutarch, 4–5, 6, 9, 11, 15, 19, 22, 27, 54, 75, 80, 81, 85, 119, 120, 122, 143, 147, 150, 152, 178–9
Pollio, Asinius, 11
Pompeius Magnus, 3
popular image, focus, 75
pornography and pornographic films, 98, 105–6, 111, 177
Portland vase, 7–8
Portrait of a Nude Woman as Cleopatra (Chase-Riboud), 115, 118–22
Portrait of a Nude Woman as Cleopatra (jazz opera), 119
Price, Vincent, 79
Propertius, 7, 8, 9

Ptolemy Alexander, 4
Ptolemy I Soter, 3
Ptolemy Philadelphus, 158
Ptolemy XII Auletes, 3
Ptolemy XIII, 3
Ptolemy XIV, 3
public knowledge, 52
pulp fiction, 36, 36–8, 39, 82–5
Purefoy, James, 42, 147
Pushkin, Alexander, 16, 78, 83, 104, 119, 122

Quo Vadis (film, 1951), 76

race, 6, 10, 16, 43, 85, 87, 90, 133, 180
racial perceptions, 180
racialization, 75
racism, 9
Reeve, Richard, 16, 19
reincarnation, 32, 35–6
Renaissance, the, 11, 85
Resor, Helen Landsdowne, 46, 48
revival, 111
Rice, Anne, 123–6, 132, 140, 162–5, 177
Rice, Christopher, 162–5
Roaring Twenties, 41
Roberts, Bette B., 124, 165
Rocky and Bullwinkle Show (cartoon), 88
Rofheart, Martha, 93
Rogers, Brett, 161
Roller, Duane, 2–3, 13
romantic epic, transition to, 67
Rome, 8
Rome (TV series), 141–50, **141**, **151**, 152, 178
Rome 2, 42
Royal Diaries (TV series), **131**
Royster, Francesca, 90, 111
Rubenstein, Helena, 42
ruthlessness, 78–9

Samson and Delilah (film, 1949), 76
Sardou, Victorien, 15, 20–5, 25–6, 27, 28, 29, 30, 36, 44, 75, 107
Saturday Evening Post, 47
Saylor, Steven, 153
Scarborough, Elizabeth Ann, 162
Schecter, Vicky Alvear, 158–9, 159

science fiction/fantasy, 85, **86**, 87, 93–4, 123, 131–5, 161–5, 177
Scooby-Doo: Where's My Mummy? (film), 174
sculptures, 114–16, **117**, 118
Second World War, 47, 50, 69, 70
self-parody, 91, 91–2
Sergeant, Philip W., 54
Serpent of the Nile (film, 1953), **76**, 77–8, 146
sexual fantasies, 98
sexual fears, 46, 48, 50
sexual imperative, the, 19
sexual predator, 20
Sexual Revolution, 84
sexual tension, 60, 61, 112–13
sexuality, 12, 13, 16–17, 36, 41, 43, 59, 66, 82, 83, 87, 105, 112–13, 118, 133, 137, 142, 158, 176
sexualization, 5, 75, 107
Shakespeare, William, 6, 11, 15, 21, 22, 25, 26, 27, 36, 61–2, 75, 91, 143–4, 145, 146, 152, 178–9
Shaw, George Bernard, 11–12, 15, 20, 25–6, 70–1, 75, 144
She (Haggard), 16, 17, 124
She and Allan (Haggard), 16
Shill, Steven, 143, 144–5, 145, 149
Sign of the Cross (film, 1932), 43, 59, 60, 62
silent film music, 31–2
silent films, 26–36, 67, 107, 124, 175
Sivulka, Juliann, 46
Smith, Jennifer, 155, 158
Society for Classical Studies, 181
Solomon, Jon, 76, 79, 89, 91
Son of Cleopatra, The (film, 1965), 82
Sordi, Alberto, 78–9, 144
Spaghetti Westerns, 82
Speed Racer, 101, 174
Spiderman, 97
spirituality, 38
spoofs, 35–6
Stamp, Jonathan, 145
Stevens, Benjamin, 161
Stevens, Dave, 136
Stevenson, Robert Louis, 16
Story, William Wetmore, 25
Story of Mankind, The (film, 1957), 79

Superboy, 96
Superman, 97
surge of interest, twenty-first-century, 139–40
sword-and-sandal genre, 75–82, **76**, 107

Tarn, W. W., 71–2
Tarr, Judith, 135
Tatum, Jeff, 9
Taylor, Elizabeth, 7, 32, 75, 89–92, **90**, 94, 107, 111, 146, 152
Taylor, John R., 71
television, 88, 106–7, 111, 128, **129**, 130–1, **131**, 141–50, **141**, **151**, 152, 177, 182
Ten Commandments, The (film, 1923), 62
Tenuta, Judy, 111
Tezuka, Osama, 99–105, **100**, 107, 177
Theosophical Society movement, 37, 38
Thomas, Henry, 57, 83
Thompson, J. Walter, 46
Throne of Isis (Tarr), 135
Tony and Cleo (Daniel), 168–9
Torres, Gina, 133
Toto and Cleopatra (film, 1963), 81–2
Trafton, Scott, 10, 16, 25, 118
tragic romance, transition from, 67
trends 1889–2022, 175–8
Turney, S. J. A., 155
TV series pitch, 182
Two Nights with Cleopatra (film, 1953), 78–9, 144, 146
Tyldesley, Joyce, 56

Uggams, Leslie, 106
United States of America, 16, 24–5, 29–30, 36, 42

vamp persona, 32–6, 38–9, 66–7, 112, 113, 137, 144, 179
vampire theme, 41, 44, 123–6, 137, 165
Vampirella, 99, 125
Varela, Leonor, 128, **129**, 130
Variety, 70
Vickery, Walt, 84–5
Victor, Aurelius, 16, 83, 104, 144
video games, 170–2, 181
Virgil, 8–9
Vores, Andy, 119

Walker, Susan, 2, 7–8
Warner, Rex, 83–4
Weigall, Arthur Edward Pearse Brome, 38, 54–6, 58, 64, 90
Wenzel, Diana, 26, 27, 44, 53
Wertheimer, Oskar von, 56, 60, 62, 62–3
White Grotesque, 90
white man's burden, 16
Wilcoxon, Henry, 59
Wilder, Thornton, 72, 175
William, Warren, 59
Windham, Dharma, 165
Winkler, Martin M., 61
women, status, 33, 39, 41
Wonder Woman (comic), 97
Wonder Woman (film), 181
Woodbury, 45–6, 47
Wyke, Maria, 2, 26, 30–1, 35

Xena: Warrior Princess (TV series), 133–4

Young, Waldemar, 62

Zane, Billy, 130